John Callaghan ... been an avid fol... shortly after th... 'milk-train run' by his rather ... Headingley. At Test match time, this involved dawn departures and long hours of queueing to see Len Hutton carry the weight of England's batting on his shoulders.

After joining the *Huddersfield Examiner* from Huddersfield College he had spells with the *Yorkshire Evening News* and the *Halifax Courier*, as well as a period of freelance journalism working for the Manchester-based nationals before settling with the *Yorkshire Evening Post*.

He has covered Yorkshire since 1972, taking over from Bill Bowes on a full-time basis in 1974. He also writes for the *Sheffield Morning Telegraph* and *Wisden* and is an occasional contributor to the *Cricketer Magazine*.

Boycott

A CRICKETING LEGEND

JOHN CALLAGHAN

SPHERE BOOKS LIMITED

30-32 Gray's Inn Road, London WC1X 8JL

First published in Great Britain by
Pelham Books Ltd 1982
Copyright © 1982 by John Callaghan
New material copyright © 1984 by John Callaghan
Published by Sphere Books Ltd 1984

Printed and bound in Great Britain by
Cox & Wyman Ltd, Reading

To my wife, Joy, who contributed in many ways

Contents

List of Illustrations

Schooldays – Boycott in the Hemsworth Grammar School team with his headmaster, Russell Hamilton.

With the Ackworth club, Boycott with his uncle, Albert Speight, and George Hepworth.

Number 45, Milton Terrace, Fitzwilliam, where Boycott lived with his mother.

Buying his first car, Boycott compares the vintage model with his new vehicle.

October 1963. Boycott, Tony Nicholson and John Hampshire.

Boycott after the victory against Surrey at Lord's in the 1965 Gillette Cup final.

Meeting the new chairman at Headingley, 1971.

Boycott and Sir Kenneth Parkinson toast Yorkshire's future, August 1977.

Boycott after scoring his one hundredth century at Headingley, August 1977.

Boycott, Herbert Sutcliffe and Sir Leonard Hutton at Headingley in August 1977.

Yorkshire secretary, Joe Lister, receiving a petition, October 1978.

Boycott talking to an admiring audience of youngsters.

Yorkshire members crowd into the conference centre in Harrogate.

Tony Vann, Sid Fielden and Reg Kirk acknowledge the cheers of their supporters.

Ronnie Burnet and Michael Crawford facing up to crisis.

Boycott hands in his nomination papers for the Wakefield district.

Preface

Yorkshire County Cricket Club completed a hat-trick of Championship triumphs in 1968, when they captured the title for the thirty-first time outright. They had also shared the major honour twice and their record was without parallel, their pre-eminence unchallenged. Since then they have fallen into dramatic decline, enduring their worst sequence of results on the field as well as a series of internal disputes entirely destructive in character. Loyalty has been at a premium.

In this period two captains, Brian Close and Geoff Boycott, have been sacked, while another, John Hampshire, resigned and eventually left to join Derbyshire, weary of all the bickering and back-biting. Two groups of disaffected members have risen up to challenge the committee, whose record with regard to man management has been the source of constant debate and who remained in uneasy control of affairs without being able to halt the slide.

Not even the return as team manager of Ray Illingworth, who quit as a player in angry circumstances, could turn the tide of events which swept Yorkshire onto the rocks of disillusionment. Year after year, the confident official forecast of better days ahead proved to be no more than wishful thinking, whistling in the dark with a familiar tune becoming discordant.

Throughout these troubled years, Boycott, appointed captain in 1971 to replace Close and dispensed with in 1978, has been the central figure — a hero to many for his great deeds and a villain to some because of a ruthless streak, an undisguised ambition and a well-developed sense of his own importance. It was an era of great change in both conditions and personnel, Hampshire's departure leaving Geoff Boycott and Chris Old as the last remaining links with that successful team of 1968. A whole new generation of players had grown up without reaching cricketing maturity or fulfilling potential.

Boycott carried the responsibility for this and the failure of the barren seventies, criticised on all sides, often by people who saw very little cricket, as the myths spread.

It is time to redress the balance. There is obviously one side to the story that only he can tell, but there is another that requires a completely independent pen. Boycott has not always been right and sometimes he has behaved badly or been misguided in his approach to others. The picture should show this. This history of Yorkshire in turmoil is, in effect, an account of Boycott's playing performance and his relationship with the club at all levels.

To put the record straight, I must say at the outset that during the years I have covered Yorkshire cricket I have come to the conclusion that Boycott was more often than not the innocent party. It might be argued, therefore, that there is a distinct bias in his favour, but I believe that the facts support the contention that he has done more to sustain the county than any other — either player or administrator.

One point needs to be stressed. Despite having to ask many searching and embarrassing questions, I am aware of no single instance when Boycott has failed to tell the truth. The same cannot be said of all those with whom I have come into contact. At the same time, the county committee is a large body and the vast majority of its members have acted, in my opinion, with the best interests of the club at heart whether they have supported Boycott or not.

The statistics are reduced to the minimum, being used solely to illustrate the various arguments pursued. They have not, however, been selected to show Boycott in a good light, nor has any attempt been made to choose either the quotes or the recollections, which are honestly presented to show things as they actually were. The opinions are based on first-hand experience gained through seeing more Yorkshire matches in the period with which we are concerned than anyone with the exception of scorer Ted Lester.

John Callaghan
March, 1982

Acknowledgements

It would have been impossible to produce this book without the help of many people. I would like to thank, in particular, the editors of the *Yorkshire Post* and the *Yorkshire Evening Post* for permission to use their files, extract some items and reproduce a number of pictures. I am also indebted to George Hepworth, Albert Speight and Terry McCroakam, who filled in the background to Boycott's formative years.

1 What You Are

Yorkshire County Cricket Club chairman Arthur Connell, putting the committee case in the strong terms demanded by a critical situation, defended the sacking of Geoff Boycott as captain in September 1978 with cutting clarity. 'It is not for what you have done,' he said, 'but because of what you are.' Like a slap in the face, it cut through all the superficial niceties in which the switch to John Hampshire had been wrapped, at the same time exposing the line official thinking had been taking for quite a while. When all the arguments about modern cricket's most controversial character have been exhausted that remark best sums up the problems which have dogged Boycott's glittering yet strangely unfulfilled career.

It also helps to explain in fourteen carefully chosen words why he never received the prize he coveted most — the England captaincy — except on temporary basis of an injury situation on a tour officially led by Mike Brearley. The man who stood for more than a decade head and shoulders above his contemporaries as a batsman has been betrayed by an inability to win friends and influence the right people. That, at least, is one way of looking at a complicated picture, but the truth is nothing like so simple, for in his darkest hour, when he was weighed down by the death of his mother after a long and painful illness and further distressed by Yorkshire's decision and the loss of the England vice-captaincy, he received a great deal of support.

Although some of this disappeared after a special general

meeting of county members had narrowly backed the committee, those closest to Boycott and, therefore, in a position
to know him best, stuck to their guns with nothing to gain
themselves. Their cause and Boycott's popularity were not
helped, however, by the misleading impression he created
during a television appearance on the Mike Parkinson show.
To many eyes he came across as arrogant and selfish — a
classic example of Boycott doing himself a disservice.

There is much of the Jekyll and Hyde in his image. A
seeker of personal glory at whatever cost to the team to his
critics, he is seen in a far kinder light by his admirers, who
regard him rather as a lone figure, defending the highest
standards of professionalism in the best way open to him.

They base their claims on his lifestyle, for he is a non-
smoker, virtually teetotal and follows an early-to-bed routine
which relegates the social side of the cricket circuit to the
bottom of his list of priorities. Boycott is also careful about
his diet to the point of being a nuisance to a legion of hotel
staff, but everything is planned to give him the best possible
chance of succeeding. Although there are many virtues in this
approach, there are snags, too.

Boycott is very much a loner so far as his colleagues are
concerned and his tunnel vision in the quest for runs has led
him to trample across the path of lesser men on a number of
occasions, believing that his presence at the wicket was of
greater usefulness. That he was usually correct did not save
him from stricture. He is not, though, alone in this, for a
crucial factor in the mental make-up of outstanding individuals
in any walk of life is a highly developed sense of self-
importance.

Modest, retiring natures may earn their due reward in the
annals of schoolboy fiction and be held in high regard over
gin and tonic in the Long Room at Lord's, but in the bread-
and-butter world of high-class competition every opportunity
has to be grasped. Even Len Hutton, idolised and imitated by
nearly every post-war hopeful, did not always endear himself
to his partners once he had earned his place on the pedestal
and, in part, the lean years of the late 1940s and early 1950s
were blamed on the special treatment allegedly afforded the
county's most distinguished batsman.

Equally, great men are set up to be shot at, a famous instance being Gary Sobers, probably the best player there has been, who as captain of the West Indies opted to bat in the middle order. His remarkable contribution to his country's cause did not save him from cruel attacks when the series was lost in Australia during the winter of 1968—69.

The popular line claimed that he had become indifferent to the team's requirements, preferring to satisfy his own needs, so Boycott is in impressive company, yet he has shown more than most that he is concerned about what people think and say. In the face of unrelenting hostility, there is more than a mere hint of insecurity about his obsession with proving himself time and again.

Where he has differed from almost every other world-class player is in his belated rise to prominence. Although he got his first game with Yorkshire's second team as an eighteen-year-old in 1959, he was twenty before he became established with the Colts. In contrast Chris Old made his senior debut at seventeen without being anything like an exception to the rule. Herbert Sutcliffe, that most correct and polished of Yorkshire and England batsmen, was describing Hutton as 'a marvel, the discovery of a generation' in 1935 when his protégé was eighteen, adding: 'At the age of fourteen he was a good enough batsman to play for most county sides.' Hutton, in one of the most remarkable innings, gave substance to this opinion with his record Test score of 364 against Australia at the Oval when only twenty-two.

In the shadow of greatness and, just as importantly, hard times, Boycott strove to build his own career, matching exceptional ability with hard work, the common ingredient in the life of the people drawn together in the mining belt around Wakefield.

There were no easy options in Fitzwilliam, where he was born, the eldest of three sons to Tom and Jayne Boycott and the demanding circumstances shaped his attitudes, making him resentful of the derision his fierce efforts to better himself attracted. He understandably believed honest toil to be more virtuous than idle privilege acquired by accident of birth, and his bitterness became the by-product of talent denied full expression as he made sacrifices on the long haul to the top of his chosen tree. Not for him the normal casual pleasure of adolescence. All his waking hours were carefully organised to fit into a distinct pattern that contained no room for frivolity.

Boycott might easily have gone to university. His headmaster at Hemsworth Grammar School, Russell Hamilton, thought so, recognising the academic competence that complemented his sporting prowess, and seven passes at 'O' level in the General Certificate of Education confirmed a keen mind, but with his father suffering from a long-term mining illness, there was not much money to spare. Putting his family first, he plumped for financial security and a job with the Ministry of Pensions, and it was around this time that another legend grew, for it has often been said that he possessed few natural athletic qualities and that his batting technique is purely artificial, manufactured by hours of practice.

As with so many apparently authoritative comments about Boycott, it is only a half-truth. In his schooldays he did practise endlessly, but in doing so he perfected an in-built skill that marked him out from his contemporaries. He shone at rugby union in the centre, in addition to revealing above-average ability as a wing-half at soccer, attracting Leeds United's attentions at one stage; but cricket was his first love and Mr Hamilton had heard a lot about him long before he reached grammar school. 'He was precise and thoughtful about everything he did,' recalled Mr Hamilton, 'and from the start I knew he had a tremendous future as a sportsman if only he were given a fair chance. He had both the concentration and the talent to make a century as a very young boy, which is most unusual.'

Although competing with and against older and stronger boys, Boycott invariably dominated matches as batsman and bowler, going on to captain his school team, then the South Elmsall side and finally the county boys in an easy progression. He also gained selection for the Yorkshire Federation, so his all-round proficiency showed through from the earliest days.

Boycott was, however, a product of his environment in which sport is given a special significance. It is more than a passing diversion because it offers the prospect of advancement. Self-made millionaires are thin on the ground in mining villages, where back breaking labour brings disproportionately small rewards, so money from a sporting career, usually in the restricted world of rugby league football, is very welcome to the few who make the grade.

Youngsters enjoy themselves while keeping a keen eye open for the main chance and, for Boycott, cricket was the potential passport to riches beyond the wildest dreams of his family and friends. No surprise then that he should apply himself so diligently. He had no plush job prospect in the city to fall back on nor a comfortable business waiting to catch him if he fell. His was a life or death struggle, with the odds stacked against him so long as he remained too proud to be servile and too talented to be ignored. His splendid uncle, Albert Speight, Mrs Boycott's fanatically cricket-minded brother, pitched him into the competitive atmosphere of the local Ackworth club as a twelve-year-old and, despite coping efficiently, he was kept firmly in his place.

League cricket in Yorkshire makes no concessions to age, the rule being that if a player is good enough he is old enough, so the young Boycott received the full treatment. No man is keen to be defied by a small boy. A nought marked his second-team debut — starting at the bottom, they called it — but in the first team at thirteen he made his initial appearance a winning one, driving the boundary that brought a three-wicket victory over Knaresborough. The outcome was his first headline, but the youthful scorer, Jeffrey Wilson, assumed that the christian name could be spelled only one way, so it was Jeffrey Boycott who got his name in the papers.

His close friend, George Hepworth shared many moments with him at the wicket and recollects: 'He always insisted on doing things properly, in playing the correct strokes. I have seen him walk away from the wicket with tears in his eyes and immediately go to work at putting things right.' With Ackworth he picked up the tips that enabled him to master tactics which were beyond his school companions. He slipped into the regular role of captain as a junior and he liked the idea of being in control.

Caution was bred into him. Every run and each wicket had to be carved out of a solid wall of resistance in the leagues, where sporting declarations are seldom considered. If you win, you have to do it the hard way. Hutton and Ray Illingworth, whose unrelenting natures forged Ashes victories in Australia, graduated from the same sort of school and were similar in many ways.

Boycott had one major trauma to survive as a boy, for a routine eye test at school uncovered his need for spectacles. This was a stunning blow, and short-sightedness is not normally a characteristic of world-class batsmen, but, supported by the indefatigable Uncle Albert he soldiered on, making the adjustment satisfactorily. Still, for a while, it was something else to worry about, together with Yorkshire's non-committal manner, as he paid studious attention to the clerical grind.

From Ackworth, he moved up the ladder at fifteen, joining Barnsley, who operated in the highly-esteemed Yorkshire League. His hesitant, exploratory steps were guided by Uncle Albert and Johnny Lawrence, whose indoor school at Rothwell became a second home. They were the two men to whom he gave his trust and to whom he owed a substantial debt. His uncle, often aching from his day at the pit, provided the early practice, hurling down a succession of overs deep into the twilight hours, and he steered Boycott neatly into the right grade at the right time. Lawrence, the former Somerset leg-spinner, offered wise counsel and the facilities for unlimited nets in the winter.

Boycott's schedule took in four visits each week to the Barnsley ground at Shaw Lane, and he made sure he was the first to arrive to qualify for two innings. As he progressed, his keen mind began to take note of the politics, particularly as he felt he was being ignored by the county. 'I stayed at Barnsley until 1961, but then Billy Sutcliffe invited me to Leeds,' he said. A former Yorkshire captain, Sutcliffe, the son of Herbert, was an influential figure and 'there were more prominent people around at Headingley,' Boycott noted shrewdly.

The change in surroundings brought advancement within seven weeks, but it is a mistake to imagine that he was unknown while at Barnsley. The county's scouting system could not miss anyone of his standing in league cricket and it is

possible that he was too well known. Aware of his un-
popularity, he withdrew into a defensive shell, so that Ted
Lester, the second-team captain in 1961, felt Hampshire was
the more likely prospect, weighing up natural stroke-making
capabilities as well as the way the two of them settled into
his side. Boycott's team-mates soon found it difficult to live
alongside his burning dedication and there were attempts to
push him out of the Colts.

One of the first complaints concerned his running between
the wickets which was allegedly governed by poor judgment
at best and downright selfishness at worst. In taking short
singles, batsmen must have complete confidence in each other.
Immediate reaction to any call is essential and there have
been many well-established partners who developed almost
telepathic understanding. Sutcliffe and Percy Holmes were a
legendary case in point for Yorkshire, but there have been
contrasting examples in which the state of the pitch and the
quality of the bowling were governing factors in one or both
minds. Boycott quickly got an unfortunate name in this
direction, being guilty some said of counting, looking to keep
the strike when conditions were favourable and to avoid it in
nastier moments.

It was also thought that he ran his own runs rather harder
than those of his partners and these suspicions have affected
his dressing-room relationships, although fact and fancy have
become dreadfully tangled. Research shows that he was
involved in only five run-out incidents with Yorkshire's
second team before being promoted, losing his own wicket
once, so that in itself should not have raised the hackles.
Rather, his unsympathetic reaction created a gulf between
Boycott and the other young men eagerly seeking to fight
their way into the first-class set-up.

Among his seniors and, at the time, betters, Boycott
defended his own interests and in his earliest Championship
matches he was at the centre of misunderstandings, with his
partners suffering the ultimate penalty. In mid-June 1962
Phil Sharpe was the victim at Northampton, condemnation
raining down on Boycott, who declined a perfectly safe run,
and that occurrence may have had repercussions at Chesterfield. Ken Taylor was run out, but the fault was not all on

one side. Boycott severely bruised his hip after falling on the ball as he dived in vain to attempt to hold a difficult catch in the outfield on the first day. This made him a doubtful starter when his side began their first innings and he had a late fitness test before opening the innings with Taylor.

The pair had put on 67 when Taylor played Ian Buxton towards mid-on and called for a single. Boycott shouted 'Wait' but Taylor kept on going, presumably having forgotten the injury which restricted his partner's mobility. Captain Vic Wilson administered a stern lecture on the need to consider other people when both running and calling as Boycott was uncomfortably cast in the role of villain, although an impartial observer noted that it would have been a sharp single at best.

Nevertheless, Boycott's reputation was not by any means undeserved and he ought to have taken the point made by Wilson more to heart, for there have been other instances which did not show him in a good light, one of the worst coming in a Test. In the winter of 1965—66 Boycott mainly partnered the aggressive Bob Barber in the series with Australia. The Warwickshire left-hander had some sparkling innings during which he was entitled to more than a fair share of the strike, yet Boycott carefully guarded his rights, whether playing well or not. The situation reached a well-publicised extreme in the fifth Test when Boycott, ill at ease with his timing, contrived to receive sixty out of the first eighty balls, managing only 15 of the 36 runs scored before running out the luckless Barber from a ridiculous call.

The carefully placed single usually represented Boycott's answer to a bowling stranglehold, with desperation sometimes leading him into blind alleys. This Test was drawn and Boycott emerged with a sound record, but tour manager Billy Griffith must have observed all that took place with mounting reservation. In isolation Boycott's horrendous miscalculation may have been no more than a minor black mark, but alongside other truths and half-truths it became swollen into a blot on his record.

There were other times with Yorkshire and England when junior players were called upon to sacrifice themselves to save Boycott, and even his most fervent admirers have had to acknowledge an Achilles heel, even if too much can be made of this weakness.

In 1962 he found himself with an albatross of mistrust hung around his neck. A confident, outgoing man might have dealt eventually with this encumbrance, but his dour defiance complicated matters. Perhaps sympathetic handling would have eased the tensions, but the Yorkshire dressing room did not include a psychiatrist's couch among its furniture. It stood as the centre of the universe in the eyes of its inhabitants. Newcomers were expected to balance the tightrope between knowing their place and matching up to requirements. Youthful exuberance has been squeezed out of many a youngster under the searching and derisive gaze of the late Arthur 'Ticker' Mitchell, as stern a coach as there has been, or by the harsh nature of Yorkshire cricket, but Boycott was equipped to handle these.

He struggled instead to deal with people and has always been bewildered by the fact that his dedication should inspire so much emnity. 'When I was a second-team player, senior officials looked down their noses at me and made rather offensive comments because I did not fit into the same mould as everyone else,' he recalls. 'I would be unnatural if I did not want people to like me, but I have always cared more about having the public respect me as a player and a person of integrity.'

The refusal to either understand or accept so clearly defined a sense of purpose is puzzling since the county always prided itself on possessing this virtue to the nth degree, but somehow Boycott ruffled important feathers and no one took the trouble to help him. Admittedly this would not have been easy, requiring an excess of tact and diplomacy as he had a habit of going onto the defensive when unsure of his ground, yet the effort should have been made because of Boycott's world-class potential.

Late in claiming attention, he made up for time lost in a style which suggests his rapid advancement might easily have created ill-feeling and, as he pressed his claims, those ill-judged singles grew in the mind, gained sometimes in the telling and the 'monster' took on another skin. It is remarkable how many people know somebody who knows somebody else who was run out by Boycott either in the leagues or with the Colts! It makes a refreshing change to hear Hepworth say: 'Geoff was an adventurous runner as a boy and I am afraid that more than once a few of us ran him out through not being as quick.' How much effect did those experiences have?

Whatever the atmosphere, however, Boycott thrived on it, quickly becoming established at the head of the second-team averages to set a trend he was to follow with the seniors, and it was in making his place secure that he gave further encouragement to the feeling that his own figures meant more to him than the team's results. In the summer of 1961, though, he blissfully ignored the sneering as his twenty-four innings with the Colts produced 688 runs for an average of 38.22 and made promotion inevitable. His stride never faltered as he crossed the next hurdle, for despite a disappointing debut against the Pakistan tourists when he made four in each innings, and other difficulties, real and imagined, he went on to top the first-team batting averages between 1963 and 1977 in an unbroken sequence, and the degree to which he dominated largely explains the increasing importance he attached to his own performance. His averages, together with those of the players who finished second, were:

1963 — Boycott 46.64	Close 35.19
1964 — Boycott 60.70	Taylor 39.62
1965 — Boycott 35.73	Hampshire 31.64
1966 — Boycott 38.55	Close 30.70
1967 — Boycott 49.35	Close 35.72
1968 — Boycott 77.23	Sharpe 33.05
1969 — Boycott 38.31	Sharpe 37.48
1970 — Boycott 51.93	Leadbeater 37.27
1971 — Boycott 105.76	Hampshire 35.97
1972 — Boycott 96.33	Hampshire 30.96
1973 — Boycott 59.46	Sharpe 38.82
1974 — Boycott 59.12	Hampshire 53.00
1975 — Boycott 73.65	Old 43.88
1976 — Boycott 67.78	Hampshire 44.93
1977 — Boycott 57.23	Hampshire 43.27

It is impossible to imagine Brian Close allowing him to play for himself in the first half of that massively impressive run, so it would have been remarkable if Boycott had not grown to feel he was the cornerstone, holding everything together, by the time he came to the captaincy in 1971, taking charge of a complete rebuilding programme, and the club ought to have been grateful for one rock to which to cling.

The formative period of his leadership was the time when the cricket committee in general and chairman John Temple in particular should have exerted themselves forcefully, initiating united effort to overcome crippling losses from the playing staff. Instead, internal squabbles spread. Boycott suffered the consequences without being able to do much about it, although in the end he found it necessary to strike a blow or two on his own behalf.

He had never been subject to false modesty, but he did look for a word of praise here and there from colleagues whose skill he admired and suddenly most of them were missing from a dressing room shorn of international experience. Far from recognising the dangers, however, the committee sat back, reacting badly when the appointment of a team manager was put forward in 1974 as a means of creating greater management efficiency. Issuing a statement through secretary Joe Lister, they fought the innovation, yet they conveniently changed their minds when ready to sack Boycott four years later.

Team spirit was under pressure in the early 1970s and there is evidence that Boycott's position was never sufficiently secure to make him certain of his authority, so discipline became ragged at the edges.

Boycott's formative years also spawned all manner of stories. It has been stated with conviction that he began in the middle-order and cried when instructed to go in first by Close. If he did shed a nervous tear that day, long ago, it was not because he feared being thrust into the unknown. With few exceptions, he went in first for the Colts and acted as opening partner for Brian Bolus on his first appearance against the Pakistanis at Bradford in 1962, going on to play seven of his nine innings in that position. His run down the order came later because there were senior alternatives to open.

Boycott is aware, almost painfully so, that the fiction is so firmly fixed in the public mind that the fact is no longer important, but one famous flight of fancy continues to cause annoyance at a considerable distance. It relates to the 1965 Gillette Cup final against Surrey at Lord's in which, of course, his brilliant 146, including three sixes and fifteen fours, earned him the individual Man-of-the-Match award. That innings is a source of pride as well as the object of wild speculation by many among the 25,000 crowd, by others who claim to have been present and by even more who apparently discovered they could lip-read while watching television.

Put in to bat, Yorkshire, in the persons of Boycott and Ken Taylor, used up twelve of their sixty overs to score 22 runs and when the latter was dismissed Close unexpectedly promoted himself to number three. He came in then, so the tale goes, to give Boycott the 'hard word' by threatening dire consequences if the opener did not improve his rate of progress. Thus, the subsequent fireworks in a dazzling stand of 192 were ascribed to the captain's intervention. Boycott's version makes more sense. 'The ground had been flooded and the start was delayed, so we all thought that, with the outfield slow, whoever had to bat first would struggle,' he says. 'In the event it was us, and we would have settled for around 170 without batting, so there were no complaints about the way Ken and I operated.

'The object was to make a sound start, which we did in preventing a breakthrough. Closey came in at three for a specific reason. We had lost to Surrey at Park Avenue in July when, on a pitch that seamed a bit, Dave Sydenham, a left-arm medium-pacer, took 7 for 32. Although conditions were not the same at Lord's, it was decided we should get a left-hander in as soon as reasonably possible in the final to counter him, and this is just what we did. In fact, when Closey came down the pitch to talk to me in the first place, it was to ask how things were going and then we had a few discussions about tactics. These dealt with the details such as who was bowling well, who we wanted to attack and who deserved most respect.'

Sydenham took 1 for 67 as Yorkshire ruthlessly dominated the proceedings, drawing their advantage from Boycott's display to win by 175 runs, but hardly anyone has heard his version.

Boycott had by then made more than one mark in the history books, as, in August 1964, he completed a rare feat that eluded both Hutton and Sutcliffe — the senior branches of the family, as well as the junior. His Test century at the Oval meant that in successive matches he had topped one hundred for county and country against the Australians. It is a curiosity that neither of the other two great Yorkshiremen had three-figure innings for the county against the oldest of England's foes.

His career was still in its infancy, though, and 1965 was a troubled season as he failed to make a first-class century. He might, therefore, have been forgiven for having some anxious moments in his and Yorkshire's first knockout final, but it is a sorry comment on human nature that his critics should use the game so freely to prop up their campaign about his allegedly selfish batting. It is also significant that they had to use considerable powers of invention to do so.

It has been similarly implied that his distinction in becoming the first Englishman to average over one hundred in a season resulted from his concentrating entirely on his own interests. This was the highlight of 1971 — his first year as captain — and the unpleasant inference stemmed wholly from his declaration immediately his average crept beyond three figures in the first innings of Yorkshire's last match against Northamptonshire at Harrogate. His action is not in dispute and he would have been less than flesh and blood had he not been aware of the figures. He does not deny that he kept an eye on his personal scoreboard, but he is open to attack only if he weakened Yorkshire's position. He did just the opposite, grinding the resistance out of the opposition with a masterly technique, and Northamptonshire were beaten by an innings and 99 runs in two days, despite winning the toss and being able to take first use of an unreliable pitch.

They were dismissed for 61 and 106 and while Boycott compiled the 124 not out he needed, Yorkshire scored 266 from only eighty-five overs to earn four points for batting. Beyond that stage there were no more bonus points available, so the declaration fitted neatly into the pattern of events. His timing was impeccable. Yorkshire's scoring rate was better than three an over, so the spectators departed in jubilant mood.

Unquestionably Boycott has been hurt by the challenging of his professionalism. In this respect he has never been prepared to make concessions. A classic example was his decision to switch from spectacles to contact lenses for the 1969 season, even though he realised that the adjustment would not be easy. He went into the matter with characteristic thoroughness, balancing the fact that a number of batsmen managed quite well with spectacles against the physical dangers. 'The idea of wearing contact lenses came to me while I lay on my back at home injured in 1968,' he said. 'I had plenty of time to think about the future, so I took it up with a leading firm of lens people in Manchester and they gave me excellent advice.' A run of low scores was the price he had to pay, but he refused to look for excuses, preferring to check for flaws in his batting and he benefited from that little bit of extra confidence.

The wind swirling dust around has caused discomfort and held up play, while a marvellous pantomime situation developed at Huddersfield in 1980 when he lost a lens and a tea-time search was conducted by a mass of willing spectators crawling over the square on hands and knees, but Boycott made the change a success. Another illustration of attention to detail is the fluttering handkerchief which accompanies his procession to the wicket and gives him a good idea of the strength and direction of the breeze.

His philosophy is best summed up in his own words. 'I look at it this way. The bowler's job is to get me out and mine is to see that he doesn't. When I am out it is my fault.' Yorkshire cricket has been his constant companion through adult life and while the marriage has often been troubled, he remained faithful in his own way, trying hard to make the relationship work. Not everyone within the county organisation can look back with as clear a conscience and it is also because of what other people were that his years in office proved so unproductive.

2 England, Their England

Boycott's strained relations with Yorkshire made purely domestic news for a long time, but his differences with those running English cricket naturally received national publicity, and it is ironic, in view of their minor standing on the Test circuit, that the Indians should figure so prominently. It is also in keeping with the way triumph and tragedy have linked hands across Boycott's career that his highest Test score of 246 not out should be followed by his omission from the England team on disciplinary grounds. The occasion of his first brush with officialdom was the opening match in the series with India at Headingley in June 1967, when his innings, stretched over ten hours against a weakened attack, helped England to a six-wicket victory but brought no praise.

Boycott went into the Test with a run of low scores at his back, including a 'pair' against Kent at Bradford, so his reaction was predictable in that he took the opportunity to play a long innings and refind a surer touch. He managed only 106 on a tedious first day, improving on the second to add another 140 in four hours, but not even the right result could save him. Soon scoring rates, like over rates, were to lose their significance, success becoming the only criterion, but here Boycott was sacrificed to the image of adventure at a convenient time through the medium of a meaningless gesture.

He remained aloof from the debate, commenting merely that he was disappointed and he duly regained his place for the third Test. Ken Barrington had also been left out two years previously for a breach of the old-school-tie ethics that were so quickly to disappear, buried under the growth of commercialism and sponsorship, so this was a minor hiccup. Nor was there anything to arouse more than mild discussion about Boycott's decision not to go on the 1972—73 MCC tour of India, Pakistan and Sri Lanka. A troublesome finger injury worried him and he had to bat in a protective stall. His memories of that part of the world were not too pleasant either, for on his way to Australia on his first visit there in 1965 he picked up a stomach complaint which kept him in hospital while the rest of the party moved on, and left him far from well during the whole trip. It is worth mentioning here that he had undergone surgery as a boy, having his spleen removed. He thought that the food, heat and conditions in India and Pakistan did not agree with him, confirmation coming from the lips of earlier travellers whose repertoire of anecdotes bulged with tales of ineffectual plumbing creaking under the strain of constant use.

In the February of 1973, however, he went to South Africa to play for the Wilf Isaac's team against school sides and to give a series of lectures and demonstrations. In ninety-nine cases out of a hundred such a trivial undertaking would have passed unnoticed, but Boycott took the full brunt of disapproval, being accused of letting down his country by scoring cheap runs off schoolboys and sunning himself when his duty was to be facing up to the Indians.

For once he was perfectly able to refute the allegations, although he could not guarantee that the bigots would listen. 'I have had an operation for the removal of my spleen and been advised not to travel to India because the climate would be harmful,' he said. 'I prefer being in South Africa doing something useful to doing nothing at home. Four other Test cricketers have declined to tour, but not a word has been said about them. People are deliberately going out of their way to harm me and this is something I do not understand.' England's captain, Illingworth, took a well-earned rest while Tony Lewis's credentials were examined and there were hopes within the establishment that the Welshman would replace the blunt Yorkshireman, who, thankfully, overcame the challenge. This was, though, another example of the way things work in cricket.

A bat-throwing incident in the Adelaide Test in 1971 proved more serious. Boycott's disgust stemmed from the decision of umpire Max O'Connell to give him run out for 58 in the first innings of the drawn game and, while the England party were less than impressed by some of the umpires, it did Boycott no good when Illingworth felt obliged to apologise on his behalf.

The great rift, which split English cricket, came on June 14 1974, when the team announced for the second Test against India did not include Boycott. Sides were taken immediately and the battle lines drawn up, with charge and counter charge echoing across the first-class circuit, but the dispute that kept the country's best batsman out of international action until July 1977, had its roots in the fertile ground of a difficult West Indies tour under Mike Denness and' fed on Boycott's desire to meet his county obligations.

Although Denness had been vice-captain to Lewis in the East, he was not the natural successor to Illingworth, who fell from grace in the wake of the West Indies' 2—0 triumph in a shortened series over here. England's cruelly exposed limitations in two shattering defeats — by 158 runs and an innings and 226 runs — had been disguised by Illingworth's expertise in the past and if he could not stop the rot Denness was hardly likely to do any better, while promoting Tony Greig stoked the flames. Denness had not been regarded as good enough to gain a place in any of the six Tests against New Zealand and the West Indies that summer and Greig's experience of leadership was limited to one season with Sussex. Both were way behind Boycott in the matter of England appearances and his feeling of outrage did not lessen after he was appointed a member of the tour committee.

He headed the averages against New Zealand with 64.00 and followed Keith Fletcher with 50.50 against West Indies, so his selection was automatic. Impartiality insisted that he had a right to be captain ahead of Denness or Greig and, like the ill-used Illingworth, he had good reason to feel aggrieved. The one casually discarded and the other foolishly overlooked were better servants of English cricket than their supposed superiors, and Boycott did not warm to the idea of being dropped down the order to number four for the third

Test in the West Indies. 'Tour manager Donald Carr mentioned the idea to me on the flight out, but I did not think much to it and thought that was the end of it until the batting order was changed at Bridgetown,' he said. England were seeking to get more out of him, but he made only 10 and 13 so the experiment had a short life.

Boycott's ingrained professionalism enabled him to deliver the goods. A total of 421 runs and an average of 46.78 left him just behind Dennis Amiss and Greig, while in all matches his 960 runs brought an average of 73.85. Boycott, Amiss and Greig represented the spinal cord of England's effort as they held the West Indies to one all and one member of that splendid trio returned home feeling badly let down by the lukewarm response his work had drawn.

Still, accustomed to the cold shoulder, Boycott carried on into his unexpected disaster against the Indians. In the cool, damp of early May, Yorkshire's match with the tourists at Park Avenue was little more than a pipe-opener, so his dismissal for small scores of 15 and 14 was of little consequence. In the first innings he departed lbw to Abid Ali and in the second fell in the same way to Eknath Solkar, a gentle left-arm medium-pacer who bowled over the wicket and who was to haunt Boycott, giving rise to a mass of complicated batting theory.

The MCC match provided the next hint of what was to come as Solkar had Boycott caught by Sunil Gavaskar at slip in each innings, the scores being 12 and 1, and the confrontation between the world-ranked batsman and the little-known seamer became page one news. Concentrating his mind, Boycott compensated with a century in each innings of the Worcester Test trial — 160 not out and 116 — and this, together with the fact that he had made the highest score of his career — 261 not out — in Bridgetown as recently as January, emphasised that low scores were not the symptoms of a complete collapse. He could make nothing of the Indians, though. The next venue was Old Trafford, which staged the opening game in the three-Test series. Abid Ali destroyed him in the first innings, Boycott being lbw for 10, but Solkar struck in the second, Farokh Engineer holding the catch behind the wicket with the bewildered batsman on 6.

The figures made grisly reading, only 58 runs for six times out against two bowlers who could politely be described as no more than honest triers at the highest level. The competence which characterised his Caribbean winter did not sustain him and he visibly crumbled. The man so few recognise, the Boycott seeking sympathy and encouragement, was bowed down by a misery of indecision and, with his county background unsettled, he turned to the chairman of selectors, Alec Bedser, making a telephone call that had far-reaching consequences. Probably neither of the principals is any longer sure of the exact words, but events ran away with Boycott, who started out in search of understanding and finished up with a rest he was not sure he wanted. Talk of pressure filled the air to saturation point and Boycott began to think there must be something in it, but all the facts contradicted this line.

As captain of Yorkshire Boycott had taken part in twenty-two Tests, scoring 1,971 runs for an average of 56.31, meeting head-on some of the best bowling in the world, so Bedser's official comment did not really add up. 'We have discussed the position with Boycott and decided, in view of his lack of confidence in his ability when playing international cricket, to leave him out.' Before the Old Trafford disaster, Boycott's last two Test innings were 99 and 112 in Port of Spain, Trinidad, so his 'lack of confidence' had suddenly manifested itself.

It existed, certainly, but selectors determined to put the best eleven into the field ought to have made greater efforts to indulge one of their most reliable run-makers. Here is a genuine insight into Boycott's make-up and the thinking of the people around him. His weakness lay in the need for re-assurance in times of stress, theirs in the inability to recognise or meet the requirement. Following his rebuff over the captaincy, the readiness to do without him as a batsman shattered his composure.

On the night the news broke, the Yorkshire team were assembled in a hotel in Bath, prior to a Championship match against Somerset. Boycott had arrived very late, drained and already displaying the symptoms of flu which was to prevent him from playing. His condition necessitated more than the chance to relax and, although the chatter of misguided comment suggested that feigned illness was a convenient alternative to facing reality, a doctor, called in the night, ordered him to bed for forty-eight hours. Boycott spent an uncomfortable time, therefore, pondering the next move while watching World Cup soccer on a portable television, provided, along with attentive room service, by a thoughtful management. A card bearing the instruction 'Do not disturb' barred the door of room 96, the occupant being disturbed enough already. 'I really wanted to play in this match,' he said as he recovered. 'With no Test commitments I had three full Championship games and two Sunday League fixtures at a stretch to put together some good innings.

'That is my main concern at the moment — refinding my best form. Everything else which has been written about me recently, my grip, my stance and being left out of the Test side, is secondary to that.' This desire dragged Boycott out of bed and into a friendly game at the nearby Lansdowne Club, who were opposed by the touring Selwyn College, from Cambridge. With utter, if subdued, certainty he put together a century at the expense of some perspiring, artless bowling before, refusing to give away his wicket to a deserving cause, he retired to the gloom of the dressing room. There, hunched over his bat gazing into space, he gave voice to the question that had burned in his mind for some months and continued to tease him as others gained preferment. 'They wanted me as a player, but not as captain. Now they seem happy to do without me altogether. Why?'

As he brooded, he came over and over to the same conclusion — he had enemies in high places. Enemies he could not touch but who hammered him at every opportunity. The feeling had been with him a long time, but he was fighting elusive foes. 'There are certain people,' he said, 'who will never forgive or forget. They keep on going out of their way to get at me and make my life difficult.' Some of these difficulties were of his own making, however, and he obviously had no chance of becoming England captain until he got back in the side as a player.

He was also vulnerable as he remained on the side-lines, for the official mind is wonderfully retentive about the faults in others while neatly overlooking its own errors. Only the most skilled politician could have extricated himself from the mess, and he would have required a cool nerve and a thick skin.

England, meanwhile, experienced no regrets, prospering against second-rate opposition and, while Boycott fretted, another handful of mud came hurtling in his direction. Some of it stuck. It began to be whispered that he had withdrawn from the England side to concentrate on his benefit following a 'difference of opinion over matters of organisation' with Roy Parsons, a Cleckheaton business man, who had been largely in charge of arrangements.

Parsons, dissatisfied with a system under which, with the best of intentions, some of Boycott's friends had been working for his fund in their own way, forwarded a letter of complaint. This arrived before Boycott went out to bat against Warwickshire at Sheffield and he did not have to wait long to read it, Willis bowling him for 15. 'Obviously this business has had something to do with my lack of success,' said Boycott, whose major concern centred on a temporary shortage of runs.

'What I really want to do is immerse myself totally in cricket. That is when I am at my best. I feel as if I have been left stranded.' He hadn't, but difficulties did crop up, mainly concerning a mammoth lottery with a car as first prize. Legal complications ruled out what would have been a big money-spinner and Boycott was rightly concerned. Benefits were becoming big business now that Yorkshire no longer controlled and invested any money that accrued, so a successful year could set a player up, providing scope to ensure the future.

Instead of being restricted to one match, subject to the vagaries of the weather, benefits stretched over twelve busy months, making claims on all the energies of the individual concerned, but Boycott had more demands on his time than most. He appreciated the value of money and was entitled to exploit the occasion to the full, yet his concern for the team limited his freedom. In the circumstances, he leaned on helpers a shade more than others and, therefore, lost sleep when he thought Parsons ready to withdraw his support.

As a quick settlement resolved the misunderstanding, it was impossible to see how Boycott could hope to profit from staying with Yorkshire. All the major events in his programme were planned and he was certain to upset more people than he pleased by limiting his activities to the county scene, thus losing support. Commonsense did not prevent the worst possible interpretation being put on the incident, but Boycott's next move made it crystal clear that money was not a prime consideration.

In September England were bracing themselves for a trip to Australia and the selectors demonstrated their flexibility by demoting Greig, giving the vice-captaincy to John Edrich and picking Boycott, who neglected to reply — a silly omission which hardly endeared him to the authorities. Finally, on October 24, he withdrew after another meeting with Bedser, who commented: 'It is basically the same problem we had in June. He does not want to subject himself to the pressures of Test cricket yet.'

There was, though, much more to it. The decision had ominous overtones, suggesting he had become disenchanted, like the willing worker on the shop floor who finds promotion barred by a disagreeable foreman or a remote management. His thoughts must have been a hotch-potch of half-formed plans and tantalising possibilities shaped into attractive but random patterns, like the bits of paper in a kaleidoscope.

There was the conviction that he had not been given a fair crack of the whip. 'There are various things which make it more difficult now for me to become stimulated by cricket, but I hope that after a rest during the winter things will improve', he said. 'I want to resolve my remaining problems and hope that the 1975 season will see me back to my best form. The authorities are obviously entirely satisfied that my personal reasons for withdrawing are good and sound.'

A well-kept secret was his mother's illness with a terminal condition that eventually brought about her death in 1978. Living with this knowledge imposed an additional strain on Boycott, who lost in the region of £5,000 through staying at home, much too sizable a sum to forego out of sheer bloody-mindedness, and not even the hatchet men chipping away at his reputation thought him so foolish as simply to sulk.

His replacement, Brian Luckhurst, of Kent, received an amazing tribute from Len Hutton, who, visiting Australia, said that the move would strengthen England's hand as Boycott was not seeing the ball as well as he had done four years earlier. Luckhurst, in his opinion, was the better player. There could be no more authoritative verdict, but did Hutton really intend to be taken literally? The kindest view is that he commented on the relative merits of Boycott and Luckhurst at that one specific instant, and then he flattered the latter.

Luckhurst took part in twenty-one Tests between 1970 and 1974, proving to be above average without making too big a mark on Boycott's yardstick, and Hutton's assessment was just one more stone hurled idly at a bowed head. A barrage of vicious abuse followed as Jeff Thomson and Dennis Lillee smashed brutally through England's bruised and broken batting with some sensationally hostile pace bowling. Thus Boycott had to withstand the taunt of cowardice out of sight of the enemy as a new Australian heroine emerged to push aside Waltzing Matilda. 'Lillian Thomson' was the girl who, in joke upon joke, chased the shaking Boycott in all manner of improbable and vulgar situations. Few stopped to recall how often Boycott had faced the fastest bowlers without flinching or noted when he made his decision to stay at home that Thomson was simply a name, a tearaway of threatening potential without any momentous deeds to his name, and there have been plenty of those in Australia. Although throughout the series of 1974—75 faint-heartedness was a handy peg on which to hang him, Boycott was still proving his enormous courage six years later to the embarrassment of such as Greig, bravely fighting it out with Andy Roberts, Joel Garner, Colin Croft and Michael Holding at forty.

The siege of Fitzwilliam on September 24 1974 turned into a one-day wonder. An army of television and newspaper men invaded the village in search of the inside story of his defection, and Boycott had plenty to say, dropping a gentle hint as to which way the wind was blowing.

'I just want to go quietly about the normal business of living. I shall be spending time at the nets, taking note of some of the promising youngsters who are the next generation of Yorkshire cricketers. I will not be coaching because Doug Padgett is doing a magnificent job in that direction, but I want to get to know these young boys so that if and when they reach the county side they will not be strangers. I have been able to see some light at the end of the tunnel and next summer I think we shall do well. There are five or six talented youngsters in the second team who have not been seen in the senior side.'

Boycott accepted that Yorkshire's poor record counted against him, being used as an excuse for keeping him out of the England captaincy, and he appreciated that prospects of bringing about the necessary improvement were slender unless he remained completely in charge. Neither Yorkshire nor England actually deserved his undivided attentions, but if he were to advantageously harness his own interests to a team cause, then the county offered the better chances. Only he could decide the next step. 'Geoff's next chance of Test cricket will be against the Australians after the World Cup next summer,' said Bedser, 'and if he wants to play then and is in form, he will be welcomed back.' As Boycott examined his options, though, his relationship with the TCCB became stretched almost to breaking point.

The strain was caused by the refusal of the Board to grant permission for a visit to South Africa with a private party sponsored by Derrick Robins, the Midlands-based cricket philanthropist. The announcement from Lord's was short and very straightforward. 'Geoff Boycott has asked for approval to play with the Robins' party. Following discussions involving senior officials of the Board and the chairman of selectors, Alec Bedser, in Australia, it was decided that this could not be given.' This ammunition was used in a cutting broadside when Bedser added that Boycott had not been ready to act as stand-by for Denness's beleaguered party 'down under' because 'of his wish not to play any cricket during the winter.'

The official reaction, while not perhaps capable of standing up to the scrutiny of the law, which later frowned so heavily on the TCCB during the World Series war, was reasonable, but Boycott also had an acceptable case. His protested innocence sounded more convincing then than later, when he had extended his rest from Tests, but the road on which he embarked was only partly of his own choosing. 'The invitation from Mr Robins came out of the blue,' he said. 'I had no idea of his intentions until I received a telephone call asking if I would be interested in going on the trip. Mr Robins said he thought it would help me prepare for the new season and that sounded sensible.

'The winter is virtually over now and, like all the other first-class cricketers, I am looking ahead. I have been training since January and I have had a few nets. Usually I go to South Africa each year at my own expense, so it seemed wise to accept the invitation. I have never had a request from Lord's about flying out to Australia as a replacement and I don't think it would have been proper for me to ask to go out. I genuinely did not feel well enough to go on the full official tour. The South African trip represented a good way of getting back to full fitness. It would not have been a strenuous tour.'

Boycott was less than pleased at being punished like some erring schoolboy kept in at playtime and, whatever the merits of the TCCB position, it hardened his attitude. England became less important in relation to Yorkshire, where he had many friends among the spectators. Popularity being as important as money to him, his benefit proved a double bonus, bringing a county record £20,639. 'This past year has been the biggest eye opener of my life,' he said. 'I have learned a lot about people — most of it good — and quite a bit about myself. Let's face it, people have been absolutely magnificent and if my fund had been only half as big I would still be grateful for the lessons which I have learned. There are always critics and I reckon I have more than my share. I try not to worry too much about that, but after a while it does start to get through.

'That is when you wonder just where you stand. I suppose I look rather cold and determined when I am batting, but that is not the whole Geoff Boycott. I'm as emotional as the next man and I can't say how much this demonstration of people's affections means to me. I have generally thought of myself as a people's player and most of my support comes from the grass roots, from those who really enjoy their cricket. Until last year I never realised just how many well-wishers I had. I hope we can win something for the Yorkshire

public next season and that I can give them something back
by playing my own part to the full.'

Therein lies the clue to his reason for turning his back on
England. He set his sights on making an impact in one area —
Yorkshire. What happened after that was largely beyond his
control, except in the narrowest playing terms. In order to
concentrate his energies, therefore, Boycott told Bedser that
he did not want to be considered again in the 1975 season,
hesitancy giving way to a clearly defined plan. 'I regard my
main task as that of leading Yorkshire back to cricket
supremacy and the next two summers are going to be important,' he said. 'For the first time in eighteen months I
have basically found peace and contentment. I am enjoying
my cricket and do not want to upset the welcome trend.
There is more to cricket than batting all day and getting runs.
I want to concentrate on developing the future of the game
in Yorkshire, where, I believe, I am best appreciated.'

At the same time, it did not seem he would have to do all
that well to persuade the worried selectors that he had a lot
to offer them, for Denness returned from Australia shell-
shocked and soon gave way to Greig. The South African's
nationality prevented universal acceptance, but he revealed
plenty of character in riding out the storm until seeing fit to
raise another himself as recruiting agent for Kerry Packer's
alternative organisation. Illingworth, a well-backed candidate
for a recall, delivered his verdict on the England captaincy:
'My own choice would have been Boycott, both because of
his qualities as a skipper which he has shown for Yorkshire
and because he is still one of the best batsmen in the world.'

With the sound of Illingworth's approval ringing in his ears,
Boycott whipped Yorkshire into shape and drove them to
second position in the Championship to make fools of his
detractors. Other individuals helped to sustain this fleeting
revival, as we shall discover, but it cannot be coincidence
that in the season he played most matches — eighteen out of
twenty in the Championship — Yorkshire enjoyed the best
placing since the title triumph of 1968. The extent to which
he dominated was underlined in 1976 when, as he stood
down injured from nine games, the side slipped and slithered
on the slopes of disillusionment. The strong hand of overseas

talent trumped Boycott's ace, exposed as it was by the absence of court cards from his pack.

During this unhappy season he began to think vaguely about returning to the England side. Yorkshire had not advanced as far as he expected and the lessons of 1975 did not seem to be appreciated everywhere. Although unhappy, however, he remained reluctant to admit he could do no more for the county and pride was an obstacle on the road back to the England camp.

He did not have a lot of time at his disposal, either, as Mike Brearley succeeded the disgraced Greig and England sorted through the debris of the Packer explosion, exhibiting an amazing aptitude for compromise that allowed the South African to keep his place in all five Tests. Brearley boasted no international pedigree, which raised doubts, and Bedser, facing up to the endless questions about Boycott's future, said: 'I am concerned with England's success and the selectors consider all players who are available. If Boycott tells us he has changed his mind then there is no possibility of his being ignored because of anything in the past. At the same time, I am not saying he would automatically be chosen. His form at the time would be the decisive factor.'

That declaration was made on May 14 1977, and within a couple of weeks Boycott telephoned Bedser, offering himself for selection on one condition. The very idea that he had the nerve to introduce provisos might give every MCC member apoplexy, but Boycott had nothing to lose by seeking to bargain.

He asked for an assurance that he would be considered on merit for the captaincy if Brearley did not make the grade. This was not forthcoming, so, although new lines of communication were established, nothing definite happened until the weekend of June 10, when the twelve for the Jubilee Test, which opened the series with Australia, were selected.

Boycott made no further moves and the subject was raised with Bedser, who said: 'Nothing has changed. Geoff has indicated that he does not want to play for England and until he changes his mind that is how it will stay.' Having been involved in a lengthy discussion with the chairman, I wrote an article in the *Yorkshire Evening Post*, pointing out that if the summer passed by without Boycott reappearing in the England ranks, it would virtually mean the end of his Test career as absence, in his case, definitely did not make hearts grow fonder.

Boycott immediately rang me to ask if Bedser had given any indication of how he would be received. 'I am not ashamed of anything I have done and I will not be made to feel the guilty party or anything like that', he said. 'As a senior England player I am entitled to some consideration.' I told him I had gained the distinct impression that Bedser would let bygones be bygones so far as his place as a batsman was concerned, but that he must expect some resistance. 'I am thinking it over,' added Boycott, 'but I will not stand for being messed about.'

Bedser, of course, could answer for nobody but himself, although as chairman he had more influence than anyone. There was also Brearley to take into account and he represented an unknown quantity in Boycott's case. It all came down to how much Boycott wanted to play again for England and before the Jubilee Test he telephoned Bedser to make himself unconditionally available. 'I have always tried to do my best for Yorkshire and England, but whatever action I take there are always those who will see something wrong,' he commented. 'I have to consider that Yorkshire are obviously weakened when Chris Old and myself do not play. That became clear last season. It is impossible to satisfy everyone, so I am content to do what I think is right.'

He received no guarantees, not even about his being selected, but that could be no more than a matter of time once he had set his mind to getting back as no other English batsman came within a mile of him for consistency or class. He had to wait until the third Test, filling in his time with a century off the tourists at Scarborough, where he was accused of being too keen to remind the selectors of his powers and not sufficiently interested in winning, but on a less than trustworthy pitch and following a first-innings collapse to 75 all out by Yorkshire, he was right to play safe. He showed up more forcefully against Somerset, adding a match-winning century at Nottinghamshire's expense for good measure, and he definitely did not kick Yorkshire when they were down or jump on the Test band-waggon because the county had crumbled around him.

They were unbeaten in fourteen first-class matches when their leading player was finally recalled by England on 24 July, having headed the county table on four occasions. His Championship average was 67.16, so the team were in very good health and began to feel out of sorts only when Boycott's selection had been announced. The Kent match at Folkestone brought their first defeat at the start of a dreadful run. Injury and illness were further handicaps as five out of six games were lost, yet it is important to realise that some players were disheartened, feeling that Boycott had turned his back on them to fight a personal battle. It does not matter whether this was the case or not, uncertainty was created as a consequence of the change in Boycott's circumstances.

These thoughts did him less than justice in the sense that he has never given below his best in any form of cricket, but his attention was again divided as he took up the task of proving himself with England. How much Boycott cared and how desperately he wanted to succeed when he eventually took part in the third Test at Trent Bridge can be gauged from his painfully slow, edgy innings. Attention to minute detail with every batting risk eliminated left him virtually stroke-less and a panic-stricken attempt to snatch a short single cut down Derek Randall with the contest evenly poised.

It was the sort of run that might reasonably have been attempted in the closing stages of a limited-overs game, with both batsmen 'set' in invisible starting blocks, or when supremacy had been impressed on weary, dispirited bowling and fielding. Coming with a Test-match innings in its infancy it broke one of Boycott's basic rules and took everyone by surprise, including his luckless partner. The blame could not be shifted. Boycott, to all intents and purposes, had taken leave of his senses as he pushed the ball gently to the right of bowler Jeff Thomson and set out on a suicidal mission.

It required an act of unhesitating generosity on Randall's part to give Boycott a chance to redeem himself. Had he paid the penalty of his folly, Boycott may have found himself out in the cold and he could see, in his mind's eye, his 'enemies' poised, ready to spring. He required another favour from the fates to confound them, for after inching along to 20 in three tortured hours, he gave a relatively straightforward catch to slip, where Rick McCosker put it down. By such slender threads our destinies hang!

There were no more errors, no further mistakes as Boycott compiled his crucial century — surpassed by Alan Knott (as England forged a winning advantage) — which gave him solid, statistical protection, transforming him from a crouching, miserable villain into a shining hero. The Trent Bridge crowd were ready to throw him in the river at lunchtime. Had they acted at the close the water would have parted to let him safely across.

Boycott's rehabilitation, confirmed by his second innings' 80 not out, was completed at his native Headingley, where he enthralled the nation by becoming the first batsman to score his one hundredth century in a Test. He stopped the daily routine in a million households around twenty past six as women with no more than a passing interest in sport put the tea back in the oven, stopped preparing dinner and left the washing-up to take care of itself; everywhere, families gathered around the television. Shop-window sets attracted pavement-blocking audiences as Boycott made the most extravagant fairy story a reality.

When he marched down the familiar pavilion steps a little before 11.30 on August 11, he had so hypnotised the cricketing world that people were ready to accept he had stage-managed the whole show, deliberately arriving in Leeds on ninety-nine hundreds.

His innings contained all the elements which had brought so much criticism down the years, yet this time selfishness was described as dedication. The gates slammed shut early on a packed, expectant crowd, whose nervousness conveyed itself in a roar of applause which greeted little more than a defensive push. It was released in a burst of emotion surpassing anything the old ground had experienced whenever Boycott pierced the field. Caught up in it, the human being inside the brittle shell of the run machine walked on air with unsteady legs at the close of play.

'I did not really think it possible, but they did,' he said,

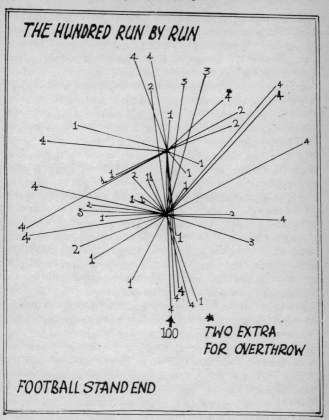

THE HUNDRED RUN BY RUN

TWO EXTRA FOR OVERTHROW

100

FOOTBALL STAND END

indicating through a window the milling throng on the field. 'They willed me to it. I have hardly slept, knowing that so much was expected of me and worrying in case I let so many people down. I know this, I bet the hall porter at the hotel is glad it's over, because I had him making tea all night.' He rested soundly enough with the record under his belt to return refreshed on the second day, when he squeezed the last drops of life out of the Australians by taking his score to 191 before being last out. Boycott had studiously stroked

47

England into an invincible position which was his broader aim. 'Test matches are won by long innings, not brief, hard-hitting ones, however spectacular they may seem,' he said. 'I reckon that if I can bat for a day and a half and make a big hundred that is half the battle. You have to work on the basis that a Test lasts five days, so there is no need to take risks. Too many batsmen can't maintain their concentration over a long enough period. They want to play all their shots. That is nice. Contrary to the many things written about me, I enjoy putting the ball away to the boundary and knowing that I have hit a fine stroke, but I try to select the right ball, thus giving the bowler less of a chance. My 191 and England's 436 here meant that unless Australia did something truly in-credible, or we suddenly went crazy, we were safe and that is part of the job completed.

'Psychologically, the other side feel the pressure of having to save the match. On a lesser scale county games are just the same, although the limit on the first innings complicates matters. Even so, I try to use the hundred overs to the full and that sometimes means employing extra care in the opening session which is not often understood.'

The selectors' script thereafter drifted into the realms of Agatha Christie, who had a practised hand in the fabrication of red-herrings and the mystery surrounding Brearley's under-study grew. Clues as to what would happen if the captain were to be injured took some finding. 'Wait and see,' said the official|voice, but Boycott had done enough to be given the vice-captaincy for the visit to Pakistan and New Zealand. Virtue gained reward and Boycott undertook his duties enthusiastically, although he had to be careful lest he trod on Brearley's toes, for the dangers of being misunderstood were apparent.

. Having been dismissed for 2 and 8 at Rawalpindi while still in the process of acclimatisation, however, Boycott set about getting the necessary practice in earnest, developing a love-hate relationship with his colleagues which counted against him in the long term. Among the tourists his determination to apply himself as much as possible out in the middle was not readily appreciated.

He batted solidly through for 123 not out against the

United Bank and 115 not out against the North-West Frontier Governor's eleven, so that he emerged better prepared than anyone from the preliminary skirmishes, compounding the felony by filling one place throughout a practice session on Christmas Eve at the Lahore Gymkhana. His mania for occupying the crease began to get on everybody's nerves. The rest of the party were, however, grateful for a teach-in Boycott provided on how to deal with leg-spinner Abdul Qadir, who took six for 44 in the second Test which England drew thanks to Boycott's 79 in the first innings, when he was run out, and 100 not out in the second. Since only Brian Rose and the obdurate Geoff Cope got beyond 20 in a timid reply to Pakistan's 275, Boycott could be said to have proved a point.

The third Test in Karachi brought the realisation of his great dream, for he became captain because Brearley's left arm had been broken in a meaningless one-day exercise against Sind. Boycott's delight at reaching this pinnacle was, therefore, tempered by sympathy for his comrade in arms and by the knowledge that political trouble hovered in the wings. Pakistan toyed with the idea of including their Packer men, Mushtaq Mohammad, Zaheer Abbas and Imran Khan, who had been released for this purpose, but the England camp objected so strongly that the possibility of a walk-out arose.

Boycott's place was at the head of this stand, but Greig, completely involved with World Series, condemned from afar, screaming: 'This is the work of Boycott and his cronies. Boycott has put the team up to this.' In fact, the England players showed consistently that they had no time for the pirate circus. They saw it as a threat to their livelihood, the few benefiting at the expense of the many, and a statement to which they all agreed read: 'The English touring team are unanimously opposed in principle to players contracted to World Series cricket being considered for selection for official International Cricket Conference Test matches.' Brearley, his broken arm in plaster, made it clear in defending Boycott that this genuinely represented the collective opinion.

If the acting captain had been greedy in the nets in Pakistan, he did his best to make amends on landing in New Zealand, standing down from the three-day fixture with Central

Districts in New Plymouth because he was worried about the batting. The gesture had little effect, but all the specialists got an extra opportunity and Boycott deserves credit for that. He had begun with a draw in Pakistan and when he got to Wellington for the first Test against New Zealand he boldly elected to field on winning the toss. How much England's first defeat at the hands of the Kiwis in forty-eight Tests reflected this act we shall never know, but two claims can be made.

Although a gale complicated the bowlers' lives, the move had been contemplated by New Zealand as well and John Wright, whose 55 made all the difference to the result in a low-scoring encounter, profited from a first-ball escape. England appealed jubilantly but in vain for a catch at the wicket and Bob Willis, the bowler, allowing his annoyance to affect his length, dropping wastefully short. Leading from the front, Boycott spent seven and a half hours over 77, and England were eventually set 137 to win. They scraped together 64 of them!

Once Boycott had been bowled off his pads for 5, the resistance bordered on the inept. Sadly he admitted: 'Any side that can't make 137 runs in the fourth innings can't expect to win,' and he called a lengthy team meeting to talk about technique. He could think of no easy way to reverse the batting failures. 'You can't change the way people play,' he said. 'You can only encourage them to play in their own way to the best of their ability and be there to offer advice if it is wanted. Every batsman struggled to make runs on the Wellington pitch. I made my 77 and John Wright his 55 because we had the character and the defensive qualities to accumulate runs. There was criticism of my slow play, but I know about cricket if nothing else and if some of the other batsmen had been content to wait for the runs, the outcome might have been different.'

He was thought too harsh and some players resented his words, but he brought about an improvement which salvaged something from this dreadful wreckage, indicating that if not entirely correct, he was not exactly wrong either. Some carping followed Boycott's decision to extend England's innings to the bitter end in the second Test, but the 418 to

which Ian Botham contributed his first century for England
turned out to be a match-winning platform and dull equality
in the 'decider' left Boycott with a record of one win, one
defeat and two draws.

The pundits enjoyed speculating during the spring of 1978,
promoting first Boycott and then Brearley as captain for the
return series against the winter's opponents. The principals,
pressed at every turn to join in the daily guessing game,
declined and Bedser put an end to the fun in May, travelling
up to Edgbaston where Yorkshire were playing Warwickshire.
He carried the news that everyone really expected and
Brearley, now he had recovered full fitness, was restored.

The chairman confessed he had 'little liking' for the delicate
mission, but Boycott's reaction pleased him, taking the
embarrassment out of the job. 'I did not relish having to
break the news to Geoff,' he said. 'It is never easy to tell a
man something like this especially when you know how
much the England captaincy means to him.

'I have to say, however, that he was absolutely magnificent.
He took it marvellously well, although obviously disappointed,
and said straight away that he would give Mike his full
support. We could hardly have taken any other course. Mike
won the Ashes last summer, losing the captaincy only when
he was hurt. It is a good thing to have two men of this calibre
for the captaincy.'

Boycott never came so close to the game's highest honour
again, being deposed as England vice-captain shortly before
Yorkshire reduced him to the ranks. He felt unfairly treated,
but stayed calm, clinging to hope where none really existed.
He remembered Greig's loss of the vice-captaincy and subsequent elevation to the top job, adding: 'I don't know of
anything I have done wrong, so perhaps I will be considered
again, you never know.' As he fell, the irrepressible Botham
soared past him on the way up, receiving promotion with a
place on the tour committee in Australia in the winter of
1979—80 ahead of a man making his fourth visit. Boycott
was an England player almost ten years before Botham's
debut for Somerset in a first-class fixture and the burly all-
rounder had not been tried as county captain when elevated
above the country's senior professional.

It strained credulity. Boycott fitted in as a reasonably happy tourist, despite odd brushes with Brearley via the Press and his inner turmoil as he pondered over Yorkshire's two-year contract in the winter of 1978.

Any number of reasons were put forward for his tour demotion. According to hearsay, he had publicly slighted assistant manager Barrington, offended high-ranking officials in Pakistan and New Zealand and upset his team-mates by asking too much and giving too little, yet if Bedser is to be taken at face value, he ended his four-Test reign as captain in credit. Bedser did not have to make that journey to Birmingham in May 1978, nor to go out of his way to praise Boycott, so the chairman's words must be taken into serious consideration as an honest and accurate representation of his opinion and we are left to wonder what went wrong.

Why did Geoff Miller get the vice-captaincy as a stop-gap in the West Indies in 1981 when the Derbyshire all-rounder, whose place on the tour had been far from assured, had minimal Test claims?

Was it, as Yorkshire thought, because Boycott remained 'too wrapped up in his own performance?' His county colleagues, under manager Illingworth and captains Hampshire and Old, tended to disprove that theory by achieving worse results without him, while he gained regular selection for England from the day he made his come-back at Nottingham, so he must have satisfied the selectors and Brearley, Botham and Fletcher, whose voices helped shape the teams they led.

Boycott did feel frustrated when his advice seemed surplus to requirements, which was the case in Australia, where Brearley did not consult him as often as he expected, and on the 1979—80 trip newspapers quickly noted the opportunity for eye-catching stories, exaggerating the gulf between the two. Boycott, they claimed, was 'fed up' and made too much of slight injuries. Brearley responded icily: 'Geoff and I have a perfectly good professional relationship. It really is extraordinary how anything to do with him is inflated out of all proportion.'

His brief and passing experience of the phenomenon left its mark, but Boycott lived with it constantly, having no chance to escape into even temporary obscurity. Headlines shadowed his every move so that he had only to sneeze to start a major flu alert.

As he departed with England for the Caribbean in the January of 1981 under Botham, Boycott was pressed into an interview at the request of manager Alan Smith and ran into trouble when he said, without rancour, that the captain rarely sought his advice. This came in reply to a question he would have avoided but for Smith's intervention on behalf of television and it was more than unfortunate that he had to suffer criticism.

In the autumn of that year his was the name the political opportunists used for their racially based attack that almost wrecked England's tour of India under Keith Fletcher. Boycott's association with South Africa might be distant and tenuous, but his fame brought the apartheid question into sharper focus and he figured on the United Nations backed black-list as much because of who he was as what he had done. As Mrs Indira Gandhi delayed a final decision on whether he and Geoff Cook of Northamptonshire, would be admitted, the banners in the popular Press screamed: 'It's up to Boycott.' Not 'It's up to England' or 'It's up to Boycott and Cook.' Only one man drew instant attention to the situation which, as Brearley observed, was remarkable.

So was the outcry which followed his return from India through ill health, an occurrence which belatedly underlined the sense of his earlier refusals to visit that part of the world. A recuperative trip to a golf course when England were going through the ritual of playing out a draw in the Calcutta Test suddenly became a betrayal, even though, up to the point of falling ill, Boycott had, as ever, led the way in applying himself to the job in hand. His years as a model tourist, using up hour upon hour in relentless practice, counted for nothing as the cry of desertion went up.

'He was not seeing things straight,' said manager Raman Subba Row, while insisting that no disciplinary action had been taken, but Boycott's Test average of 44.57 together with the top aggregate, indicated that he saw things straighter than any of those who were upset by his action. Boycott, although seeing nothing wrong with taking gentle exercise after three days in bed — he wandered around a few holes at the golf course and did not play a round — apologised, but another brick settled firmly into place on the barrier which separated him from the others.

His isolation — mental and physical — stemmed from the ever-present suspicion that his efforts were not appreciated, that his best would never be good enough, and he was rightly upset when newspapers arrived from England proclaiming that Fletcher had ordered him to get a move on. The captain immediately said he was sorry and that his comments had been misunderstood, but the hurt had been inflicted.

It is, however, wrong to label Boycott a bad tourist. Bedser, as a tour manager, reckoned his attitude 'just about right,' adding: 'There are occasions when he gets a bit depressed and is inclined to flare up.' Boycott's insistence on sticking to the truth even when unpleasant may, therefore, be marked down as an on-going mistake.

After Illingworth, the last outstanding England leader, there has been a captain who wanted to make the West Indies grovel, a captain who hummed classical music, a captain who threatened to see heads roll and two captains who got into the team on the grounds that they had special qualities of leadership. In that company, a captain with his mind on avoiding defeat at all costs and winning if possible, risking bruising a few egos in the process, could have held his head as high as his standards.

As an England cricketer, Boycott expects five-star treatment and is ready to be awkward if it is not forthcoming. In the old days amateurs from the upper strata of society adopted similar stances without disturbing the smooth rhythm of life. The son of a miner from an obscure village in Yorkshire was permitted no such liberties.

His consolation came from his batting and the records duly fell. 'I have not made a habit of thinking about them, but it is nice to do something like this,' he admitted after overtaking Colin Cowdrey as England's top scorer at Old Trafford in 1981. 'I have always thought that if I kept my form and played long enough the runs would look after themselves.' He might have added that his career should have looked after itself as well, but it never did, although he went on to overtake Sobers at the head of the world's list of Test run-makers.

3 Uneasy Inheritance

The matching millstones of a glorious tradition and inadequate playing resources were to hang around Boycott's neck throughout his term as Yorkshire captain, adding to his problems because they were so rarely appreciated. The enormously impressive past contained an unrivalled number of Championship triumphs, and the county's nurseries, places such as Pudsey, Farsley, Kirkheaton and Lascelles Hall, were famous throughout the world. There have been many eras in which Yorkshire would cheerfully have tackled any Test team without fearing defeat, and their massive representation in cricket's Hall of Fame gave rise to the assumption that the Broad Acres endlessly produced sides of exceptional merit.

The unshakable faith in a divine right to win was, therefore, widely held and what might otherwise have been a harmless exercise in self-deception put an unrealistic burden of blame on Boycott when he found himself unable to turn the tide of events which was sweeping his team into the depths of despair.

The popular line was based on the county's dominance for more than a decade, with the Championship being won six times in the 1960s and the Gillette Cup captured twice for good measure. The lean years between 1949 and 1959 were forgotten. The breaking up of a truly great side as early as 1968 and its disintegration in more ways than one by the time Boycott assumed command were ignored.

Everyone is entitled to an opinion, but Boycott deserves the courtesy of the facts. The loss of Illingworth, Fred Trueman and Taylor in 1968, followed by Jimmy Binks in

1969 and Close in 1970 was crippling. They had over a century of Test 'caps' to their credit and it proved impossible to replace their battle-hardened qualities. However Yorkshire manipulated their senior squad, boys took over from men in a playing sense.

The side-effects were as deadly if less immediately apparent, so although the built-in professionalism and instinct for survival held things together for a while, the consequences were waiting just around the corner. The angry manner of Illingworth's departure and the badly-timed sacking of Close did far more than deny Yorkshire the skills of two out-standing all-rounders. These separate yet inter-linked actions created anger among the public and confusion generally, so that in some cases a sense of direction was lost. Many people pondered on the way two magnificent servants had been lost to the county and wondered what might happen next.

Illingworth asked for his release because the county were not prepared to offer a contract and, in challenging the status quo, he represented the broad view of all the players.

Yorkshire had traded profitably for more than one hundred years on the passionate desire of almost every boy to qualify for the dark blue cap with the proud white rose, an artificial contrivance bearing eleven petals, one for each member of the team. They demanded and received willing, unthinking devotion. Illingworth's voice cried anarchy in their ears. At the same time he negotiated from a position of strength, for, without regularly attracting the biggest headlines as either batsman or bowler, he quietly established himself as one of — if not *the* — best day-in-day-out county cricketers since the war. His figures were impressive — 14,829 runs for an average of 28.46 and 1,390 wickets at a cost of 18.17 runs each — and he earned them the hard way, proving time and time again to be at his most resourceful when the going was next to impossible.

Yorkshire took no account of this, indicating that when he went he could take with him anyone else who was not satisfied. That, more than anything Boycott did or did not do, brought about the unwelcome Dark Age. Speaking at the heart of an improving and grateful Leicestershire, Illingworth pointed the finger. 'Looking back on my years as a player with

Yorkshire, I feel bitter about certain individuals,' he said. 'I would be lying if I did not admit this. The way we were treated and things like that were not good.'

Bitterness existed in other hearts, too, which though not given publicity, smouldered and burned, and the younger players sometimes found it hard to cope with public expectations in the prevailing atmosphere. Other counties would have recognised the symptoms, having lived with them for many years before finding a cure in the importing from overseas of ready-made remedies. Yorkshire were both patient and doctor, unable to cope with the illness, unwilling to prescribe the most drastic medicine.

The lack of rapport between the committee and its employees was emphasised by Illingworth after he had extended his career far beyond his most ambitious hopes as captain of Leicestershire and England. Retracing the path which had led him to Grace Road, he said: 'I knew, even in my best years, that one or two fools on the committee were still wanting to play Geoff Cope instead of me. I faced the secretary with it man to man, but he would not admit it. I probably started the movement towards more progressive thinking, for by my going and one or two others leaving, they suddenly found themselves in the cart.

'I probably made things more right for Yorkshire than they have ever been. Now they haven't got a side to go with it.' No mention of Boycott there, just a down-to-earth assessment of the position. 'They haven't got a side.' As Illingworth saw it, Boycott faced a long, uphill haul.

There was dramatic confirmation in the drop from first to twelfth, Yorkshire's lowest placing in the Championship, in 1969, although too few took notice of this unpleasant evidence, preferring the illusion, created by victory over Derbyshire in a sub-standard Gillette Cup final, that all would soon be well again. There was something to look forward to in the development of Chris Old as a dangerous fast-medium bowler, so people were happy to sit back and wait for the best of the ten Colts who figured in that summer to emerge as fully-fledged cricketers capable of filling the gaps on a permanent basis.

Knowing smiles appeared as Yorkshire managed something

of a revival in 1970, climbing to fourth in the Championship, but they were near the bottom of the Sunday League and had been hurried out of the Gillette Cup amidst flurries of snowflakes at Harrogate in April. These signs of cracks in the foundations of a once strongly-based first team prompted Close to express his fears. 'The source of young blood in Yorkshire has dried up and to a large extent I blame the leagues,' he said.

'Almost every league is playing limited-over cricket, which is as different from first-class cricket as chalk from cheese. I find that when we get youngsters in the county side because of Test calls and injuries the first thing we have to do is teach them to think, because in league cricket a batsman can be starved out.' Close had come to this conclusion with a comparatively settled and experienced group of players around him. Boycott gained command in a much worse position. Close's was a familiar theme, but a fair comment nonetheless and one that echoed ominously as Boycott struggled to fashion success from very ordinary raw material.

Standards in local cricket definitely declined, with few specialists coming forward among the bowlers as the excess of pace and spin steadily gave way to defensive medium-pace and the pot-hunting mentality. Yorkshire, in relying exclusively on home-grown talent and denying themselves access to the 'transfer market', were at a disadvantage. Illingworth, on his return to the club as team manager in April 1979, made efforts to harness the production line more effectively only to run into a stonewall.

Close's opinion, important as a guide to the resources at Boycott's disposal, was significant from his own point of view as well, for he had hardly got the words out of his mouth when Yorkshire sacked him in the most startling of upheavals.

They gave his often expressed dislike of limited-over cricket as their reason, but it was a thin excuse at best, and none of the senior players had anything other than contempt for the Sunday League, which, despite bringing in badly needed money, never earned respectability among the participants. No one, therefore, set much store by the official statement, which dressed up as tidily as possible the brutal fact that Close, after twenty-two years, got a few hours to choose between resigning and being sacked. In preferring the latter he displayed more character than many of those running the county's affairs and angry reaction inevitably followed.

The depth of feeling must have shaken the committee as the wind of change rattled the windows and hammered at the doors of Headingley. A Yorkshire County Cricket Club Action Group was formed, causing a lot of embarrassment, while the subsequent weakening of resolve within the club substantially affected Boycott's prospects.

Close's salary was paid up to 31 March 1972, which gave him breathing space, but Yorkshire's timing looked thoughtless to say the least, giving rise to conjecture. Admittedly in mid-September Close, who had been worried by a damaged shoulder, talked about retirement, but by then, according to custom, he had been retained for another year.

His depression resulted from the aches, pains and strains of the season and, after his dismissal, he quickly asserted that he had been looking forward to another two or three years as captain. Like Illingworth, he also went on to do a job for his country although rejected by his county.

If Yorkshire were merely unhappy with his indifference towards the one-day game, why did they not take action sooner? Why wait until the replacement had flown to Australia? These questions together with the attendant arguments were a source of acute concern to Boycott, who, 12,000 miles away, was the key batsman in Illingworth's line-up as England steadily ground out an Ashes victory. As the new captain he could do no more than hope everything would be sorted out by the time he returned home, spending some of his spare time wishing he could have achieved one of his major objectives in pleasanter circumstances. He was too emotionally involved with Yorkshire cricket not to be lifted by his appointment, but too much of a realist not to be familiar with the problems.

Not least of these centred on Sharpe's position, as the stocky batsman stood senior in all but ability, having earned a cap in 1960 and filled in as official vice-captain in 1970. This was a weighty consideration, his appointment being a complete break with normal practice.

Yorkshire had not had a vice-captain since 1932, when Brian Sellers served under Frank Greenwood and, whenever necessary, the senior professional deputised, Binks having stood in for Close in 1969. The wicket-keeper's departure left Doug Padgett as senior professional and the committee did not even take the trouble to inform him of their decision. 'The first I heard about it was when I was stopped by a man in the street,' he said. 'I do think the committee might have given me a telephone call to put me in the picture. It appears that Phil is being given the experience so that he can take over the captaincy at some time. My main disappointment is the committee's attitude in not telling me themselves.' Yorkshire secretary John Nash explained: 'The committee now believe that somebody should be designated to do the job so that there are no doubts.'

Sharpe then must have thought he was being groomed as Close's successor as he led the team in six of their twenty-four Championship matches in 1970, with Boycott playing under him, his record being three wins, two defeats and one draw. There was nothing wrong with that, so nobody could follow the thinking when Yorkshire overlooked him for the top job and dismissed him from the minor role, which went to Don Wilson, who was also touring with Illingworth.

Sharpe accepted the rebuff with typical fortitude. 'Good luck to him. I'll give him all the support I can.' It was, however, a blow to his pride, consigning him to a kind of limbo, and speculation increased when it became clear that Boycott had not been a unanimous choice. Wilson, it transpired, had his share of support.

Good will appeared to be in short supply, with too little thought being given to the club's well-being on the field, and it would have taken leadership of the most dynamic kind to immediately solve all the problems.

In this respect both Yorkshire and Boycott were unlucky. The activities of the Action Group appeared to unnerve the committee, with nobody prepared to risk rocking the boat. After being so nearly sunk in a storm of their own making, they wanted a trouble-free passage. One consequence of the turmoil was the resignation of Sellers as chairman of the cricket sub-committee.

After ruling his players with the proverbial rod of iron during fifteen years as captain, Sellers continued to be entirely his own man when taking higher office, leaving himself open to the charge of assuming too much power. His readiness to forge and implement policy was not in itself a bad thing with a large and unwieldy committee at his back, but the day of reckoning had to be faced over Close and Illingworth and, in keeping with his gutsy reputation, he offered himself up for sacrifice to the Action Group, thus saving other faces. Two new men came into positions of central authority at the same time, therefore, John Temple becoming cricket chairman to team up with Boycott. A different man to Sellers entirely and lacking the standing which automatically went with a notable playing background, Temple saw himself as a pacifier, using persuasion rather than force and he obviously had a tricky path to tread.

Yorkshire could not afford any more disturbance with their whole operation coming apart at the seams. The team was doing badly, the committee were under fire and the finances were in poor shape, 1970 having been the most disastrous year in their history with a deficit of £8,109. Strong men trembled, the weaker fainted away, and the committee cannot escape responsibility for the circumstances in which Boycott began the task of restoring the club to its former eminence. Those with the best interest of Yorkshire cricket at heart ought to have been more vigilant and positive in embarking on a weeding out process. They, not Boycott, had the means.

What he wanted most of all was a right-hand man and a word here and there of appreciation from other than the youngsters, who would look up to him anyway. Having to rely so much on himself, he sought eagerly for a reliable 'sounding board' for his ideas, a thinking cricketer equal off whom he could bounce his thoughts. One was provided by Lester, by then scorer to the first team, whose experience as a hard-hitting middle-order batsman shortly after the war and as second-team captain equipped him to offer welcome advice. Lester, however, carried no real weight and Yorkshire ought to have given him greater authority by making him team manager if the committee could not find the time to turn up home and away to assist with the running of the side. Often correct in his judgments and in the guessing game which is part and parcel of being captain, Lester never pressed his point because he acted unofficially and in not making further use of him the county committed another mistake. Lester could have ensured the necessary continuity during Boycott's Test absences, but the chance was missed, even though he continued as a confidant, an old head full of wisdom with knowing eyes that picked out the odd things so easily missed on the field.

Boycott did not allow the war raging on the home front to become a distraction, preparing himself by batting with a brilliance that put him firmly at the head of any world list. A superb Test record contained 657 runs for an average of 93.85, while he piled up 1,535 runs in all matches — eighteen short of Wally Hammond's total, which was the best by an Englishman in Australia — before disaster struck. Australian pace bowler Graham McKenzie hit him in a limited-over game in Sydney on February 8, breaking his arm. It was a sickening blow to Illingworth with the series still in the balance and to Yorkshire, who were short of good news, but most of all to Boycott, who arrived home less than two weeks later with his arm in plaster and his aspirations in the melting pot.

As if he and the county were not under a big enough handicap already, the prospect of his missing the early weeks of the season loomed large. Boycott made the best of a bad business. 'I kept my mind on the important job of playing for England while in Australia, but now I can give all my time to Yorkshire,' he said en route north to meet the committee and put forward one or two points which included a note of caution.

With nothing to be gained from promising too much too soon, Boycott measured his words carefully during his address at the pre-season luncheon. 'It would be easy for me to say we will win a trophy, but all we can do is to play positive cricket,' he said.

'We hope to be one of the best fielding sides in the game and will try one hundred per cent because nothing else is worthwhile.' Illingworth also preferred to wait and see. On his return from the New Zealand leg of his winter journey he said Boycott should do well, adding, though, that he had personality problems to overcome, and it was in the tricky area of human relationships that Boycott faced an immediate test.

The pattern for the 1971 season was set in the first two weeks. Yorkshire made the most miserable of starts and failed to bring about a recovery, while Boycott's inspiring debut as captain acted as the prelude to his best summer as a batsman. Suggestions that individual honour came at great cost to Yorkshire gained substance from well-known and supposedly informed commentators, but were nonsense.

Boycott at once found himself picking up the pieces of an innings defeat in the opening Championship fixture with Kent at Bradford, where he must have been tempted to deliver a stern reprimand about the feeble way in which Yorkshire simply gave up the ghost. The question of the poorest eleven to represent the county at first-class level would generate as much heat as the often indulged pastime of naming the best, but in May that year the one which faced the reigning champions had obvious claims. It was: Sharpe, Woodford, Padgett, Hampshire, Dalton, Hutton, Old, Bairstow, Cope, Wilson and Bore.

Boycott was still recovering from his broken arm, Barrie Leadbeater had cracked a bone in his hand, and a strained leg tendon forced Tony Nicholson to rest, but, after making generous allowance, Yorkshire's surrender, total and abject, brought shame on the county. Their most devoted apologist found nothing to comfort him as Kent won with humiliating ease. Under close scrutiny, Wilson's leadership did not emerge from the wreckage too well. His tactics had to take account of a miserable first-innings score of 93, but he fell onto the defensive too easily, yielding the initiative when his one hope lay in counter-attack. While Kent applied persistent pressure with seven close catchers for Derek Underwood, Yorkshire's concern centred rather on saving runs. No Underwood lurked in their ranks, although Mike Bore was to try and imitate his style, but bowlers need the backing of the captain if they are to go all out in the quest for wickets, so Wilson's emphasis on economy was misplaced.

Boycott, the frustrated spectator, made a note of this,

recognising the case for a considered balance between attack and defence and rarely had his handling of matters in the field queried. A dreadful attendance, mocking the brilliant sunshine, warned the club of general unrest.

On the Saturday only 526 paying customers supplemented the gathering of members, while receipts amounted to a miserly £245. Boycott, the major attraction and the outstanding player, reacted swiftly, hurrying back to action sooner than had been imagined and possibly before it was wise, his action governed by the most honourable of motives. He ran the risk of failure with his arm not quite right, but he chose to lead by example, which makes it all the more a pity that his calculated risk was soon forgotten, along with the grandeur of his dashing stroke-play.

The irony is that, in the final analysis, Boycott's feat of averaging over 100 in 1971 became a plank in the case against him. The magnitude of the achievement really put it outside the normal scope of discussion. It was the subject of admiration by ninety per cent of the cricket-watching public, and rightly so, for only the legendary Don Bradman and, completely artificially, another Australian, Bill Johnston, previously completed an English season with a three-figure return. Johnston scored 102 runs to average 102, contriving to be not out in sixteen of his seventeen innings on the 1953 tour, but Boycott battled through the dangers of thirty innings, scoring 2,503 runs — 74 more than Bradman, who, however, had the better average, 115.66 to 100.12.

Those who devalued Boycott's performance used not only his neatly-timed declaration against Northamptonshire at Harrogate but also the overall pattern of his batting to denigrate him.

Boycott was censured in many an after-dinner speech for devoting the season to this one act of self-fulfilment and it all sounded so convincing with the wine drowning memory as well as sorrows and the cigar smoke clouding the issue. It was a long, long time between May and the winter months.

He made a most forceful entrance in the second Championship fixture, conjuring up out of thin air a three-wicket victory over Warwickshire at Middlesborough. The Acklam Park pitch was in its most benign mood and Warwickshire missed pace bowler David Brown, who had been injured in the first innings, yet Yorkshire's last-day requirement of 267 runs in 170 minutes appeared excessive. Without Boycott it would have been impossible.

At ease and yet fiercely demanding, he strolled to fifty in an hour, going on to his century with a savagely struck six in one hundred minutes. He stood at the crease driving, pulling and hooking, giving not the semblance of a chance and refusing to allow even the slightest restraint. Helpless and weary, the bowling degenerated into insignificance and the fielders dispersed in a far-flung circle around the boundary.

Boycott's share of 161 amounted to 110 when he heaved a catch to deep square-leg in pursuit of another six and he left behind a sense of gleeful anticipation of further pleasures to come as Yorkshire collected the points. No innings ever served a team's needs better and he wisely grabbed the chance to make his position clear. 'My instructions from previous captains have been to give the innings a start,' he said as the dressing room rocked gently in tune with the celebrations. 'Now I feel I have to give an example to the rest of the lads. If they see me poking about they might think it is difficult. I may get out occasionally, but I think I will serve the team better by playing the innings the tactical situation requires. I would like to think, for instance, that I helped John Woodford to play so well here.'

The uncapped batsman from Little Horton shared the honours with a century of his own that day and obviously everyone benefited if Boycott continued to operate with such ringing assurance.

The normally astute Brearley must not have noticed this, for he then set Yorkshire 212 runs in three hours in the Middlesex game at Headingley, which presented no problems, Hampshire being Boycott's companion in a spendid entertainment. Invited to double the scoring rate in an otherwise drab contest, they cantered home with five overs and eight wickets to spare, the captain setting the pace and shaping the twin endeavour.

What could not be despatched powerfully was steered carefully. Middlesex had no opportunity to break the partnership, with not a single mis-hit in evidence, while the running

between the wickets rewarded complete trust and understanding. It was a brief and tantalising glimpse of all that
might be, assuming a willingness on all sides to give and take.
This meant that Boycott would have to be tolerant of weakness in others, who, in turn, had to turn a blind eye when he
reacted badly to set-backs. Neither party proved sufficiently
adaptable to make it a workable arrangement, however.

Even so, Boycott generously stood down from the un-
demanding friendly with Oxford University, explaining: 'I
want the others to get some practice. My arm aches a bit, but
it's all right really and I would like to continue with the run of
good form I have found. It's more important, though, for
some others to get that sort of advantage at this stage.' So
they did, with runs coming in profusion from poor bowling
in an exercise that admirably served its purpose as well as
bringing victory by an innings and 177 runs.

By the end of May, therefore, Yorkshire were by no means
in bad shape. They had won two and drawn two of their five
Championship engagements and, if the Sunday League form
was still a bit wobbly, things had improved.

Boycott's work in the field also brought him some merit
marks from the more thoughtful observers as attention to
detail paid dividends. 'I have always tried to put myself in the
captain's position whenever I have played, right from the
start when I was just a schoolboy playing with men much
older,' he said. 'That is the way I believe you learn. There
were times in the early days when the captain would do
something and I would not understand and perhaps think he
was wrong. That's when I really watched and worked out the
whys and wherefores, because not even the good, sound ideas
always come off, and it is a mistake to judge only by results.
The higher up the ladder I got the more subtle the lessons
were, yet they were there just the same, and now I have
become captain myself I try to get my team to put forward
their ideas.'

This steady application, plus his cultivated eye for what
opponents favoured and could and could not do, enabled him
to work out a sensible containing policy in the limited-over
matches, and while Yorkshire remained anchored in the
bottom half of the Sunday League table they generally kept

the other side's innings within reasonable bounds. Boycott could and should have had his genius fitted into the collective framework and failure in this respect is not his alone. Yorkshire hovered on the brink of prosperity so long as he held the reins, but as soon as he let go the steering faltered.

Unfortunately things did not run smoothly, for by some strange, bewildering thought processes some senior players decided that he was not doing the job properly, or, more accurately, to their gratification. They did not define their grievance exactly, but broadly it related to his supposed self-interest.

Boycott, at the same time, could not avoid the wrong sort of publicity, although initially the victim of a cynical declaration by Derbyshire's Buxton at Chesterfield. After the second day had been lost to rain and the start of the last further delayed, Buxton called a halt to Derbyshire's first innings at 82 for five, following on to deny Yorkshire bowling bonus points. A loudspeaker announcement cleared up the confusion for a small band of spectators as the match drifted to a farcical conclusion, but the incident drew attention to a loophole in the system, leaving Boycott feeling cheated and wondering about the repercussions had the roles been reversed.

Shrewdly he withheld comment, but he was less prudent at Old Trafford during the Roses clash, getting into trouble for talking too freely. A major incident blew up out of a casual conversation on the first day, overshadowing the actual contest, which ended in a muddling draw after Boycott had been taken ill.

Lancashire were bowled out for 168, to which Yorkshire replied with 43 for 2 in two hours off thirty-two overs. Boycott, in company with many Yorkshiremen, thought that Peter Lever and Ken Shuttleworth expended their energies unfairly wide of the stumps and said so, duly appearing in the headlines next day. Part of a captain's job is to make himself available to the Press and Boycott had been the subject of enough attention to know the rules of this particular 'game'. The furore could not have been entirely unexpected and he was careless in allowing himself to be taken off guard. 'Representatives of the Press came to ask me about the run-out incidents in which I have been involved during the last few matches,' he said as the inter-county row broke about his head, with Lancashire demanding a retraction. 'I explained this, but then, completely unofficially and talking about the game as a matter of interest, I made reference to the Lancashire bowling, which other people, like me, thought ill directed. I am sorry opinions meant to be off the record have been published, embarrassing Lancashire and two of my England colleagues.'

The Achilles heel! Boycott had been run out on that same day by Clive Lloyd as he tried to combat the negative bowling by stealing a dangerous single to ease the tension that builds around a stationary scoreboard, his wicket being Lancashire's justification.

He was also run-out in an earlier match against Middlesex in the first innings, but another weakness — the tendency to say too much and to trust the wrong people — did him more harm. Lancashire chairman Cedric Rhoades rightly expressed annoyance, yet he gave sound advice. 'Geoff will have to learn what to say and when to say it.' As thick, yellowing files in a thousand newspaper offices around the world testify, Boycott struggled to deal with the less than scrupulous side of the media in which there are journalists well aware that his name makes news and underwrites extravagant expenses. Many of the stories which earned him his notoriety followed off-the-cuff remarks or confidential asides and if his critics had suffered from similar goldfish-bowl pressures, the sort which hounded George Best into unpopular corners, they might have shown more sympathy for Boycott. Harried into error or marginally misquoted, he could seldom defend himself once the story had been splashed across the sports pages.

A balancing factor is Boycott's facility for withdrawing into a protective shell which cuts him off from the niceties of life that cost so little yet are worth so much and hardly had the cease-fire sounded across the Pennines when he got on the wrong side of Bedser, who was not pleased to find himself in the dark about the illness which overtook Boycott at Old Trafford and kept him out of the first Test against Pakistan.

Suffering from nervous exhaustion brought on by worry over the Lancashire dispute or concern at the activities in those darker corners of Yorkshire, Boycott went to bed on doctor's orders and did not bat on the last day of the Roses game. Bedser did not, however, discover the extent of his incapacity until he telephoned his Fitzwilliam home. Mrs Boycott contacted the Yorkshire secretary, who did his best to pass on the message without success, so responsibility could be spread around a little, but most of the blame settled on Boycott as he slept on in Milton Terrace, blissfully under sedation.

Nor was he popular with England, who were batting to avoid defeat, when he decided he had recovered enough to lead Yorkshire to an innings victory over Nottinghamshire at Headingley, scoring 169 and handling his team faultlessly before catching up with the tourists at Bradford.

In beating Nottinghamshire he stuck to the pattern with which Close acquired a few enemies up and down the country, building a huge first innings total to squeeze the resistance out of the opposition, and he did not hesitate to give Pakistan a strong dose of the same medicine, guaranteed to kill not cure. The visitors' team manager reckoned that the fixture could be set aside for practice and foolishly made this public knowledge, pleasing no one and upsetting a lot.

Rain made the conditions pretty miserable as Yorkshire won the toss and batted on and on, much to the delight of the Park Avenue humourists, who enquired politely and regularly as to whether the Pakistanis were enjoying their fielding practice. They very definitely were not and, despite some fine bowling from their captain, Intikhab Alam, who raised the lurking spectre of Yorkshire's age-old fallibility against leg-spin, the tourists were steadily reduced to a rabble. They showed so little interest that eventually the umpires lectured them in the manner of a boxing referee stimulating a reluctant fighter.

Boycott called a halt at 422 for nine and Pakistan, on 140 for five with the follow-on looming, were in danger of defeat when the weather washed out the whole of the third day. The policy might have been vindicated but for the rain, yet Boycott came under fire for 'killing the game', to which charge he replied: 'All I am interested in is playing cricket positively and with imagination.' The professionals and the serious students of cricket knew exactly what he meant.

Two other matches merit close attention, the first coming at Sheffield in July, when Boycott made a challenging declaration to prevent the contest drifting into stalemate. These are the most finely balanced of calculations and, as we have noted, Boycott made a mockery of some earlier mathematics.

Unless the wicket is deteriorating, allowing turn or giving uneven bounce, the advantage must lie with the batsmen, who can choose between pressing on in an attempt to win or blocking out for a draw once their main chance has disappeared. An assured, experienced captain, with the support of confident bowlers, can skilfully lure a side onto the rocks, as Yorkshire did so often with Close at the helm, but it was a relatively new trick for Boycott to master and his gamble went down as Mike Procter hit a winning streak.

The powerful South African hammered 111, leading Gloucestershire cheerfully to 201 in 135 minutes, and a four-wicket defeat made a big impression on Boycott. Yorkshire would have struggled to bowl out Gloucestershire in slightly more than two hours, but the way in which they lost raised some queries in his mind. If he were to lead Yorkshire out of the wilderness, he thought, the attack would have to become more reliable when the chips were down.

The uncertainty that existed to an unwelcome degree was confirmed at Hull in Boycott's absence. Yorkshire, on an unreliable pitch, needed 150 in the fourth innings to beat Essex and they reached 135 for six, coming within touching distance of getting something right without him. Then two wickets fell quickly and they lost their nerve, making no effort to get the runs from the last two overs.

Boycott's form commanded respect at any time. That he produced it throughout the 1971 season against such an unsettled background borders on the unbelievable. His outstanding innings from the point of view of size was 233 at the expense of Essex, but the range and quality of his stroke-play brought greatest credit. He hit eleven centuries for Yorkshire and since he finished as the target for sinister allegations, the matches in which they were compiled must be studied to discover the extent to which Yorkshire were compromised.

He was, of course, the match-winner against Warwickshire, Middlesex, Nottinghamshire and Northamptonshire, so on we go to Colchester in late June. Here Boycott batted for six hours and twenty-five minutes for his 233 — over half Yorkshire's 421 for four declared. Essex, forced to follow on 204 behind, narrowly escaped defeat by an innings, with Stuart Turner, badly missed before scoring, helping Robin Hobbs to hold out.

Boycott carried his bat through a completed innings for the third time, taking 182 off the Middlesex bowling at Lord's, and, with Fred Titmus getting some turn, Sharpe's 36 stood out as the next best score in a drawn engagement which, in the light of a second innings collapse to 157 all out, must have brought defeat but for Boycott. His 133 against Derbyshire at Scarborough included the shocking running out of Sharpe, who was sent back with lordly disdain when fully committed, but Yorkshire accrued their highest number of bonus points, five, and the visitors spent two gruelling days doggedly hanging on for a draw.

Although honours were more even in the Sheffield Roses match, Lancashire rarely experiencing anxiety, Boycott's 169 came out of 320 in a day and his partnership of 186 for the third wicket with Hampshire was the best in that context since the war. A green and seaming pitch awaited Leicestershire at Bradford, where Nicholson scythed through the opposition, taking five wickets in a total of 204 all out to leave Boycott in casual command, helping himself to 151 while sharing a stand of 182 to match Hampshire blow for blow, run for run, and there were four batting points as a bonus.

Boycott's other two centuries were made in lost causes which he prevented becoming utter disasters.

Hampshire had eight wickets in hand at Bournemouth, although they scored no more than 332 runs. Yorkshire were shot out for 96 as the ball turned sharply, Boycott's share being 40, and 233, out of which he had 111. Overall he contributed 151 against the 167 of his ten team-mates, becoming the first man to 2,000 runs in the process. The gulf in ability and application was even more pronounced at Edgbaston, with Warwickshire's winning margin of 22 runs being restricted by Boycott's solo. In reply to Warwickshire's 354 for eight, Yorkshire lost six wickets for 45 in a complete capitulation. Lumb (1), Sharpe (6), Hampshire (0), Johnson (0), Hutton (4) and Bairstow (9) came and went, giving no hint of permanence, but Boycott carried his bat through another completed innings, his 138 preventing the follow-on and charting a possible escape route.

In the second innings, chasing 284 in four and threequarter hours, Yorkshire made a splendid start, Lumb keeping Boycott company while 134 runs were collected, but the rest obligingly folded, the captain's 84 being unchallenged. He had 222 of the 477 runs coming from the bat, so in none of those eleven innings which were the hard core of his record-breaking average did Yorkshire lose out.

On the contrary, Boycott invariably raised the tone of the proceedings, preventing his less able colleagues from being utterly exposed, and the comparison added up in much the same way in the Sunday League. Yorkshire gained four of their five victories under Boycott, with Wilson and Padgett managing just one success between them in five matches. Boycott finished as the leading Yorkshireman in the official averages with 443 runs for a figure of 49.22, although he came second behind Leadbeater in the county list which accepted qualification on fewer innings.

His sparkling 93 proved too much for Warwickshire, while he claimed top score of 54 out of 147 in the 39-run triumph over Sussex at Hove. A splendid 73 in a total of 169 put an impressive stamp on the season as Northamptonshire were beaten by 30 runs at Bradford, so here, too, he was the difference between the moderate and the downright bad.

In the third Test against Pakistan at Headingley, he passed another milestone, sharing his one hundredth century partnership in his 422nd innings. He was measured against the senior branches of the Hutton and Sutcliffe families as a matter of course. Sutcliffe reached the landmark in his 457th innings, Hutton in his 414th. Along the way Sutcliffe scored 19,344 runs, Hutton 19,220 and Boycott 19,899. The doubts which existed were destroyed by every fact.

Yorkshire ended up thirteenth in the Championship and fared badly in the one-day competitions, but David Bairstow arrived on the scene as an accomplished and competitive wicket-keeper in the traditional mould, while Hutton improved with his medium-pace bowling to earn selection for England, weakening the county yet standing out as a source of pride. Boycott's last, defiant gesture was the 124 not out which ensured his three-figure average and, since decisively defeated Northamptonshire mustered very few more in two completed innings, its quality could not be denied.

The controversy surrounding the occasion was unworthy of either the man or the county he served so impressively and the much-discussed triumph over Northamptonshire had an additional significance. It ended a sequence of seventeen matches without a win — the longest in Yorkshire's history.

Padgett retired at the end of the season, taking charge of the second team and concentrating on coaching. In going he severed another link with the great days. He also took with him a wealth of experience which enabled him to develop the youngsters but which, as a result, was denied on a day-to-day basis to Boycott.

4 The Managing Director

Boycott's cause was, to all intents and purposes, lost by th
end of September 1971. The fight continued, of cours
stretched across seven more bitter years, during which h
enjoyed a handful of heartening successes while steadil
losing ground, but the inescapable fact was that if he coul
not swing the balance his way by his efforts in that fir
season he had no real chance of ever becoming totall
accepted. He could have done nothing more. He had co
founded prediction by harnessing his rate of progress to th
demands of the situation and, virtually single-handed, save
Yorkshire from the indignity of finishing at the foot of th
Championship table.

Cruelly blunt in his dealings with people on occasion
Boycott gave offence, but that did not detract from h
position as the most important figure in the county, entitle
to special consideration because the club were utterl
dependent on him.

Despite this, the mutterings and mumblings persuaded th
committee to hold an enquiry which, however, yielde
nothing. It was one thing to complain with Boycott out c
earshot and another entirely to face him, especially when th
disaffected failed to match words with deeds, and those i
charge, being well aware of the problem, had a duty to ac
vigorously. This was the moment to back Boycott or sac
him, but they hesitated

The committee could profitably have studied the average
which were the most accurate guide as to who had done wha
and they make interesting reading:

74

CHAMPIONSHIP AVERAGES 1971
Batting

	INNS	NOT OUT	RUNS	HS	AVGE
Boycott	24	4	2,197	233	109.85
Sharpe	27	3	823	172*	34.29
Hampshire	37	4	1,118	183*	33.87
Johnson	7	0	165	53	23.57
Padgett	33	1	727	133	22.71
Leadbeater	30	5	564	69	22.56
Woodford	20	1	417	101	21.94
Lumb	5	0	106	65	21.20
Dalton	13	1	221	119*	18.41
Hutton	25	3	398	47*	18.09
Bairstow	34	5	438	67*	15.10
Old	24	5	270	28	14.21
Nicholson	21	7	192	33	13.71
Wilson	20	4	141	37	8.81
Cope	19	5	91	16	6.50
Bore	19	4	60	16	4.00

* indicates not out

Bowling

	O	M	R	W	AVGE
Hutton	479.3	130	1,038	57	18.21
Wilson	472.1	187	979	49	19.97
Nicholson	646.5	184	1,411	53	26.62
Bore	538.3	192	1,184	44	26.90
Old	442	103	1,184	42	28.19
Cope	444.3	145	1,084	37	29.29

Yorkshire's greatest weakness is exposed. Although Hampshire topped 1,000 runs, neither he nor Sharpe was consistent, Padgett disappointed his many admirers and the rest hardly made an impact. Only Hutton came near to matching Boycott's standards among the bowlers, being rewarded with his five England 'caps', and adding to the serious draw-back of limited ability was Old's worrying run of injuries. The Middlesborough seamer broke down several times and finished the season needing a knee operation which meant that he hardly filled the role of strike bowler vacant since Trueman's departure.

After Boycott, Hutton came next in importance, therefore, looking the one man who might replace Illingworth as the successful all-rounder without whom Yorkshire's prospects of winning anything were remote. Cope, whose potential as an offspinner had been a factor in Illingworth's calculations when he asked for the security of a contract, lacked the weight of stroke to make the necessary runs, while Old's solid effectiveness with the bat was a thing of the future.

Boycott, then, had good cause to seek a meaningful association with Hutton, but, in this, too, he was to be unlucky. The young university star did not fulfil his promise, never again rising to the heights of the England team, although called up in the twelve or thirteen, and his shortage of runs and wickets, together with business involvement, minimised his influence.

Nevertheless, Hutton became the focal point — albeit innocently — for the mischiefmakers, who saw in him an alternative captain. He possessed exactly the right credentials with suitable social standing, so, spurred on by his brief rise to prominence, a group began to advance his cause, whispering Hutton's qualities and Boycott's alleged limitations whenever and wherever they discovered an opportunity.

Hutton, born not so much into a different background as a different world to Boycott, enjoyed the wealth and privilege that his distinguished father's skill and subsequent commercial enterprise brought to the family. Almost two years Boycott's junior, he grew up free from the anxieties which featured so prominently in the other's battle for recognition. Repton and Cambridge moulded a man of wide-ranging ability, with a degree and accountancy qualifications offering him vast scope outside cricket, and he moved into the Yorkshire side almost as a matter of course.

Hutton's debut, at the age of nineteen, came in an Old Trafford Roses clash in August 1962, but he did not concentrate his attentions, winning a Cambridge Blue which restricted the time he could give to the county. This scarcity of regular involvement did not hold him back, for he gained his 'cap' in 1964, by the end of which season he had scored

723 runs and taken thirty-four wickets for Yorkshire. These did not amount to a glowing recommendation, nor did the easily gained distinction persuade Hutton to play more often. After breaking his nose in a motoring accident in 1965, he hardly appeared at all in 1966 and 1967 because 'There was too much coming and going to settle.' This philosophy found no echoes in the single-minded Boycott with his nose to the county grindstone, so it was the logical extension of consequence that they should find it almost impossible to meet on common ground.

They got at cross-purposes on their first meeting as opening partners in a second-team match at Bridlington in 1961, Hutton scoring 49 out of 70 for the first wicket in his cheerful, uncomplicated way and then sitting through Boycott's slow grind for his first century for the Colts. From that day Hutton regarded Boycott as one-paced, but when his selection for England came in 1971 he paid splendid tribute to his new captain.

As he celebrated he gave Boycott a lot of credit for his general improvement and for reviving his interest in the game. 'Only this season have I really felt satisfied,' he said. 'As a younger member of the famous Yorkshire team of the 1960s, I felt I was just making up the numbers. Now I am involved in making things happen. Geoff readily asks the players for advice, encouraging a lot of free speech in the dressing room. Whether he takes the advice is another matter, but it makes you feel involved and that is a good thing. It gives me added responsibility and I feel more in the game. From watching others do the talking I have become an important part of the team. Under Close it was different. He consulted the players, but they were always the same ones and the rest of us were left out of it.' This unsolicited testament has to be set against the grumbling and is clear proof that Boycott made a genuine effort to establish harmony.

Obviously it would have been nice for him to talk things over with such as Close, Illingworth and Binks, but they had gone, so he made the best of it by trying to carry his team along with him, seeking to win both respect and popularity, and it is impossible to understand the rumblings of rebellion unless envy is accepted as the reason.

77

This is far from unthinkable. There had been instances in the 'good old days' when disagreements and petty jealousies led to furious rows and catches being dropped deliberately and it is quite possible to believe that, with Yorkshire enfeebled, Boycott's fame and standing with the public, became a source of irritation.

By late July the manoeuvring to edge Boycott out of office was a badly kept secret, with an anonymous committee member telling Trueman 'His removal will have to be handled as delicately as a military operation.'

The claims that the captain persistently received one hundred per cent backing are, therefore, easily refuted. At every turn there was opposition. Some of the evidence is hearsay, for the anti-Boycott lobby specialised in the hidden assassin technique and one man's word conflicted with another's. I can, however, vouch that there were people of trust within the club pushing for Hutton as captain as late as 1974. I learned that season that I could do myself a lot of good with a section of the committee by using the columns of the *Yorkshire Evening Post* to pave the way for a change of captain. Typically, a request for direct quotes prompted an immediate change of subject.

With no official England tour, Boycott left the politics behind and flew to South Africa for a three-month warm-up to the 1972 campaign, scoring three centuries in his first five innings for Northern Transvaal to create a very favourable impression.

He soon attracted a big following and his frequent net practices in Pretoria, where he undertook some coaching, drew enthusiastic audiences, whose approval contrasted sharply with the mixed reception at home, and it was not uncommon for him to provide eagerly awaited entertainment twice a day.

Meanwhile, back in frost-bitten Harrogate, Trueman launched a fierce attack on Boycott, bringing up again his declaration against Northamptonshire with emphasis on the fact that it came when his average climbed above one hundred.

In knocking Boycott's achievement, Trueman warmed to his theme. 'What did we get?' he asked, bristling with righteous indignation. 'Somewhere near the bottom of the batting bonus points league. I think it is disgusting.' Two points sprang to mind immediately while the invective clung on the walls.

Yorkshire under Close had always put the emphasis on winning matches, collecting bonus points as an after thought, so they were not geared to the pursuit of them when Boycott assumed command.

Yorkshire admittedly gathered an inadequate forty-seven batting points, with only three of the other sixteen counties faring worse, and this was not good enough. But what happened in previous years? Yorkshire claimed forty-nine points in 1970 under Close and a far more 'disgusting' thirty in 1969, while in 1968, when Trueman himself played and they won the Championship, the total was forty-six from twenty-eight matches — four more than in the reduced pro-gramme of Boycott's first year. So what was all the fuss about?

Forty-four of Yorkshire's batting points in 1971 came from the seventeen games under Boycott's leadership. With Wilson and Padgett in charge the team collected three points from seven fixtures! They put up a series of woeful displays in the process and it is enlightening to study the first innings' scores from those seven matches, remembering that bonus points were awarded for every twenty-five runs over 150 in the first eighty-five overs. Yorkshire's totals were:

		points
v Kent	93 all out	0
v Worcestershire	160 all out	0
v Somerset	181 all out	1
v Worcestershire	170 all out	0
v Kent	89 all out	0
v Glamorgan	353 for 2	2
v Essex	91 all out	0

A catalogue of shame, relieved only the once, at Swansea, where Yorkshire batted so slowly they were severely barracked by the Welsh crowd. Boycott, indeed, comes out of any serious analysis with credit, and on his return from South Africa he discussed the whole business, sensibly restating the opinion generally held in Close's time. 'I have heard comments on batting points this winter as if they were a vital factor in winning the Championship,' he said. 'They are really part of it and need to be regarded as such. It must be remembered that poor pitches inhibit batsmen, who get suspicious and lack the confidence to play shots.'

He loyally refrained from drawing attention to the short-comings of others, an example which could usefully have been followed.

Yorkshire, slowly sweeping away the cobwebs which had decorated their headquarters for so long, belatedly stream-lined their operation in 1972.

All twelve members of the cricket committee had enjoyed a say in selection which was demonstrably wrong and under pressure from a variety of sources sub-division created a smaller group consisting of Boycott, Padgett (as second-team captain), Temple, Sellers, Sutcliffe and Frank Ambler, a man who devoted a lot of his energy to keeping an eye on the second team. Although the personnel changed and the doubts about Boycott found expression in this small area, it was a good idea with obvious merit so long as the individuals concerned could find time to watch most of the matches, if only on a rota basis.

Unfortunately, things did not work out quite so well, although remarkably, considering the underlying confusion, Yorkshire made a wonderful start to their 1972 programme, qualifying for the knockout stages of the new Benson and Hedges Cup and climbing defiantly to the top of the Championship table in early June with fifty-one points from four matches.

They won three of the four group ties in the 55-overs-a-side Benson and Hedges event after getting off to a flying start with a nine-wicket victory over the 'old enemy', Lancashire, at Bradford, where Boycott chipped some of the gloss of the picture by taking to task Man-of-the-Match adjudicator Bill Voce.

The former Nottinghamshire and England fast bowler decided that Lancashire's Barry Wood had earned the award by scoring a gritty 31 in a total of 82 and taking one wicket for 13 — Boycott's — in eight overs. Wilson, with his haul of five wickets for 26, had arguably better claims, but it was not a matter worth arguing about and, while Boycott felt he did his job by taking up cudgels on his colleague's behalf in the cause of justice, he did not do himself a lot of good. Still he acted in good faith and put his head on the block for someone else, a gesture deserving appreciation.

Nothing else went wrong, so Yorkshire enjoyed the luxury of losing to Nottinghamshire in the final zone game without it affecting their progress. Boycott was in splendid form, although over-cautious in his Championship declaration against Derbyshire — memories of Gloucestershire and Procter? — and he began to nurse hopes of producing something tangible. Old and Nicholson bowled well, the former having had a second knee operation, the Benson and Hedges run continued and a solid challenge for the Sunday League title satisfied the members besides attracting paying customers through the turnstiles — sweet music to the ears of the treasurer. Boycott savoured a dream in which he received the Benson and Hedges Cup at Lord's, but it was transformed into a hideous nightmare by one wickedly destructive delivery from Warwickshire's Willis that shattered his right hand.

The fateful moment marking the end of Yorkshire hopes for a season and Boycott's for much longer arrived in a Gillette Cup tie at Headingley. He was 12 when Willis struck him on the middle finger of his right hand, crushing it against the bat handle to cause an injury representing the first pebble in a landslide that buried so much splendid work and left instead a pile of rubble. In a spectacular collapse three of the next four Championship matches brought defeat, twice by margins of more than an innings, as Boycott helplessly stood by, neither use nor ornament, as they say in Yorkshire, his pained presence being an unwelcome reminder of how much the team missed him.

While the loss of momentum generally was bad enough, the most serious set-back occurred in the Benson and Hedges Cup final, in which Leicestershire swept home with five wickets and seven overs in hand against a side led by Sharpe as Wilson was another casualty. The Yorkshire players spent much of the day looking figuratively over their shoulders, wondering what Boycott was thinking or what he would have done. Their nervous excuse for an innings never got established.

Ten overs of the new ball brought 21 runs and the loss of two wickets, followed by injury to Leadbeater, who retired after being struck on the wrist and returned to make a top score of 32.

Johnson added a dogged 20, but there was simply no substitute for Boycott and a total of 136 for nine gave the bowlers precious little margin for error. Surprisingly Yorkshire used up their ration of fifty-five overs, the only team Leicestershire did not bowl out in the competition that year, so much of their application was negative, and had Boycott played in so low a scoring game he would have been vilified.

Defeat was a blow of monumental proportions from which the county never really recovered and success at that moment must have sent them in an altogether different direction. Sport permits no certainties and no one can categorically state that Yorkshire would have won had Boycott taken part, but, considering all the angles, it is no exaggeration to insist that he was half the team. Whatever the conspiracies might suggest, the players operated more efficiently under his skilful direction, while his scoring power in the earlier period of prosperity underlined his worth. His pre-injury record was:

Benson and Hedges Cup — 217 runs for three times out, average 72.33.

Sunday League — 175 runs in four completed innings, average 43.75.

Championship — 605 runs for seven dismissals, average 86.43.

The untiring Johnny Wardle, with his left-arm spin shortly after the war, and the fiery Trueman in his prime, shouldered back-breaking burdens in the dependence of their colleagues without being as important to their respective sides as Boycott. He also possessed the coolest head in a crisis, his field placings being dictated by that extra degree of study, so while Leicestershire, responding to Illingworth's astute guiding hand, may have won in any case, Boycott would have made things ten times harder. It is just as realistic to think that Yorkshire were equipped to extend their Championship run as well, despite Test calls, had Boycott not been hurt. The heart, however, went out of the players and in his enforced idleness he became utterly convinced that his role was central to any advancement.

Wilson's injury weighed less heavily in the balance and his vice-captain's unreliability as a slow bowler was a constant source of concern. Sharpe, however, felt the axe first, losing his place in late July, Wilson's turn coming as the poor results continued. Nicholson took up the responsibility as captain fleetingly in a rain-ruined fixture with Sussex and, as this stretching chain of command rattled under the strain, the wonder was that Hutton stayed in the background.

With his name bandied about in high places he seemed the obvious choice as captain, yet he found himself serving under four others. It was all very confusing, especially as he remained on the shortlist for so long. We shall presumably never know why the committee exhibited so little confidence, but Boycott saved them further heart-searching by recovering in time for the return game with Surrey, who had beaten Yorkshire by an innings and twelve runs little more than two weeks previously. As if by magic they reversed the result. Surrey had one change in personnel, so it can safely be inferred that Yorkshire's dramatic upsurge brought a nine-wicket win. Boycott scored no more than 23, next to nothing in his book, yet the team tackled the job with a rediscovered pride and purpose. A downtrodden shuffle gave way to a determined stride and one man, misunderstood and so often reviled, was the reason.

Boycott finished at the head of the first-class averages, helped Yorkshire to their best Sunday League placing of fourth and steered them into a cup final, all in the shadow of Test duty and injury, performing a minor miracle, but the vexed question of bonus points cropped up again on cue, thirty-nine being regarded as unacceptable. Gloucestershire, who finished third, and Northamptonshire, in fourth place, were, however, among the five counties faring worse and he emerged better than his three deputies from a thorough examination.

Twenty-eight batting points accrued from the ten Championship games in which he led the side, the other ten producing only eleven. There were five points from Sharpe's three matches and six from Wilson's six, while Nicholson's single fixture was badly affected by rain. Beyond dispute, the critics hung Boycott for the crimes of others.

In the Championship he compiled six centuries, the other three-figure innings coming from Dalton, with 128 off the Middlesex attack, and Hampshire, who took 111 at the expense of Glamorgan and added 103 against Middlesex. Although playing fewer innings than most, Boycott scored 1,156 runs, over 400 more than Hampshire, for an average of 96.33, and his big scores nearly always brought considerable benefit to the team, starting with an aggregate of 115, easily the highest of the match, as Gloucestershire were defeated by 126 runs on a lively Middlesborough pitch that defied the skills of all other batsmen.

His first century arrived at Taunton, where the weather bit deep into each of the three days and killed off all hope of positive cricket, and then the Headingley Roses game provided the setting for one of Boycott's most masterly displays. He contributed 105 to Yorkshire's 253 for eight, outpacing all his partners to make 82 out of 119 for the first wicket with Sharpe and one hundred out of 147 altogether in another rain-ruined draw.

His 100 at Worksop denied Nottinghamshire the possibility of a rare success over Yorkshire for while his runs came from 181 balls, with thirteen boundaries, the rest of the side struggled painfully in the face of hostile and accurate bowling from Barry Stead, eager to prove his old county had erred in releasing him. Only after Bolus had prolonged Nottinghamshire's reply to 228 into the third day, gaining a lead which ensured stalemate, did Boycott indulge in practice, giving the scarcely considered spectators value for money by means of another fluent knock that would have served as a series of illustrations for any text book.

Yorkshire fared badly without him against Northamptonshire and Surrey, being shot out for 96 and 133 at the Oval by Intikhab, whose leg spin utterly confounded them, so his return to Championship action at Grace Road was important, especially as he hit 204 not out, but he still found himself in the firing line because Yorkshire got no more than one batting bonus point. The familiar barbs were sharpened for the occasion, even though Boycott operated in great pain after being hit on his injured hand by McKenzie, who had an unhappy knack of causing him grief. Despite this, Boycott reached his century out of 139 and his second hundred occupied two hours, which is good going by any standards. The upshot was that he gave Yorkshire a chance of success when otherwise none existed and but for a brave rearguard action by Mick Norman Leicestershire might have gone down.

Boycott's 121 at Chelmsford — he scored 207 altogether — did not deny Essex, for whom Fletcher hammered a decisive unbeaten 139 against the clock, but his runs were an integral part of a very good contest.

In the Sunday League he matched enterprise with reliability, piling up 256 runs for an average of 32. Nothing special there, yet only Leadbeater, with a surprising spurt which carried him to the head of the national figures — 440 runs (55.00) — and Lumb did better for Yorkshire. Based on the evidence of hard facts, therefore, Boycott's standing looked essentially secure and after two years there was no evidence to back up the persistent assertions that he put himself first and the team second. The sniping continued for all that.

In doing remarkably well, Boycott had to overcome more than the loss of form among his senior players and the main worry concerned Cope's action, the offspinner having been banned for 'throwing' following the Warwickshire match at Sheffield at the end of June. Replacing Illingworth, an arduous assignment in itself, became a crushing burden for the sensitive Cope as he struggled under a great weight of responsibility that disturbed his rhythm and accentuated a natural jerking movement.

Had he not been the only offspinner of anything like county class or had Illingworth's departure not been so precipitate, Cope would have had more time in which to straighten out the kink. Instead he tackled the job as best he could while under suspicion and when he finally received his suspension, Yorkshire's alternative was Bore. This necessitated two slow left-arm bowlers operating in tandem and their differing styles did not compensate adequately for the lack of someone to spin the ball the other way. Bore, seldom getting the right sort of chance, never quite came through and at that stage in his career was not really a front-line attacker.

Nicholson, on the other hand, figured prominently, so his leg injury which developed into a thrombosis in September 1972 drained vital strength from the team, while Hutton's announcement that he would be unable to play on a full-time basis in 1973 piled on the agony.

In this respect none of Boycott's troubles were of his own making, but in speaking his mind on a whole range of subjects he pursued an unwise, if honest, policy. His anxiety to become more involved in the decision-making persuaded him to campaign openly for an appointment as a sort of managing director with a broadly defined function which included sole charge of all cricketing matters — very much the position eventually filled by Illingworth.

'A committee should exist as a safeguard, just in case the managing director went off his nut,' he claimed, seeing the need for greater on-the-spot authority, particularly at away matches, when power sharing with distant and difficult to contact officials limited his ability to maintain full control. Years ahead of his time, however, he fell foul of the traditionalists, who had no intention whatsoever of delegating any of their rights to a common player.

Similarly, he upset a lot more people by advocating the taking away of fixtures from Bradford and Harrogate in order to centralise activities at Headingley. Anger and outrage sprang up all round — as they did in 1981 when Illingworth pressed the same arguments and the county took a policy decision to make more use of their headquarters — but Boycott's suggestion made sense. It cost Yorkshire a lot of money to carry the first-class game to clubs whose members gained free admission, but emotional attachments to uneconomic venues stood in the way of progress for many years, shielded by the system of district representation on the ruling body. This had allowed local interests to hold sway to the disadvantage of the county and Boycott banged his head against a solid wall of passionately held opinion. An outcry arose without giving voice to many constructive replies.

J.P. Burnhill, the president of the Central Yorkshire League, leapt in with both feet. 'It is a good thing Boycott does not bat with the handle in his mouth,' he exploded. 'Unless the county committee take action about recent

86

public remarks by Mr Boycott then I say they have gone from strength to chaos.' Why? Why should extending Boycott's influence or taking extra games to Leeds cause chaos? These ideas were hardly the stuff of which revolutions are made, far-reaching though they may have been, and they merited careful thought, but Coun. F.A. Rotherham, the Mayor of Harrogate added his weight to the onslaught.

'One admires Boycott so much as a cricketer, but saying what is in your mind and what is helpful to cricket is very different. I don't think he was very helpful on this occasion.' Boycott's sole concern, though, was with the future of Yorkshire cricket and he remained ever ready to put forward imaginative plans for committee consideration.

One example involved the complicated business of moving their activities up and down the county, a major snag being the shortage of suitable covering at some venues. Boycott, fretting over the long delays, wanted some action. 'I pointed out that we should make the effort to help the grounds on which we played by transporting big covers by lorry to the various centres a few days before we were scheduled to play there. It sounded expensive, but I think there would have been extra receipts to cover the costs once the public realised there was a better chance of seeing play. I mentioned this several times to the committee, but nothing was done.'

Boycott's frustration stemmed not simply from having his suggestions ignored. He visualised himself as the man in the middle, with one foot in the dressing room and the other in the committee room, linking the two. He had faith in his administrative ability and it says much for his desire to serve the club that he wanted to do more than just captain the team on the field. He felt entitled to a hand in organising the future on all fronts. Wickets happened to be a case in point, for the Yorkshire players did not always get pitches to suit them in their home matches.

Other counties prepared wickets to favour their strengths and with an eye on the likely composition of the opposition, but Yorkshire made do with what they were given and one groundsman admitted off the record that he followed orders from his employers to ensure that all the county games on his square lasted the full three days to guarantee the bar and refreshment takings. Fine for the club concerned, but very hard on Yorkshire, whose prospects were obviously diminshed. On such issues Boycott readily stood up to be counted, accepting the tag of troublemaker.

Ten years later Illingworth and Old, as captain, were making the same complaints to emphasise Boycott's merit, although they slipped down the ladder of popularity in their turn, too.

Whether they liked it or not, Yorkshire had no option but to reappoint Boycott for 1973, for their hands were tied by the absence of an acceptable alternative. They revealed that the cupboard was bare by announcing they intended to nominate his deputy on a match-by-match basis, an admission that Sharpe and Wilson no longer commanded automatic selection. The granting of his benefit came as a bonus to Boycott, who, however, realised his task was getting harder rather than easier. The after-effects of his illness bore down on the gallant Nicholson, while Hutton turned his attentions to the world of commerce. Old, like Boycott, had acquired Test status and never since the confused period before Lord Hawke had Yorkshire looked such a ragged outfit.

5 Under Fire

The hard-won right to contracts, a legacy of the Action Group's activities, caused a new wave of controversy to sweep through Yorkshire in the winter of 1972—73. Boycott, asked by the rest of the squad to negotiate general terms before they settled individual details, drove a hard bargain, and it is interesting to note that he played his part entirely to their satisfaction. As with any new venture, many points required ironing out and the actual signing was delayed in his case. Soon rumour of a dispute sped hot from a thousand lips and less than two weeks after his reappointment and the news of his benefit, Ladbrokes offered six to one against him playing for Yorkshire in the coming season.

Meanwhile, Illingworth, happily committing himself to another three years at Grace Road, had something relevant to say. 'I have enjoyed my cricket with Leicestershire. There is a different atmosphere from that in Yorkshire,' he said, talking about an era in which trophies had been won and in which Boycott was no more than a junior member of the Yorkshire side, doing as he was told.

Boycott flew out to South Africa, leaving the county to deny that any rift existed. 'There are two small points to be settled,' insisted secretary Joe Lister. Still, the question of money was interesting. Could Boycott expect to be paid more than his colleagues and get £200 for each Test appearance on top?

In purely statistical terms he could, and the differences were quickly settled by a meeting between his solicitor,

89

Duncan Mutch, and Arthur Connell. The following Press release was agreed: 'Yorkshire County Cricket Club and Geoffrey Boycott have now reached complete agreement as to the contract terms and look forward to the future when they hope that there will be seen to be a continuation of the progress of the team following last year's marked improvement. Geoffrey Boycott feels that he will be leading a team of enthusiastic players who have the opportunity to lay the foundation for the re-establishment of Yorkshire cricket.'

For some reason the word 'enthusiastic' disappeared before it reached the media which puzzled both Boycott and Mutch. Did the county not agree that the players were enthusiastic? If so, then it was up to the committee to find out why and take the appropriate steps. There is no record of anything being done along those lines. Did they not want to make public any enthusiasm which existed? Apparently not, although to the logical mind nothing but good could come from advertising the fact that everyone was keen and ready to do their best.

From all angles the omission was perplexing, confirming Mutch's belief that something had to be done to improve relations, so he met Temple and Lister to discuss ways in which complete mutual trust could be achieved and there was a friendly exchange. Unfortunately in some areas the suggestion arose that if Boycott and Yorkshire had parted company before the start of the 1973 season there would have been public backing.

From this it is reasonable to assume that Boycott's departure had been discussed, if only unofficially, or, at least, considered as a real possibility in one or two minds. The sentiments took a lot for granted, though, and were hardly realistic. The vast majority of members and supporters had neither knowledge of, nor interest in, the politics behind the scenes. Events on the field concerned them, so they appreciated Boycott as the best player and the best captain.

In his first two years in charge Yorkshire won only one of the seventeen Championship matches he missed and lost eight, while his superiority as a batsman stood out like the Alps on Salisbury Plain. The spectators whose devotion to a troubled cause deserved far greater consideration drew consolation from pride in Yorkshire's policy of using entirely home-grown material and from Boycott's brilliance. When defeat brought jibes from the jubilant followers of other counties, they fell back on Boycott's talent to defend their own honour and it is extremely doubtful that they would have stood quietly by while he went on his way.

The near riots of 1978 and 1981 are a tribute to the high esteem in which the customers held him and, in any case, having granted him a benefit, the committee had burned their boats and the show had to go on.

The bizarre pattern of results which developed as the 1973 season progressed further stressed the reliance on Boycott. Yorkshire struggled miserably through the early weeks of the Championship, showing very little form, but they won six of the first ten Sunday League games, laying the base for a title drive which carried them into second place behind Kent in the final reckoning. This unexpected success was based entirely on the runs which flowed from Boycott and Hampshire, who both averaged over 55. Hampshire, with 668 runs, broke the record aggregate for the competition and Boycott, in fewer outings, proved he was by no means a one-paced batsman by matching that fluency. His 444 meant that he and Hampshire were responsible for 1,112 Sunday runs, while the other fifteen players called upon managed 1,086 between them, and the next man in the statistics, Hutton, had an average of 19.80!

Boycott provided the initial inspiration with the most spectacular of centuries — 104 not out, to be exact — against Glamorgan at Colwyn Bay in April, his runs coming out of a total 186 which was 24 too many for the Welsh side. Dashingly enterprising, he eliminated risk without allowing the bowling to impose compensating limits and he could be forgiven an abberation when, in the nineties, he ran out Johnson, who threw away his wicket by responding to the call for a suicidal single.

It was a blemish, but not a serious one, and Boycott continued in a rich vein with 72 not out as Nottinghamshire were beaten by seven wickets. Subsequently he and Hampshire plundered 160 in 28.1 overs against Warwickshire, Boycott's share being 67, and having picked up speed he kept his foot firmly on the accelerator whenever possible. He made his one mistake in the farcical ten-over slog at Worcester, where the match started in heavy rain which prevented the issue being contested over a sensible distance and ensured conditions more suited to mud wrestling than cricket when the pointless exercise got underway.

Boycott elected to field on winning the toss and Worcestershire frantically slogged their way to 95, rather more than he expected. For some reason his mind went numb, for instead of dropping down the order to make way for the bigger hitters better equipped for the waterlogged rough and tumble in which it was essential to get the ball into the air, he went in first as usual and succeeded in getting in everybody's way.

Chasing a target of ten an over, Boycott, as though hypnotised, contrived eight scoring strokes in eight overs, the soggy ground denying his strokes more surely than the fielders, while his partners slipped, slithered and cursed him and Yorkshire lost by 24 runs.

'I tried, but I couldn't do anything about it,' he apologised, and his reluctance to improvise, to take liberties with the orthodox, remained a part of his mental make-up to which few of his detractors drew attention, possibly because a lot of them saw too little cricket to notice. They busily dealt with what they regarded as the more obvious.

For the only time in his eight-year reign as captain, Boycott did not take part in a Championship victory, Yorkshire winning three matches under Sharpe, who, despite everything, found himself standing in as acting captain for two more seasons, and thus was born the notion that the team did better when he was away. The fact that it did not stand up for one moment to any sort of impartial scrutiny made no difference. Something that should have been welcomed as a sign of developing strength in depth and an important advance turned into a source of discord.

Injury and England calls limited Boycott to eight Championship outings, yet he managed two of the seven centuries credited to Yorkshire, finishing comfortably at the top of the averages. Mention must be made of the batting bonus points, for although Yorkshire were restricted to twenty-eight — Derbyshire alone had fewer — sixteen came from those eight matches in which Boycott played. Twelve came from the other twelve matches.

Sharpe and the improving Lumb hit two centuries each, while Johnson got one, but otherwise the batting did not distinguish itself, a number of sorry collapses disfiguring the scoreboards. Leadbeater, awarded his 'cap' back in 1969 in the expectation that his almost flawless technique would entitle him to a permanent place, never translated promise into performance, losing his position with an average of around fifteen, and Yorkshire were grateful for the robust work of Bairstow, who responded to the receipt of his 'cap' by blossoming into a solid striker of the ball. Old also offered hints of the all-round skill which eventually served the county so admirably, but no one could get away from the fact that Boycott held the key. Confirmation came on June 30, the most embarrasing day in Yorkshire's history.

Before a disbelieving gathering at St George's Road, Harrogate, Durham grabbed glory as the first minor county to beat first-class opposition in the Gillette Cup and a number of things contributed towards the disaster as the part-timers, including Old's international rugby union playing brother, Alan, comfortably passed Yorkshire's 135 all out with five wickets and a little under nine overs in hand. Old bowled badly for a Test choice and Boycott committed a tactical blunder, finding himself with four overs of his most likely bowler unused after relying on Howard Cooper and Phil Carrick, who contained without threatening when economy had no merit.

The game really swung Durham's way, however, as a result of a single delivery from Stuart Wilkinson, a medium-pacer of no known pedigree. It came with Yorkshire, who had won the toss and decided to bat, on 18. Boycott, in excellent, watchful command, had just square-driven a boundary with calm control when the fatal ball hurried down the pitch. It straightened a fraction off the seam to beat the bat and hit off and middle stumps, carrying Durham to the heights and plunging Yorkshire to the depths. The shock waves would have been no greater had W.G. Grace appeared in a fiery chariot. The earth went spinning from its axis. The laws of nature were suspended.

Boycott's team-mates came and went in a dazed procession, hustled on their way by delirious young men, who acted like pools winners and felt they had done something as clever as selecting eight draws on the football coupons. Boycott's lapse brought the house of cards crashing down and shame spread like a plague.

Bravely stepping into the breach, Temple tried hard to minimise the extent of the catastrophe, saying: 'I am disappointed rather than disheartened. One day we look very good and then we have other days when we look a mediocre side, which we are not.' A good try, but not good enough. There was plenty of evidence of mediocrity which demanded but did not get attention.

A season-long analysis revealed the bowling to be no better than the batting, in spite of the persistence of Old and the courage of Nicholson, who fought his way back to something nearing fitness, patiently assisted by the county's too-little-appreciated physiotherapist Colin Kaye, and took sixty-three wickets. The spin was virtually non-existent, with Wilson dropped and Cope taking six wickets at 42.33 each on his return with a remodelled action. Carrick's twenty-two victims cost 45.86 runs each and Bore had thirty-eight wickets for 32.00. Hutton's contribution amounted to nine wickets and 65 runs, so it was not surprising that the Sunday League satisfaction balanced dismay at fourteenth place in the Championship — Yorkshire's worst.

Incredibly, former Yorkshire captain Ronnie Burnet joined a campaign for a change of leadership, although his statement contained a lot of wishful thinking. 'Something has got to be done very quickly to rescue Yorkshire,' he said. 'The first thing is a change of captain. I do not wish to go into the merits of Boycott as a captain, but the very fact that he is away from the side so often because of England commitments is reason enough for making a change. He has no chance to build up the sort of team spirit Yorkshire need to get them through the current crisis. I would suggest that Richard Hutton be invited to take over the captaincy immediately.

'I'd also like to see the selection committee picking the strongest available side and, as far as I am concerned, that would include playing experienced men like Don Wilson and Doug Padgett. They could provide the experience and Hutton would do the rest . . . it must be obvious to anyone that the one thing the team needs now is experience and fight.'

Since Hutton, in considering his business interests to be more important than cricket, would represent a return to the days of the amateur captain in spirit, he was unlikely to rally a group of disgruntled professionals. Nor were Wilson and Padgett equipped to improve playing performance. Every reasonable guideline led to the conclusion that Boycott stood alone as the man with the very qualities Burnet sought, experience and determination. Given consistent backing he possessed the qualities to make something happen and Burnet, like so many, approached things from the wrong end. He should have been asking why the rest of the contracted squad achieved so little.

Burnet was, though, a powerful personality and attracted an audience. So did Sir Leonard Hutton.

He said: 'I must admit the biggest trouble seems to be the lack of team spirit, although I do not know much about Geoff Boycott as a captain.' No one, however, took the trouble to define team spirit. Its strength or, indeed, its presence is generally difficult for outsiders to gauge and its effect is impossible to calculate, particularly among professionals to whom any game is more than a sport, so it proved impossible for Boycott to answer back. Team spirit usually varies according to the nature of the personnel concerned rather than their ability and divisions existed to a marked degree in a lot of successful teams. Most of the youngsters in the 1970s got on well enough together and a number of those in a position to know accepted the dressing room was happier then than in the past when the participants kept conflict out of sight of the amateur captain.

Burnet, not then on the committee, received no significant support as the players, temporarily realising where their best interests lay, closed ranks and backed Boycott to the hilt. Nicholson led the chorus of protest. 'I have never heard such a load of rubbish. Despite the fact that we are not doing well, the atmosphere in the dressing room is magnificent, much better than in the 1960s when we were winning the Championship. I reckon the Yorkshire dressing room is the best in the country.'

Hampshire lagged little behind in rallying to the cause. 'The captain has my full support and the support of all of us. We are disappointed at not doing well, but the cameraderie is really something. It is a pleasure to play in this side, even if we all realise that our results are upsetting a lot of people. It is about time the record was put straight so far as Geoff is concerned.'

Bairstow and Carrick, representing the younger element upon whom Boycott allegedly poured disdainful scorn, also professed their contentment. 'It is as though people were talking about a different club,' said Carrick.

The player's opinions are the ones worth considering. To deny there were problems is to be at odds with reality and some members of the team probably kept their tongues in their cheeks, yet it is important to acknowledge that they could have been less fulsome or hidden behind the refuge of 'No comment.' They didn't and it was misleading that the attack on Boycott got a lot more publicity than the unsolicited reply with preceded an unequivocal statement from Temple, who thundered: 'I absolutely deplore the unsubstantiated comments which have been made about the captain. It is up to everyone to support the captain and Geoff Boycott has my wholehearted backing.

'I have no reservations at all about his captaincy on the field. He does a first-rate job.' Anyone who wondered about the inclusion of the words 'on the field' did not have to wait long for enlightenment, for Boycott promptly tripped over his broader ambitions. Heartened by the general vote of confidence, he allowed his three-point plan, aimed at restoring the county to the top of the tree, to appear in the *Sunday Mirror* in an article by Ted Dexter, who developed what Boycott regarded as a normal cricketer-journalist conversation. The plan was constructive rather than sensational.

Boycott argued that Yorkshire should acquire their own ground because facility for practice depended on the approval of the various ground authorities and he claimed Leeds had exercised their right to withhold that approval. He also wanted to break with tradition by taking on a ground-staff or at least to extend the coaching system and, thirdly, he asked for a place on the cricket committee, something that was his by right anyway. 'It is still considered right and proper if the players get on with playing the game while someone else makes the important decisions,' he said.

His theme, punctuated by sensible, balanced observations, refuted firmly the attacks made upon him, and much of what he said Illingworth repeated at a later date.

His concern at the declining league standards was shared in every knowledgeable quarter and he illustrated his point with reference to Stephen Coverdale, an eighteen-year-old who had deputised for Bairstow against Nottinghamshire at Bradford but who did not keep wicket for his league club first team. Without whining, Boycott finally emphasised the advantage other counties enjoyed from the presence of imported stars, and the article presented a fair picture of Yorkshire cricket. It brought a stinging rebuke from Connell, who dispatched a stern letter.

A member drew the committee's attention to the newspaper and, reminding Boycott of the expressions of loyalty expressed the week previously, he wrote: 'You are quoted in the Sunday Press as making public criticisms of the committee and its policy and, in particular, implying that you do not have the opportunity to express to the committee your views on general cricket matters. This, I think, you will appreciate is not true. The contrast in the attitudes of the committee and of the club captain cannot have escaped your notice. Mutual trust and mutual loyalty between the committee and the captain of the club are essential and the committee cannot tolerate public criticism of the committee or its policies by its captain. You are free to make whatever criticisms you wish to the committee direct, but not through the media.' A friendlier, hand-written postscript about Boycott's fitness did not lessen the impact of this severe reprimand.

A man-to-man exchange must have been more satisfactory to both parties and Boycott waited for two weeks before replying to express his concern. 'I must at once emphatically deny that I have been in any way disloyal,' he wrote. 'I am sure you all know my main ambition has always been to lead the county team back to its rightful position in the various competitions — to the top; and I also think you will realise that I have always sought to achieve my objectives by dedicating all my efforts to their fulfilment. This principle applies to my present job. If any member or members of the committee have any doubts about my loyalty I would want to meet them and talk it out.'

Turning to the article, Boycott denied it contained any suggestion of troublemaking, adding that while he could not control the Press, he had done his best to gain the confidence of most cricket commentators. He continued: 'I hope that on reflection you will be able to agree that nothing that I am quoted as saying in any way reflects disloyalty to the committee. On the contrary that it emphasises my determination to do whatever I can for Yorkshire cricket. There are two points which I wish to make before ending my letter. First of all, as county captain, I must make myself available to the Press. This is part of the job to which I was appointed by the committee in rather dramatic circumstances when on tour with the English team in Australia.

'I feel that it would be right for the committee to accept that I do my best to be loyal to them, the team, the club and to Yorkshire cricket in general and to bear with me if, on occasion, I get misquoted or misinterpreted, for this can happen to any one of us, whether a member of the team, a member of the committee or an official. Secondly, I do have very definite ideas about how we can achieve our main objective — the resurrection of Yorkshire cricket at county level. I believe we have made real progress towards this in the last twelve months and I think it should be possible to make continued progress and to build our resources into a really first-class team.'

This plea from the heart confirmed that Boycott remained slightly uneasy in his relationship and the danger of his judging others by the same high standards he applied to himself still existed. An indication of the pitfalls came in the fixture with Nottinghamshire at Bradford. Leadbeater, after a fielding error, made an excellent stop and Boycott, with his hands shoulder high, clapped the fielder and turned to the crowd as if to say: 'That was alright. Let's give him a hand.'

A well-intentioned reaction? It contained an element of sarcasm that was not missed. A quiet word or a nod would have been better, just as a simple chat with Boycott would have been beneficial as and when the necessity arose.

The committee's refusal to implement their own regulations, however, blocked the lines of communication. Liaison between the captain on the circuit and the administrators in their offices was not helped by the unexplained failure to invite Boycott to cricket committee meetings. He did not receive a copy of the minutes, which might have made life easier for him, and the committee were on distinctly dangerous ground.

According to the official year books issued by Yorkshire from 1948 to 1959 the first and second-team captains were listed as members of the cricket committee, irrespective of whether they were treated as such. They were, of course, amateurs, but when Wilson replaced Burnet in 1960 an adjustment occurred. The year book from then up to 1971 stated: 'The first and second-team captains are ex-officio members of the cricket committee.'

The words are clear. There is no room for error. Boycott was entitled to attend committee meetings in 1971 'by virtue of his office' and while Yorkshire argued otherwise they were clearly in the wrong. The position slightly altered again in 1972, with the creation of the selection panel, for then Boycott could reasonably be confined to decisions surrounding the composition of the side, but the committee appeared unable to understand their own publication. That is why Boycott possibly annoyed them in extensively advertising his interest although his technical expertise and on-the-spot knowledge should, in any event, have been used to the full.

Yorkshire finally bowed to logic, Boycott being invited to attend his first cricket committee meeting on November 26, 1973. He communicated his pleasure to the chairman. 'I do so wish to say how delighted I was to be invited to join the cricket committee and how much I appreciate all you have done to bring this about. I would like you to know that I shall do everything I can to serve in the best interests of Yorkshire County Cricket Club and I sincerely hope that I will be of some help to the committee in years to come.'

SUB-COMMITTEES

The following Sub-Committees have been appointed for the year 1971 :

Finance Committee

Mr. B. H. BARBER
Mr. C. G. BUCK
Mr. A. H. CONNELL
Mr. M. G. CRAWFORD
Mr. J. H. DICKINSON
Mr. R. L. FEATHER

Mr. W. E. HARBORD
Mr. L. LEWIS
Mr. G. J. SELLERS
Mr. N. SHUTTLEWORTH
Mr. G. H. SMITH
Mr. E. H. UMBERS

Cricket Committee

Mr. F. W. AMBLER
Mr. J. D. H. BLACKBURN
Mr. M. G. CRAWFORD
Mr. R. L. FEATHER
Mr. R. E. HAIGH
Mr. C. HESKETH

Mr. F. MELLING
Mr. A. B. SELLERS
Mr. H. SUTCLIFFE
Mr. W. H. H. SUTCLIFFE
Mr. J. R. F. TEMPLE
Mr. N. W. D. YARDLEY

The First and Second Team Captains are ex-officio members of the Cricket Committee.

Grounds and Membership Committee

Mr. F. R. ATKIN
CAPTAIN J. D. W. BAILEY
Mr. W. E. BAINES
MR. J. D. H. BLACKBURN
Mr. C. R. CLEGG
Mr. A. H. CONNELL
Mr. J. H. DICKINSON
Mr. G. D. DRABBLE
Mr. R. E. HAIGH
Mr. S. B. HAINSWORTH
Mr. W. E. HARBORD
Mr. C. HESKETH

MR. G. P. HIRST
Mr. L. LEWIS
Mr. J. T. LUMB
Mr. H. J. MCILVENNY
Mr. F. MELLING
Mr. A. B. SELLERS
Mr. G. D. SHIRES
Alderman C. J. SIMPSON
Mr. E. H. UMBERS
Mr. H. WILLEY
Mr. C. R. YEOMANS

The President and the Hon. Treasurer are ex-officio members of all the Sub-Committees.

The page from the Yorkshire County Cricket Club yearbook of 1971, which clearly states that Boycott, as captain, was an ex-officio member of the cricket committee.

100

This, together with the smooth and rapid settlement of his contract, marked a brief interlude — a period of relative calm — without giving the impression of total peace. That never came, but, afforded some respite, Boycott brought a semblance of respectability back to Yorkshire in the next few years, although his personal standing plunged as he resolutely turned his back on England.

6 In Exile

Boycott arrived home from a gruelling winter in the West Indies to face the long slog of his 1974 benefit programme weary and dispirited, despite averaging 73.85 in all matches in the Caribbean and 46.78 in the Tests. It was a sad start to a year that involved pressure, frustration and disappointment in equal measure, a year that brought a difference of opinion with his organiser, exile from the England team, heated exchanges involving cricket chairman Temple and another half-hearted rebellion among players whose loyalty flew as a flag of convenience.

The season declined into the unhappiest of his captaincy, with an eventual record benefit of £20,639 offering belated compensation, as confirmation of public goodwill, for the bruises inflicted on his bristling ego.

While Boycott employed his talents far away in Antigua, another ex-Yorkshire captain, Vic Wilson, who had not been noticably close to the action, took it upon himself to comment on the state of the county. 'Personally, I think Boycott should be replaced,' he told his audience at the Sessay club's annual dinner. 'Magnificent run machine that he is, there should be a team spirit with everybody fighting for everybody's place.' As the old red herring floated to the surface again, Wilson went on to contradict himself in one sense.

'When Ray Illingworth left Yorkshire, that was when the fortunes of the county side changed and started to go down hill,' he said, getting his argument back onto a firmer footing, but he then continued: 'There is nothing the matter with the ability of the players, but it is obvious that not everything is running as smoothly as it should.' This sentiment simply flew in the face of reason, for the scorebook revealed that there was obviously a lot wrong with the ability of the players, and if all these so-called experts on Yorkshire cricket had troubled to see sufficient matches or just examine the figures they must have seen that without Boycott's runs there would have been precious little to theorise about. There were, however, too many not qualified to hold an opinion let alone express one.

Unfortunately for everyone Boycott, sooner or later, had to bow to the laws of nature which insisted that he could not continue to carry the team on his back without some reaction. In three magnificent years after taking over from Close, he scored 4,150 runs for the county, averaging 90.21, but he was vulnerable, worn down, like a boxer, by the relentless body punching to which his morale had been subjected. Brash, occasionally aggressive arrogance camouflaged the pain inflicted by wounds driven deep into his back and by the indifference with which his efforts in the West Indies were received.

A slight hesitancy crept into his practice back at the Headingley nets. It passed almost unnoticed but still worried him. With the rhythm not quite right, he discovered difficulty in adjusting to the light after the bright sunshine of the West Indies. He anticipated the difficulties that lay ahead as he got off to an edgy start, despite a run of acceptable scores and a century off the over-matched Cambridge University students. Never exactly in tune, he waited for the crisis while working desperately hard to avert it with relentless application in the nets and out in the middle.

Yorkshire qualified from their group in the Benson and Hedges Cup, and, for all the talk, their concern at losing Boycott's services to MCC during the zonal tie with Nottinghamshire at Trent Bridge was genuine. Action spoke louder than words and the sly suggestions that they did better without him made no impression on the committee, who appealed vainly for his release from the representative engagement after being parties to the agreement which limited MCC to one man per county. When the chips were down everybody wanted Boycott all right.

Yorkshire overcame the disadvantage to win at Nottingham in drizzling gloom, thanks to resourceful batting from Lumb and Old, but there was no respite for Boycott, who fell out of form and under the spell of Solkar.

Seven first-class innings outside the unconsidered university games brought 75 runs, which worried Boycott far more than his benefit because Yorkshire steadily compiled their worst opening sequence in the Championship since the war, going eleven matches before finally beating Nottinghamshire at Worksop. Injury to Hampshire, who broke his thumb in the Benson and Hedges competition, loomed large as the batting failed and went on failing with horrendous regularity. It is against this depressing background, then, that we have to take sides in the row between Boycott and Temple which stemmed from a dull Roses draw at Headingley.

Whatever blame attaches to Boycott, all his actions in a watchful, uninspired contest were conditioned by fear. He fielded first on winning the toss for two reasons. The Leeds groundsmen used the relaid portion of the square for the first time and how it would play was a matter of guesswork, while he had no real faith in his own batting, never mind the less capable others. The wicket turned out to be of low bounce and little pace, so Lancashire found responsibility for shaping the last day's play unwelcome, David Lloyd settling for a target of 244 in 147 minutes plus a minimum twenty overs in the last hour. Yorkshire did not take up the chance, Boycott scoring a sedate, unbeaten 79 out of 124 for three in fifty-four overs to earn Temple's displeasure, which was forcefully expressed.

Talking to the Press, he said: 'We always discuss previous matches at our selection meetings and I shall want to know why we did not make a better attempt at winning. When you win the toss and put in the other side you accept an obligation, it is as simple as that. We just did not set about getting the runs.' The cricket chairman apparently did not know of the official ban on public comments, outlined in Connell's letter to Boycott less than a year previously. 'You are free to make whatever criticisms you wish to the committee direct, but not through the media,' he was told, so the converse surely applied and Temple stood in breach of an agreement. Boycott was entitled to think that one law existed for him and another for the officials, and he answered Temple thoughtfully.

'In the same circumstances, I would do it again,' he said. 'I have to weigh up all the possibilities and then make the decisions. I am surprised at this kind of criticism in one way, yet I realise that some people might express disappointment without taking everything into consideration. It is no use rushing at an innings because we want to win a match. We want to win every match, that goes without saying, but I also have a responsibility to make sure, if possible, that we do not lose. I consulted the senior players, as I usually do. We talked about it and agreed that it was not a justifiable risk unless things went our way early on.

'Our batting has not been too good lately. Nobody, myself included, has been getting runs and it was a lot to expect of us to suddenly come right. If we had lost three or four quick wickets going for the runs the chances are that we would have been beaten, and how many people would have thanked us for that?'

Only a few argued with Boycott. Fielding first by choice imposes no obligation, of course, and never has, and Yorkshire faced the prospect of having to maintain a run-rate far in excess of anything that had gone before. In addition, while they batted in a steady drizzle and poor light, Lancashire bowled a meagre ration of eight overs in the first half hour, continuing to rely largely on pace when they had the opportunity to tease Yorkshire with flight and spin. David Lloyd also understood the practicalities.

When Boycott marched off to the Test trial, the enquiry was held up and then further postponed for one reason and another until it faded from the memory, but the damage had been done to the image of the club and its captain, who followed the approved method by writing privately to Temple. He still believed that mutual trust was being rebuilt, if slowly. Referring to the Roses match, he said that the adverse publicity demonstrated how careful both of them had to be and how important it was to maintain a united front.

Reversing the commonly accepted roles, Boycott, the

aggrieved party, went a long way towards patching up the quarrel, although adding that at least one member of the committee said too much in public and should be stopped.

On top of all this came his traumatic break with England, but once his system got over that shock, he quickly settled back into a familiar groove, hammering Derbyshire for an unbeaten 149 and scoring a defiant 63 in difficult circumstances at Middlesborough, where Middlesex adapted readily to a bowlers' pitch to win by eight wickets. A spectacular 107 by Norman Featherstone wrecked Yorkshire, but he chanced his arm and no one equalled Boycott for quality, a sure portent of better things to come.

Sadly, Yorkshire did not share his regained prosperity and by the end of June languished red-faced at the bottom of the Championship table with the future no brighter than the immediate past. To make matters worse, Boycott fractured the middle finger on his right hand at Leicester, McKenzie yet again doing the damage. Hampshire's recovery marginally softened the blow, giving the middle-order the necessary stability, but a savage mauling at the hands of Worcestershire at Hull, where the margin of defeat in fractionally over two days was an innings and 83 runs, sowed the seeds of further discontent.

A number of players expressed their dissatisfaction with Boycott to the committee, although few had grounds to complain about anyone else in view of their own feeble records, and Temple was moved to issue another statement as speculation mounted. 'The question of Boycott and any change in the captaincy has never been raised at any committee meeting this season,' he said.

Spiteful tongues wagged to the effect that Boycott planned to retire once his benefit money was safely gathered in, leaving Yorkshire to their own devices — a fate, incidentally, they thoroughly deserved. Repeated with noisy frequency, it demanded a denial, and Boycott issued one, sitting on the grass just outside the boundary fence at Hull, a lonely figure as his beaten team departed.

'Why should I want to give up?' he asked. 'Yorkshire cricket is still my life and I never want to play for any other county. That would not be the same thing at all because I

106

believe in and care about Yorkshire and Yorkshire alone. I
know there are people who want to force me out and I know
who many of them are. I intend to play for the county for as
long as I can.'

Colleagues who had backed Boycott so loudly less than a
year before shifted their allegiance perceptibly and Hampshire,
in the car park of the Hull Crest Motel on the last morning
of the Worcestershire match, said briefly: 'I have nothing to
say about the position with Boycott. I supported him before,
but it's up to him now.' One thing, though, was crystal clear.
Boycott could not be blamed for the plight in which Yorkshire found themselves as the batting averages at that stage
in the season illustrated conclusively.

YORKSHIRE'S CHAMPIONSHIP BATTING AVERAGES
as at 9 July 1974

	INNS	NOT OUT	RUNS	HS	AVGE
Boycott	11	3	415	149*	51.87
Hampshire	7	1	236	87	39.33
Leadbeater	15	2	361	92*	27.76
Lumb	13	2	289	123*	26.27
Hutton	16	2	292	102*	20.85
Bairstow	15	1	254	56*	18.14
Sharpe	18	1	295	41	17.35
Cope	12	2	149	43	14.90
Carrick	7	2	71	44*	14.20
Old	7	0	96	35	13.71
Squires	15	1	182	67	13.00
Nicholson	11	5	76	17*	12.66
Johnson	7	0	66	36	9.42

Without playing anything like the highest number of
innings, Boycott scored over 50 runs more than anyone else
and only four other batsmen averaged better than 20. Hampshire's 39.33 stood as the solitary acceptable figure other
than his own, for really anything less than 30 leaves a lot to
be desired in a specialist batsman. Sharpe slithered along the
downward path which ended in his release, while England
rugby union winger Peter Squires, who always gave the
impression of being a useful striker of the ball, and the con-

scientious Johnson achieved nothing at all, despite fielding
with athletic brilliance in the covers and at mid-wicket. The
catalogue of near disaster underlined that Yorkshire's playing
strength did not match up to requirements.

Laying even a small proportion of the responsibility for
this sorry state of affairs at Boycott's door dangerously
missed the point, and cautiously the more thoughtful considered the possibilities of signing an overseas player on a
strictly one-off basis to spread the load. Anticipating resistance they reckoned that the risk of temporarily alienating
the membership was worth taking, subject to the right man
being found. Briefly a small group pondered over pushing the
issue, with South African Eddie Barlow in mind, and this
highly efficient all-rounder might have joined Boycott to
form a winning partnership, but things drifted on due to a
shortage of the nerve that redirects the course of history.

In relation to the internal disquiet, another relatively
minor yet impressive incident deserves mention. Yorkshire's
game against Warwickshire at Abbeydale Park splashed to an
early conclusion as heavy rain swept the exposed ground
throughout the second day, driving everyone into the sponsors'
tent to enjoy the warm, dry hospitality. Everyone that is
except Boycott, Carrick and Arthur Robinson, who spent a
drenching hour in the soddened nets. Those watching from
convenient shelter cast Boycott in the role of volunteer, since
he did all the batting, and the other two as pressed men,
having to bowl under orders. Not a bit of it. The left-arm
spinner shrugged off the rain and explained his eagerness to
take part in what appeared a foolhardy exercise.

'The one thing about bowling to Geoff is that you learn
something all the time. We were out there for my benefit as
much as his. He told me one or two things I wanted to know
and pointed out small errors he had noticed from a batsman's
point of view during matches.' Robinson, an unfailingly
cheerful left-arm medium-pacer from Northallerton, echoed
the sentiments.

Boycott's good points as a team man have so regularly
been overlooked or missed altogether, but another welcome
move brought him back into the team for the Gillette Cup tie
following the Hull debacle.

He underwent the ritual of a long net at the Anlaby Circle ground before declaring himself fit, despite experiencing pain. 'I could do to rest a bit longer,' he said, 'but I want to show the right sort of example. Things are bad and perhaps a Cup win would make it easier for the boys.' Hampshire's unbeaten 87 turned out to be the match-winning performance against the county of the same name in the Gillette Cup tie — a fitting outcome — but Boycott provided the inspiration, particularly in handling his reduced resources in the field when Hutton limped out of the attack with a pulled muscle in his back.

The all-rounder bowled one over and while Leadbeater operated splendidly as an emergency seamer, the whole side responded well to the captain's thoughtful lead. Yorkshire won by 41 runs to upset the odds impressively and Boycott did his best to use the victory as a morale booster. 'This shows what we are capable of,' he said. 'We are a much better side than our position suggests and I think we can go on to better things now.'

This they did, Boycott master-minding and Hampshire starring in a tremendous triumph at Worksop, where Robinson reaped the reward of his labours with a hat-trick and Yorkshire enjoyed the best of the weather to sweep home by an innings and 69 runs. This first Championship success of the season was particularly valuable since it ended a sequence of forty-three first-class away matches without a win stretching back to July 28 1970, when Boycott's unbeaten 260 helped to beat Essex by an innings and 101 runs at Colchester.

Of those games, seven were played under Close, twenty-one with Boycott as captain, nine with Sharpe in charge and six under Wilson and Yorkshire were pleased to stop the rot. The form hinted at a smattering of potential for the rest of the season which was not lost on Boycott as his personal plans remained in the balance.

He did not reply to an invitation to tour Australia in Denness's party, although indicating privately that he wanted to go. He was unsure because he knew Yorkshire's poor record counted against him in the smarter circles when the England captaincy came up for discussion, even though his frequent absences affected it, and he recognised the possibility of proving something if he stayed in charge throughout the full campaign.

Three factors helped to sway his final decision — his mother's condition, a cricket committee meeting on September 12 and a weariness of spirit which expressed itself as a physical illness.

At the committee meeting, former England wicket-keeper Don Brennan asked whether Boycott could guarantee that he would not revert to the way in which he played at the start of the season if he lost form again. Brennan also wondered if he would play under another captain, while Sutcliffe raised the suggestion that he might do better as a batsman if he were not captain. This when as top Englishman in the national average with 1,783 runs (59.43) he finished fourth behind Clive Lloyd, Barry Richards and Glenn Turner.

Robin Feather, a Bradford representative on the Yorkshire committee, drew attention to the uncertainty surrounding Boycott's Test obligations with some thoughts on whether the team would appreciate having one captain all the time, barring injury, but on a confidence-sapping majority vote Boycott was reappointed for 1975.

On September 24 he withdrew from the tour party 'for personal reasons' permitting, however, the vaguest hint of a plan taking shadowy form to escape. It was based on the slight upsurge in the second half of the 1974 season. Hampshire's blistering power had a lot to do with Yorkshire's brighter moments and he scored 157 not out and 158 in the victories over Nottinghamshire and Gloucestershire. In that Gloucestershire game at Harrogate they introduced a new medium-pace bowler in Steve Oldham, who made his senior debut ten days before his twenty-sixth birthday almost as an after-thought, and it is an accurate reflection on the extent of Boycott's difficulties that he came into the side because there was nobody else. Injuries seriously limited the county's options, which were reduced to virtually nothing when Dennis Schofield, a medium-pace seamer from Holmfirth in the Huddersfield League, found his firm reluctant to allow him further time off work. For various reasons several other alternatives did not answer the call so Oldham was a last-minute choice.

Although a regular second-team player, Oldham had wandered into no man's land when he and Yorkshire bumped into each other to their mutual benefit. He possessed a lively pace and earned regular employment without really becoming an automatic selection or making a great impact, although when they parted company in 1979 he took the decision and moved on to Derbyshire.

Boycott slipped out of the limelight for a while, but he still headed the three-day and Sunday League averages, scoring over 500 first-class runs more than his nearest rival. His dominance of the Sunday scene was such that his average of 40.33 left him the only one above 30, so those who approached the committee with submissions about his competence as captain revealed an amazing shortsightedness.

He alone prevented their frailty being cruelly exposed. Hutton, for example, took part in the discussions, but in what was to be his last season he averaged 18.80 with the bat in first-class games and his 24 wickets cost 25.83 runs each. Similarly in the Sunday League his figures were 17.37 and 23.16 respectively which put him at a distinct disadvantage when talking about relative merits.

Towards the end of the season, Yorkshire, led by Boycott, comprehensively outplayed Sussex at Headingley, Derbyshire at Chesterfield, and Surrey at Bradford, while honours were even at Scarborough in the draw with Kent. Also there were some moments in the Sunday League to inspire hopes of better days, leaving Boycott anxious to exploit the situation.

One thing seemed clear from the outside. He could not pick and choose. He must stay either inside the England camp or cut himself off altogether, and this he did, so that his horizon shrunk to encircle the domestic scene, which was far from calm.

Some players grumbled about the financial terms, three of them seeking a meeting with the committee to negotiate an increase, while Sharpe, Wilson and Hutton all departed for reasons which were not made exactly clear. As another chunk of experience disappeared, the rather surprised Sharpe coming to terms with Derbyshire, Yorkshire ought to have been weakened and the future did not look bright superficially, yet Boycott hid his dismay very well. He faced a tough battle against discontent, scheming critics and a system enabling every side but his own to be strengthened by overseas talent, but he was ready to test his and the county's mettle by means of a bold thrust.

Wisely he refrained from broadcasting his plans. He believed he had plenty of information concerning these undercurrents in Yorkshire and asked to meet the president, Sir Kenneth Parkinson, and the chairman in an attempt to establish a working relationship at all levels. Far from being divisive, Boycott, albeit as an act, in part, of self-preservation, tried to unite the warring factions and included on the agenda for this secret meeting, eventually held on February 18 1975, were:

1 — How to establish trust.
2 — The possibility of eliminating disloyal elements.
3 — Elimination of all signs of public dissent.
4 — Control of publicity concerning team selection and individual playing performance.
5 — Establishing firm but fair team discipline, supported by the committee collectively and committee members individually.
6 — Improvement of selection procedures and announcements.
7 — Improvement of practice facilities and arrangements and their enforcement.
8 — Improved contract arrangements.

Boycott and Mutch immersed themselves totally in this project, but there is little evidence of self-interest and they stood to gain nothing much themselves. A bit of peace for the captain perhaps and very little else. The discussions occupied some three and a half hours during which Boycott frankly outlined the areas in need of attention and Connell wrote: 'I am sure our meeting was very worthwhile. We can, I think, only proceed by general exhortation and education, but this there will be.'

Before leaving the trials and tribulations of 1974 we will pause and study the partly completed jigsaw with one key piece quietly fitted into place. Towards the end of the summer, I met an old friend in Reg Haigh, the one-time Huddersfield representative on the county committee and then a vice-president. As the son of the famous Schofield Haigh, who shared the glory of Hirst and Rhodes, he had long and illustrious links with Yorkshire, serving for many years on the cricket sub-committee. Normally he was the soul of discretion, faithfully keeping the secrets that were part and parcel of his life, but for once his feelings got the better of him. Declining to contribute towards one of the many collections taken for Boycott, he proclaimed fiercely: 'I wouldn't give him twopence. He only got the job in the first place because some of them lost their courage at the last minute. A lot of us didn't want him in the side, let alone as captain.'

Said with passion, the sentiments came from the heart and represented a conviction which was entirely his business, but it could only have been cricket committee members who had lost their courage at the time of Boycott's appointment — and Close's sacking — so what would have happened if they had remained steadfast? Wilson for captain! The assumption is unavoidable, but there is nothing to indicate that things would have been any better and the obvious inference from this tit-bit of off-hand conversation is that Yorkshire were in a quandary as they fired Close.

Regretting this minor betrayal of confidence, Haigh declined to comment further, but his words confirmed that Boycott's promotion represented uneasy compromise at best.

Boycott wintered well, preparing his notes for the February meeting, fulfilling his carefully calculated quota of net practice and planning to make the best use of what he had got. Although logic prophesied a further decline for a Yorkshire team weighed down by the loss of three more England cricketers, he banked on youth and enthusiasm more than compensating, together with the regular supply of runs from his own bat.

Ironically, Hampshire, who went on the controversial Robins' tour of South Africa from March 1 to April 2, severely damaged his right ankle in which he experienced discomfort for a long time, but, notwithstanding all the complications, Yorkshire made nonsense of prediction by steadily climbing up the table rather as if a load had been lifted from their shoulders. Second place in the Championship rankings would have been welcomed as a near miracle by many counties and, since the gallant Nicholson managed only seventy-three overs and six wickets, it more than sufficed, even in Yorkshire, to silence all opposition to Boycott.

It is arguable that this remarkable development in the one year that he played regularly was the long arm of coincidence, but it is better sense to admit that his talents counted for more than those of Sharpe, Hutton and Wilson put together.

He set the ball rolling with a defiant battle cry. 'I believe that if we start the new season where we left off last year, when, for two months we had a more or less settled side and played very well, it should not be long before we are winning one of the four major trophies. Some of our youngsters are no longer inexperienced in terms of opportunity in the first team, so now is the time for them to turn in performances that command established places.

'When Yorkshire gained their first county Championship under Lord Hawke, he said "I could have won nothing unless I had the loyal support of the team and one of the best committees it was possible to serve under." I sincerely hope to be able to say something like that in the future.'

Yorkshire had a difficult opening programme, taking in games against Surrey, Kent, Worcestershire, who were the defending Champions, Lancashire and Leicestershire, so Boycott called a team meeting to discuss the overall approach, another shrewd move, aimed at involving everyone and building a feeling of togetherness. The players sensibly opted for caution, contenting themselves with avoiding defeat in the first month and justification of such modest ambition came at once, untidy bowling and fielding marking a rain-ruined draw with Surrey.

Boycott endured the extra annoyance of being turned down by the Leeds club when he asked for a Yorkshire League game in the search of practice. Having already agreed to accommodate Cope, Leeds were in a difficult position, but Boycott did not like it, insisting that not enough consideration was given to the county. His spirits soared again with a much better all-round effort at Dartford, where grim resistance on a tricky pitch plus a high standard of bowling almost fashioned a victory of traditional quality and he then had the satisfaction of reaching a personal landmark.

Worcestershire basked in the distinction of being the only county against whom he had not recorded a century, so he arrived at the beautiful cathedral ground with an extra incentive. By a quirk of circumstance, it was only his ninth innings against Worcestershire and he took the precaution of having the champagne on ice. It stayed there for quite a while as rain brought the first day to a premature end with Boycott barely warmed to his task. Adding to the sense of the dramatic, the Action Group disbanded, leaving behind £400 for the use of the county club, a warning that many eyes were fixed on Yorkshire's activities and a stinging exit line. Jack Mewies, a Skipton solicitor, their spokesman, said he felt they had made the right sort of impact. 'We got Yorkshire to admit that Close was badly treated and we also got rid of Sellers as cricket chairman, though in view of what has happened since I am not sure that was altogether a good thing. We hope they are not going to chuck out any more players who are capable of doing well in the county side.'

When Boycott resumed at Worcester, he was superb. The pitch offered the bowlers every chance, which they eagerly accepted, but only at one end. As John Inchmore and Brian Brain extracted vicious lift and later Ted Hemsley, Norman Gifford and Ian Johnson made the ball turn, Boycott operated with such unruffled calm that two members of the team went out for more champagne — at his expense!

He savoured the nineties at leisure, loitering over a succession of singles to arrive at one hundred without nervous haste, but the other side of his nature immediately shone through as he punched the air vigorously and threw up his arms in a giant V-for-victory sign. Typically, substantially longer minutes of solid application followed his moment of pure joy. Self-satisfaction gave way to dedication and where others might have thrown away their wicket to celebrate, Boycott turned his attention instead to winning the match.

'Of course I was pleased, very pleased,' he said at the party in his room at the Giffard Hotel. 'That is only part of it though. As Yorkshire captain I have to do my best for the side, which is what I did.' His best grew into 152 not out in a total of 278 for eight wickets declared, with the next highest score Lumb's 29, and when Worcestershire limped to 124 for six he had brought Yorkshire a marked advantage. From that point, as the wicket dried out in an entirely friendly fashion, the game ran away from Boycott, who stepped back into the more familiar role of villain by delaying his declaration until Worcestershire required 273 in 110 minutes. He accepted the derision of the crowd with an air of resignation that fitted him like an old coat.

He had seen and heard it all before and there was no necessity for him to explain anything to his opposite number Gifford, who passed on a sympathetic parting word. Given time and a fair hearing Boycott might have persuaded the spectators that he had never been in a position to win and, therefore, saw no reason to risk defeat. Yorkshire's second innings concluded with an unbroken fourth-wicket partnership of 83 between Hampshire and Old, who collected the runs in an hour against defensive fields so easily that Worcestershire fancied their chances in any reasonable run chase. Boycott also acknowledged that the other side would not view in a favourable light the concession of points to the title-holders and while he erred on the cautious side in some instances, usually he simply bowed to the inevitable.

Maybe as a reaction to the armchair experts, who always thought they knew better, or perhaps in an attempt to show that he did not mind being 'one of the boys', Boycott played the wildest innings of his career at Canterbury in the Sunday League, lashing out so furiously that he frightened his team mates half to death and they crashed to a six-wicket defeat. His share of 115 amounted to 24 hysterical runs and mercifully he abandoned the experiment with the long handle there and then.

Recovering from this rush of blood, he held Yorkshire together effectively as the first part of the plan carried them into June unbeaten in the Championship. That was all that could be said, though, for they were fourteenth in the table which did not look good, no better than halfway up the Sunday League and out of the Benson and Hedges Cup having lost in the quarter-finals. This latter disappointment was no fault of his, for his scores in the limited-overs compe-

tition had been 47, 51, 54, 59 and 58, the highest for Yorkshire on each occasion, but his worries surrounded his master
plan which hung limply on the drawing board.

It would have been so easy for everything to collapse about
his ears, with Old going away on World Cup duty and his
pace attack in the willing but ordinary hands of Robinson,
Cooper, Stevenson and Arnie Sidebottom, yet Boycott did
more than muddle through. He created circumstances in
which Yorkshire thrived to the delight of his friends and the
dismay of his enemies.

The significance of his refusal to play for England became
apparent, for without both him and Old the team would have
been a desperately patched up affair, but he had already
dedicated himself to the county by informing the selectors
he did not wish to be considered for the World Cup or the
four-match Test series with the Australians.

'I hope we can win something, because we have the ability.
If people think I have let them down by not playing for
England, I am sorry, but I have thought very carefully about
this. It is not something I have decided on the spur of the
moment. I don't think of myself as a quitter. I have worked
too hard for that and too many people have shown their
faith in me. I have realised that the prestige and money you
get from playing for England really is not everything. This
season I have been determined to enjoy myself in trying to
bring some success to Yorkshire and that is why I do not
want to play for England. There is nothing sinister in my
decision, though there are those who will invent an ulterior
motive, I suppose. Not many really know me. Perhaps this
year I will change some opinions. At any rate, I can try.'

All this went down well in a dressing room different in
character as well as personnel, for relationships were raised to
a happier plane with a cheerful acceptance of the captain's
'little eccentricities'. An easy-going attitude developed,
boosted by a spendid win at Bristol, where Gloucestershire,
defeated by an innings and 122 runs, barely carried the
contest into the third day and captured only two Yorkshire
wickets while surrendering twenty of their own.

Nor was it eroded by failure against Middlesex at Scarborough, where Yorkshire had the worst of a rain-affected

pitch. Boycott's unbeaten 175 could not prevent the visitors, who carried the older heads, winning by 20 runs, but this was the only defeat of the season and Yorkshire went on to out-play Warwickshire handsomely at Edgbaston by nine wickets.

Boycott scored 462 runs for an average of 115.5 and York-shire won two out of three matches during the period of the World Cup. England's loss, Yorkshire's gain and in considering the period when the side turned a corner it is informative to reflect on the players who did the trick. The line-up was Boycott, Lumb, Leadbeater, Hampshire, Sidebottom, Bairstow, Carrick, Stevenson, Cooper, Cope and Robinson. Stevenson went on to earn his England 'caps' and Sidebottom, despite more than his share of injuries, became a first-class competitor in every sense, but in 1975 they were merely highly-rated juniors.

As individuals, Yorkshire hardly excited the imagination, but thoughtfully guided by Boycott they worked as a unit. With Old back, they duly defeated Hampshire and the move up the table gathered momentum, attracting the detractors to the barricades of blind prejudice. The wreckers dismissed a string of workmanlike performances because of the quality of the weakened opposition and this was, to be accurate, a half-truth.

Gloucestershire missed their Pakistan Test stars, while Hampshire lacked Gordon Greenidge and Andy Roberts, from the all-conquering West Indian World Cup squad, and Richards, who declared himself unfit. Still they suffered no more than Yorkshire in having to rely on more local skills and it was funny how excuses were made for them but not for Boycott and his men.

A further indication of the nonsense to which he was subjected came at Harrogate as Somerset and Close scrambled to a draw with their last pair at the wicket. They made 423 for seven in the first innings, thanks to a superlative unbeaten 217 from Viv Richards, so Yorkshire's frustration was eased by a degree of self-congratulation, but the knockers, single-minded to a man, lashed Boycott for a declaration setting Somerset 300 in three hours.

Close, fuming at either his side's collapse to 116 for nine or the fact that Boycott enjoyed the better of the exchanges, complained about negative cricket. 'If he had set 85 an hour we would have had a go, and I know who I would have backed,' he moaned. Boycott, too, knew whom he would have backed on those terms as well, so he asked rather more and got as near to success as he dared to hope.

The next fixture has a minor place in history, marking Hampshire's active appearance in the first-class captaincy stakes. He made his debut in this direction at Bournemouth in the final match of the 1974 summer, but got on the field solely to inspect the saturated turf, the abandonment coming without a ball being bowled. Boycott, nursed a strained wrist tendon through his purple patch, but gave in to the pain and dropped out of the fixtures with Sussex at Hove and Derbyshire at Chesterfield and Hampshire, as he took over, was not exactly enchanted at the prospect.

He got off to a winning start, Yorkshire grittily taking full advantage of some bad captaincy by Greig to edge home by two wickets on a pitch from which the ball reared and spat on the last day, thus adding confirmation that some of the old qualities were being discovered.

Hampshire's worst fears turned into reality at Chesterfield, however, when he won a toss he wanted to lose and reluctantly batted on a green pitch that suited Mike Hendrick down to the ground. Yorkshire nudged and pushed their hesitant way to 146 and the acting captain wished he could have debated the pros and cons of putting in Derbyshire. Boycott appreciated exactly how he felt, for there would have been plenty wise after the event if he had fielded first and lost. Rain spared the team's blushes without disguising a flaw in the system.

While Yorkshire busily restored self-respect, England got rid of the luckless Denness, who suffered the inevitable penalty for a first Test disaster in which Australia finished an innings and 85 runs to the good. For an hour or two Boycott wondered if the captaincy would have come his way had he not opted out and he got the vote from Illingworth, who recognised virtue when he saw it and who had a first-hand example of the fighting heart transplanted into Yorkshire cricket by the lonely surgeon in the Gillette Cup clash between his old county and Leicestershire at Headingley.

Boycott, although less than one hundred per cent fit, again put the team first and played, his 24 being bettered by just two other batsmen in a low-scoring encounter. Yorkshire, held to 109, reduced Leicestershire to 86 for nine before McKenzie and Ken Higgs inched their team into the second round in what turned out to be a dress rehearsal for the Championship run-in.

More important than any single result, however, was the way Yorkshire pulled at last in the same direction, a co-ordination of effort not seen for many years, and Illingworth was quick to praise when he could have sneered. 'With only 109 runs to play with they made a magnificent effort,' he summed up. 'I do not want to see it happen, but if Yorkshire were to recruit one top overseas batsman they would probably be an outstanding side.'

This testament to an outstanding recovery brought out the point Boycott's critics conveniently avoided — overseas players — and it is apparent that one man paid the price for a massively supported principle. At the same time, Boycott slipped up, being talked into playing the unproven Alan Hampshire, John's younger brother, in the Cup tie and then complaining about the mistake afterwards, but no real damage was done, and Yorkshire experienced the heady delights of topping the Championship at the end of July when they earned eighteen points from another fine display. Surrey were defeated at the Oval by 35 runs, Carrick bowling Pat Pocock to conclude a persistent bit of cricket through which the often discussed team spirit shone like a beacon. Boycott had little to say as the vast Oval dressing room rang to the sounds of excited horseplay, but his self-conscious enjoyment of the occasion allowed little doubt about his thoughts.

He accepted then that Leicestershire, with games in hand, were favourites for the title and they duly edged out Yorkshire, who won six of their last eight games and stood up to the tension marvellously. Boycott put together his last Championship double-century — 201 not out — as Middlesex were vanquished and everything finished in a blaze of glory at Middlesborough, where the happy-go-lucky Essex suitably filled the role of sacrificial lambs.

Victory by 59 runs was Yorkshire's tenth of the Championship season and their total of fifty-six batting bonus points brought general satisfaction, for only five of the other sixteen counties did better. Boycott scored 1,891 runs for an average of 72.73 in the three-day competition, nearly 500 more than anyone else. Remarkable consistency ensured that his average never dipped below 67 throughout the campaign and his brilliant first-wicket partnership with Lumb was at the heart of the county's batting.

One of the saddest aspects of the troubled years concerned the way in which serious differences rose up between Boycott and Lumb. The latter, without endearing himself to the supporters, appeared regularly in the side as the one batsman after Boycott and Hampshire upon whom the county could rely. Favouring the leg side and rarely spectacular, Lumb advanced by stealth, creeping up on the scoreboard almost unobserved, although it was a shortage of speed about the field that usually brought the wrath of the customers down on his head.

Despite his doubts about Boycott, however, Lumb's best season was 1975, when he opened the innings regularly with his captain.

They fashioned six century starts to Championship innings, averaging slightly over 64 together as they provided the type of platform which made Holmes and Sutcliffe so feared and respected. Lumb collected 1,396 Championship runs and 1,532 altogether in all first-class matches for an average of 41.40, which stood as his best long after bitterness had crept into the relationship.

Yorkshire's fifth place in the Sunday League owed plenty to Boycott's 666 runs, a total only 23 short of the competition record held by Barry Richards. He had seven half-centuries in fourteen innings, only once failing to get into the 20s and averaged 60.54. Hampshire chipped in with 627 runs (48.23), with Lumb's 222 runs leaving him a distant third on aggregate.

Boycott's facility for pressing on enabled him to put his name to another record at Scarborough. A rare 99 made up slightly more than half the 186 he put on with Hampshire to set a new Sunday best for the first wicket as Gloucestershire suffered a pounding and an 11-run defeat. In every possible way Yorkshire prospered in the wake of his triumphant progress, but two matters spoiled an otherwise trouble-free year. The first concerned an incredible outburst from John Edrich, the Surrey captain, who launched an outspoken if badly researched attack on Boycott and Yorkshire, his anger being occasioned by the England situation.

'I think it is wrong that while the rest of us do our duty and are proud to do it, whether the going is tough or not, Boycott, who made his name with England and currently tops the national averages, should be able to opt out and carry his county to the top of the table. If Yorkshire win the Championship this season, it will be unfair to other counties who consistently give their best men for England duty.' Noble sentiments, but entirely misplaced.

Edrich spoke after three Surrey players, including himself, had been called up, but he did not get around to mentioning that Pakistan Test men Younis Ahmed and Intikhab, as members of the Oval staff, gave Surrey a regular advantage over Yorkshire, who did not complain. Unwittingly, though, he touched on a significant aspect of the Championship.

Glamorgan (1969), Hampshire (1973) and Worcestershire (1974) all captured the title without providing one player for England, so the cost of patriotism was too expensive for some, and in 1975 Yorkshire's Old and Hampshire played Test cricket. Boycott's record with England stood unchallenged in the post-war era, for he opened the innings sixty-four times — one more than Len Hutton and eighteen more than Edrich, the other two on the right side of the forty mark. On every count Edrich was unfair, but if Boycott was innocent in that instance, there can be no appeal in the face of a guilty verdict over a breach of club ethics.

Before the cricket committee had the chance to consider awarding any 'caps' Boycott publicly tied their hands by foolishly saying he did not intend to make any recommendations along those lines. 'Several youngsters did well and that is very pleasing for everyone concerned,' he said. 'But Yorkshire "caps" are awarded for persistently high levels of performance over a period of time, not on the strength of one encouraging season. The ones who have done well should be told so and rewarded financially but I do not think a "cap" must follow automatically. It has to be something for which a player strives continually, always raising his performance until it is clear that his "cap" has been earned over a long and consistent period.'

These sentiments were in keeping with the high standards Boycott saw as the long-term solution and he knew well enough that 'caps' had been awarded too quickly in the past, 'devaluing the coinage'. They should, however, have been saved for the committee meeting and the other members of that body were furious that he usurped power so casually, facing them with a *fait accompli*. If they awarded a 'cap' — and Carrick, with 79 first-class wickets at 21.17 came into the reckoning — it would be marked down as a slight on the captain, besides publicising another division in the camp.

In backing Boycott, they acquitted themselves better than he did and he was also wrong when bluntly stating that the team still had a long way to go. This he did after an unwilling appearance before the cheering enthusiasts at Middlesborough as feelings ran high, almost as high as expectation. His balanced, calculated response to all the rejoicing struck the wrong note, and it was neither the time nor the place to be talking of more toil and tears. Yorkshire cricket had been down in the doldrums for so long that its followers deserved a break from grim reality.

These shortcomings hardly affected his standing with the public, however, and for a while he basked in unqualified hero-worship. He missed only two Championship and two Sunday League fixtures in a triumphant procession and the split decision which gave him another year as captain in 1975 was translated into a unanimous one, although, by accident or design, two of his most outspoken critics failed to turn up for the meeting on October 10.

Boycott had turned the tables comprehensively on his detractors, who consistently attributed Yorkshire's decline to his leadership. The Championship return of only one defeat was the best for Yorkshire since 1946 so that something positive resulted from his self-imposed Test exile.

The light flickering at the end of the tunnel little over a year previously shone brightly, and he thought the title could

have come Yorkshire's way with better luck with the weather.
'I can't remember one instance when it has helped us,' he
reflected. 'We would probably have beaten Glamorgan on a
turning wicket if the match had not been spoiled by rain and
we were in good positions against Leicestershire at Bradford,
Worcestershire at Worcester and Surrey at Leeds when the
weather intervened.' Nicholson's retirement left the seam
bowling cupboard rather bare, however, spotlighting the un-
certain patches in the background. Old was an outstanding
seamer, but Cooper and Robinson fitted in as supporting cast,
so much depended on how Stevenson and Sidebottom coped
with extra demands.

Boycott, keenly aware of the need to maintain and channel
the spirit and enthusiasm feeding on the fruits of success,
spent the winter waging a long, hard, unsung battle on the
team's behalf over the rates of pay. Bearing in mind the
possible implications of a Government wage freeze taking
little account of the cricketer's complicated and precarious
lot, he thought advice should be sought to design an acceptable system. As the committee refused to accept readily his
proposals, the danger arose of at least two players leaving.
Anxious to ensure a decent standard of living for his men,
Boycott stuck to his guns, squeezing some concessions to
bring about a satisfactory conclusion.

A long and very carefully worded letter to the chairman
went a long way towards raising the club offer — another case
of Boycott's value as an intermediary and of his work in the
common cause. Cricketers' salaries are not straightforward
because they are usually paid over six months, leaving them
free to supplement their incomes from a variety of sources in
winter. Some, of course, are luckier than others here, and
quite a few Yorkshiremen bemoaned the fact that the committee did not do more to make their lives easier. 'You get a
lot of promises from them, but at the end of the season
nothing ever happens,' complained one. 'Surely with all these
businessmen about there should be a few jobs going to tide
one or two of us over. Not all the lads want to go overseas to
play more cricket. You get a bit fed up playing day in day
out for most of the year and staleness creeps in, but they
can't afford to do anything else.'

So Boycott collected another merit mark without any attendant publicity and the first weekend of the 1976 season began on the most encouraging note. It ended in all-encompassing depression, for the forty-eight hours encapsulated a nine-wicket win over Kent in the Benson and Hedges Cup, a six-wicket defeat at the hands of Surrey in the Sunday League and, worst of all, injury to Old, who broke down with knee trouble that was to cripple Yorkshire.

As they tumbled down to an uncomfortable eighth in the Championship and a miserable fifteenth in the Sunday League, it was easy and convincing to dismiss 1975 as a flash in the pan, but that did not take account of the mishaps which included Boycott being badly hurt. The blow which broke a bone in his right hand in the Sunday 'battle of the Roses' at Old Trafford on May 16, fractured the controlling vertebra in the spinal cord of the county's resistance. He stood down from nine successive Championship games between May 19 and July 18 while Hampshire presided over five draws, two wins and two defeats and some more unrest became apparent.

Old took seven wickets at 44.14 in four Championship outings all the season. The promising Sidebottom, who dislocated his right elbow assisting Huddersfield Town in the Football League and then got hurt in the famous West Indies confrontation on a dicey pitch at Abbeydale Park, managed 44.3 overs and six wickets. Eighth place in the final Championship table represented neither disgrace nor failure to the fairminded, therefore, although that troublesome variable, team spirit, all right at the start of the season after Boycott had won the extra money, gradually disintegrated. The set-back at the hands of Combined Universities in the Benson and Hedges Cup at Barnsley did not help.

Although they lost the toss and, with it, a rain-affected tie to Surrey at Bradford, they considered themselves certainties to qualify from their group when, thanks to Old's all-round efforts, they crushed Sussex at Hove. The minnows from Oxford and Cambridge, thrown into the big pool to make up the numbers, duly arrived at Shaw Lane without a point to their name. They departed with the most famous scalp of all hanging from their belt, while Yorkshire held an angry inquest behind a firmly closed dressing room door.

Hampshire made a very surprising decision by pairing the young Bill Athey, who made his debut only three days earlier, with Leadbeater, whose well-known correct style inhibited his range of forcing strokes. Leadbeater used fifty-three deliveries to collect 24 runs, Athey received ninety-four balls from which he laboured to 30 and after this crawl Yorkshire panicked. Old and Hampshire, swept up in it, got themselves out without scoring before Johnson organised a sketchy resistance and carried the score to 185 for seven. That should have been enough, but Old, who complained of pain in his left leg after being hit twice by Sarfraz Nawaz in the course of a gallant century at Northampton on the Wednesday, got it into his head that bowling short offered the easy route to victory and Hampshire could not persuade him otherwise.

The completely unknown Gajan Pathmanathan struck 36 from four overs by the England bowler with contemptuous precision and nothing much mattered after that.

Boycott, looking very thoughtful, watched it all from the tea room, breaking off occasionally to sign autographs. He saw all he had carefully built falling down, but he stayed out of the way on orders. 'They don't want my opinion, so what can I do?' he asked. 'I kept out of the dressing room to give John a free hand, but I think I could have helped. It does not make sense to me to have me here and not use my experience.'

Possibly there and then, surrounded by friends, neighbours and some former team-mates from his formative years in the Yorkshire League, he toyed with the idea of returning to the England side, but a lot happened before he crossed that distant bridge. One occurrence related directly to his links with the England selectors and the captain, Greig. Barrington and Sir Leonard Hutton, who were on the selection panel, turned up at Hove for the Benson and Hedges tie and, while Boycott was dismissed for six, exploratory talks took place. Nothing concrete developed, all concerned maintaining a discreet silence, but so long as they kept lines of communication open the position remained open-ended.

While Boycott filled in the idle hours with tantalising day dreams and theories as to how matters might most quickly be put right again, Yorkshire continued to struggle. Things did not go all that well before his injury and at Ilford, Yorkshire, bowled out for 113 and 228, lost by nine wickets to end a run of nine wins and five draws. Boycott himself made only 9 and 2, the first time since the Bramall Lane Roses match of 1973, when he scored 9 and 6, that he had failed to reach double figures in one innings of a Championship fixture, and only century-maker Lumb did anything among the others.

That occasion allowed another insight into the care Boycott took over handling individuals. With Yorkshire forced to counter-attack by the nature of the wicket and their feeble first-innings batting, he gave the new ball to Robinson and Cooper, who posed no threat. Oldham prized out the first three Essex batsmen, suggesting that his extra pace entitled him to open the bowling. Boycott did not agree. 'In a one-match situation that might be right,' he said, 'but I have to think about Robinson and Cooper, who have earned their seniority. How would they feel if I relegated one of them to first change? How would they bowl? What would be the reaction among the others?

'There is more to being captain than just looking at one situation and deciding what to do. I make sure that everyone feels part of the team with a specific job to do and, at the moment, Robinson and Cooper are my two top quick bowlers.' All the same, Boycott soon displayed his flexibility by using Oldham with the new ball, but his commendable efforts were not enough and when he was out of action the bowling fell apart, Hampshire experiencing difficulty in co-ordinating the attack and his field placings.

In three successive one-day games 617 runs were conceded and only eight wickets taken. Yorkshire never recovered. Hampshire, in his benefit year, scored runs in magnificent profusion, but he did not possess Boycott's surer touch as captain, so that almost everything painstakingly put together in the previous year came apart.

The Headingley Roses match illustrated the problem accurately, boring all and sundry to distraction as Lancashire scored 201 for seven declared and 27 for one to Yorkshire's 141. Although the weather did not help, Hampshire, if he is judged in the same harsh light as Boycott, allowed Leadbeater to linger for two hundred minutes for 28 in an innings that could be defended only at great cost to other reputations. If

Leadbeater played to orders, Hampshire had no faith in the rest.

Yorkshire lost six Sunday League engagements, despite scoring more than 200 runs in each of them, four under Hampshire and two under Boycott, both of whom bordered on despair at the bowling inaccuracies with which they had to contend. Boycott recovered from the broken bone in his hand at the end of June, only for his return to be further delayed by a recurrence of the disc trouble that kept him out of action for half of the 1968 season.

'I have had a few long nets and although the hand is painful and nags the longer I bat, I could put up with that. The back, though, is something different. The truth is that I could not field, so although I might make a few runs I would be an embarrassment.' A realistic appraisal of his own capabilities did not bring total approval.

A substantial victory over a Kent side minus seven regulars did not diminish the size of the growing crisis nor the need for more committee involvement.

Temple, Brennan and Sutcliffe, however, journeyed down to Wellington for the Gillette Cup tie with Shropshire obviously intent on hardening the team's resolve. They knew that defeat would be a disaster of greater proportion than the one at Harrogate and they dispelled, in passing, the rumour that Yorkshire had imposed a time limit on Boycott, threatening to terminate his contract unless he quickly regained fitness. Pausing before he administered a general pep talk, Temple said: 'To suggest that Geoff Boycott might be replaced is totally wrong so far as I am concerned. The committee, together with the rest of the county, want him back as soon as possible.'

This welcome involvement on a day-to-day basis might have filled the void left by Boycott's injury. Shropshire were comfortably beaten, but there followed a thoroughly wretched effort at Worksop. On a turning pitch, Nottinghamshire comfortably amassed the top score, 263 for seven, in the fourth innings to win a contest they seemed resigned to losing from the time they conceded a first-innings lead of 106. Yorkshire bowled and fielded as if in a bad-tempered trance.

Boycott reappeared for the second-round of the Gillette Cup in which Gloucestershire provided the opposition. He did not feel quite ready, but a breathless one-run triumph over Middlesex at Bradford fell short of the convincing evidence required to allow him a longer rest. The sixty-over competition was Yorkshire's last chance of gaining success to bridge the gap with 1975, but Boycott made his effort in vain.

Although he picked up 38 from fifty-five deliveries to send Yorkshire on their way to 232 for nine, Zaheer, fitter and more fluent, dominated the stage, his 111 carrying Gloucestershire to victory by four wickets as Boycott spread a defensive net that could not contain the flood of runs. Understandably he tried to regroup, to get a solid base, so he made caution his watchword to the stage at which he ringed the boundary with fielders in the Sunday League. He claimed erratic bowling forced his hand, yet his reaction magnified the weakness, giving the attacker few economic options. Boycott contended conceding boundaries drained confidence and undermined accuracy, but Yorkshire showed up better when pursuing a clear, positive objective and, while he walked a tricky line, he could have given a bolder lead. This was demonstrated at Grace Road as Yorkshire lost by 152 runs shortly after lunch on the third day.

Rhodesian Paddy Clift did the hat-trick to spearhead a drive that removed Yorkshire in the first innings for 85 — 157 behind. After checking the weather forecast, which promised a continuation of the sunshine, Illingworth declined to enforce the follow-on, mystifying the spectators by batting a second time to leave Yorkshire a target of 380. He reasoned there was nothing to be gained from having to bat last in the event of Yorkshire making something of their second attempt, and Boycott's soundest tactic would have been a vigorous assault on Leicestershire. Instead he tried to contain and did nothing for morale.

To balance this though, he produced an innings to rival that against Warwickshire at the start of his captaincy, beating Glamorgan by seven wickets at Middlesborough virtually off his own bat. On a benign, easy-paced wicket, Glamorgan's scores were 349 for seven and 320 for three, Alan Jones helping himself to a century in each innings and then setting

Yorkshire a target of 318 in 190 minutes. He made few friends around the ground, it being generally accepted that such a task belonged to the realms of fantasy, and Yorkshire's initial response did little to appease the spectators, who spent the tea interval condemning the Welshmen.

In the late afternoon sunshine, however, Boycott cut loose to hammer the bowling all over Acklam Park, racing to 156 at a deceptively easy pace. Like a finely-tuned engine, he accelerated smoothly without straining. Jones gambled on Yorkshire accepting risks in pursuit of their objective, but Boycott refused to take them. 'People often do not understand how to calculate a team's chances when they are chasing a target,' he pointed out. 'They look at the runs, divide the time into them and come up with a figure of so many an hour. That's fair enough, but I go into it much more deeply. I study the opposition bowling and try to work out who will send down most overs, who can come back for a second spell and who will tire quickly and become vulnerable. I base my projected run-rate on these observations. Sometimes I realise that 70 an hour is out of the question because there are two very quick bowlers who will keep going for a couple of hours or thereabouts and bowl about twenty-eight overs in that time. Then again, 80 an hour can be well within reach because I find a bowler easy to handle or because only one of the front-line bowlers is dangerous. It all boils down to how many deliveries I am likely to receive from whom and no one can score against pacemen bowling wide of the stumps. Spectators ought to stop and consider these things when they are trying to tell me what to do.'

The summer ended on a melancholy note at Scarborough. Yorkshire, trapped on an old-fashioned turner by the immaculate Indian spinner Bishen Bedi, lost by 198 runs, but there was a worthy footnote. Nine Yorkshire batsmen recorded first-class centuries amid the ruins of so many crumbling innings. Boycott, Lumb, Johnson, Hampshire, Leadbeater, Old, Bairstow, Athey and Jim Love shared this distinction with the considerably more famous sides of 1921, 1926 and 1955.

Boycott, having said too much too soon about 'caps' before, now believed that, despite the many set-backs, a change of heart was called for to lift flagging spirits. He wanted Robinson, Cooper and Carrick to be honoured on the field during the last Scarborough fixture when a substantial crowd would create the proper sense of occasion and the players and public could join in a special ceremony. He explained this in a letter to Temple, adding: 'I am sure if this is done, it will be in the best interests of the team and will show that the committee and I appreciate loyalty and endeavour.'

In the absence of a favourable reply, Boycott asked that the normal end-of-season selection and cricket committee meetings be brought forward, delaying his departure on a private trip to Australia to make himself available.

'This meeting rejected all my suggestions for "caps",' he complained. 'Mel Ryan, Padgett and I voted for my suggestions and Sutcliffe, Temple and Brennan against. Temple exercised his casting vote against us, so the motion was dead. I then wrote to the president and the chairman from Heathrow before I caught my plane to ensure that my ideas were considered at the next meeting of the cricket committee.' Boycott, thus, left matters in the air, keeping in touch from a considerable distance with the aid of Ryan, the former Yorkshire medium-pace bowler, who replaced Haigh as the Huddersfield representative.

Ryan, relatively new to the committee, having been elected in 1974, staunchly defended Boycott's interests at the cricket committee meeting on October 5. The minutes reveal that after reappointing Boycott as captain and dealing with the contract terms to be offered, 'discussions then took place on the question of awarding county "caps". Both M. Ryan and G.H. Dennis felt that a county "cap" should be awarded to A.L. Robinson. Mr M.G. Crawford proposed, seconded by Mr F. Melling, that "caps" should be awarded to both Robinson and Carrick, and this was carried by eight votes to four.' The four who voted against Boycott's recommendation were Temple, Sutcliffe, Brennan and Feather.

Ryan wrote to Boycott on November 7, penning some stinging comments about the committee and telling him he had been made captain again for all the wrong reasons. He also commented: 'It is time you had people around you who are working together for the same end.' In twelve months Yorkshire tumbled from the heights, carrying Boycott with them, and he was far from happy as he wintered in the warmth of Australia. He had demonstrated in the clearest way that he was the cornerstone, holding up the whole edifice of Yorkshire cricket, yet he found neither widespread acceptance nor total security.

7 The Prodigal's Return

A cricketer first and a politician second, Boycott developed an aptitude for the complex art of subtle manoeuvre as a matter of necessity during the long wrangles with authority. Nevertheless, he got his priorities sorted out for his visit to Australia, where he played Grade cricket at Waverley with impressive results. He strung together five centuries in his first ten innings, averaging over 200 for a spell and, as ever, attracting attention on all sides.

He also indulged in a commercial exercise, taking in things other than cricket, but his attention never wandered far from the main theme in the rhythm of his life and he earned respect. John Chapman, the Waverley secretary, had no axe to grind and nothing to gain from expressing an opinion on Boycott, so it is all the more valuable for being unbiased. He said: 'Frankly I did not know what to expect. I had my reservations about him, but now I am proud to think he has become a friend. The zeal and the absolute dedication of the man is beyond belief. It has taken the team a while to get used to his style of run-getting, but we are on our way now. This togetherness is best summed up by the fact that Geoff came out here for only three matches originally but will stay until the end of the competition in March.'

This contradicted the dogma that Boycott was difficult to get on with and too selfish·for the good of the team and he arrived home for the spring nets of 1977 with his batteries fully recharged. This was just as well, for he faced the two most testing years of his career.

It began quietly, Boycott achieving a nice balance in his pre-season address. 'Our big strength is that we have a lot of very promising youngsters, but our weakness is that we have relatively few experienced players and if they are injured or out of form it throws a lot of weight on young shoulders. I can see a lot of young Yorkshire players, some of whom many people have not yet heard, pushing for England places in the next few years.' Time bore out his prophecy, Athey, Love and Stevenson all earning international honours and, while quite a lot had been heard of them then, they were in their cricketing infancy.

Yorkshire could not, however, have made a much worse start, for they were out of the Benson and Hedges Cup by the end of an autumnal April. In this second game Boycott brilliantly collected 102 from only 149 balls in a brave attempt to compensate for Old's absence with a bruised hand.

The England bowler declared himself unfit, but Boycott might have pressed the matter and taken a chance with him if he had been surer of the backing of the high command. Old, equally, may have risked breaking down if the threat of repercussions, however slight, had been removed. Yorkshire lost the match largely as a result of some uninspired bowling and played on for no more than the sponsors' money against Minor Counties (East) and Essex. Ironically they received the Gold Award for the outstanding player in all four zonal ties, Boycott being honoured three times as his side's major strength.

The Sunday results were also worrying, although Boycott stood out as an exception to the gloomy rule, but Yorkshire did somewhat better in the Championship. Old, bowling with controlled hostility, captured sixteen wickets at 10.56 in the first four matches, one of which brought victory, and three draws were entirely the fault of the wretched weather. Old was never fully fit again that year, so it was as well that Boycott chipped away persistently at the suggestion that he won too few games to be a truly great batsman.

His facility for accumulating without slogging came in useful at Bradford. Yorkshire were set to score 213 in what amounted to thirty-nine overs to beat Northamptonshire and succeeded admirably, sped on their way by an opening stand of 135 from only twenty-five overs by Boycott and Hampshire, the captain tailoring his 74 exactly to fit the shape of the proceedings.

Yorkshire travelled down to Cardiff at the end of May to oppose Glamorgan as the Championship leaders, but with Boycott, Old and the cricket committee out of step. Old's assignment specificially concerned the Sunday League fixture after he had talked over his fitness with a committee representative in Bradford. A quick look at the flint-hard Sophia Gardens pitch convinced Boycott that Old should also turn out in the three-day game, while the concensus of Glamorgan feeling was that he must be a match-winner in the conditions. Old, however, stuck to the decision made 220 miles away. He did not think he could cope physically with the longer course and Boycott had no reason to expect wholehearted sympathy if he made a stand and things went wrong. Fate has a habit of accentuating the ridiculous, and Old, unable to bowl, of course, galloped about for most of the Saturday as substitute for Carrick, who nursed a king-sized headache and a lump to match from a blow on the head at short-leg as Alan Jones pulled powerfully.

Sidebottom starred in another pantomime. He put together his maiden century in a last-wicket stand of 144 with Robinson — four short of the best for the county — and tragically ran himself out with suicidal deliberation, but Yorkshire, in their most convincing mood, duly wrapped up a third successive Championship triumph. Memories of the opening weeks faded.

Their best opening sequence for eleven years in the Championship, three wins and three draws, kept everybody reasonably happy, even though the expansion of Kerry Packer's World Series operation cast a long shadow over the game as a whole. The Packer case is too long and involved to be gone into here, except in its relevance to Boycott. Stories had been on the rounds for some time when the news broke on the English scene in early May of a privately-arranged series of games in Australia. Thirty-five players signed three-year contracts to compete under the Packer banner.

The list included Greig and had been composed by him in collaboration with Ian Chappell. It did not include Boycott, who refused an invitation to join the 'pirates'. Within days

Greig lost his England captaincy, opening all kinds of doors, and Boycott suddenly emerged as the hero of the hour. The rebel had found a cause and, not for the first time, he put money second in taking his stance.

Boycott knew that considerable wealth could come from the deal, for he represented a high-priority target for Packer, who, in challenging the structure of the established game, aimed at offering an attractive package for the Australian market. He freely admitted his initial interest.

'When I was in Australia during the winter, I was approached by Kerry Packer and asked if I would join an international team to play against Australia next winter,' Boycott explained. 'I agreed to do so and shook hands on the deal. At the time I thought we were talking about a single series. However, when Packer's representative, Austin Robertson, delivered the contract it was immediately clear to me that if I signed I could be forced into a situation whereby I would be in conflict with my county committee and the Test and County Cricket Board. I therefore decided that it would be impossible for me to sign the contract in that form, despite the high financial rewards proposed. On no terms would I be ready to throw overboard my responsibilities as the Yorkshire captain or the trust that has been created at all levels of Yorkshire cricket.'

He stressed that in his opinion the Packer contracts were dangerous to the counties, ensuring the sponsor's complete control over the players, and subsequent events confirmed his honesty. It also says a lot for Yorkshire cricket that both Old and umpire Harold Bird also rejected advances from Packer. The counter claims that Boycott wanted to be captain of the world eleven and feared the quick bowling that featured in World Series made no impression on anyone who studied the position, but the advent of Packer made him think.

Brearley, by no means a proven Test batsman, came in for Greig, and, despite Yorkshire's flickering promise, frustration and disillusionment were poor companions. He listened carefully, therefore, when Bedser said that there were no major obstacles preventing his return to the England side if he made himself available.

Boycott's form, which could really be taken for granted,

would be the decisive factor, and, as he made up his mind to return to Test cricket, he maintained an average in the 60s with effortless ease. Yorkshire's four-wicket victory over Somerset stemmed from his first innings 139 not out and his second-innings 60. In the first place he stood firm to prevent a collapse and then he and Love, who assisted notably, plundered 98 from twenty overs of the new ball to lead an exciting chase towards 149 in thirty-one overs. His century off the Australians at Scarborough set him up for another at Lord's. Here he negotiated very hostile bowling by Wayne Daniel, who posted two fly slips on the first evening, but he lingered through ninety-six overs for his 117, being well below his best partly because he did not trust a less than full-strength line-up to deal with the strong home attack.

Yorkshire's heavy defeat on an unpredictable Sheffield pitch in the return game tended to prove his point after he had resumed his international career, and he rounded off his pre-Test selection burst with a wonderful display in crushing Nottinghamshire at Trent Bridge. Yorkshire raced to a fourth-innings 323 in 280 minutes to win by five wickets. Only once before — in 1910 — had they made more in similar circumstances and Boycott's contribution was 154, compiled with strokes of the highest quality.

Although at times he drove his admirers to distraction by retiring into a protective shell, he was motivated as much by collective as individual preservation and when his recall to the Test team was announced on Sunday, July 24, Yorkshire's Championship position looked healthy. They were the only unbeaten side in first-class cricket with six victories and eight draws and shared fifth place in the table.

Throughout this run they fielded first every time, on seven occasions by choice, and against Kent they broke the sequence in more ways than one. Much to his disgust, Boycott lost his wicket in the early stages after winning the toss and choosing to bat, and he apparently became dispirited as he sat un-happily in the corner of the dressing room.

He did himself a further disservice by bowling at the wrong time in the televised Sunday League fixture at Canterbury. Boycott's medium-paced in-swingers reappeared after a seven-year break in that season and he had a spell of 8—2—15—1 against Nottinghamshire at Trent Bridge. He bowled so well that the shock of seeing him wheel away in his cap was soon absorbed, amusement giving way to respect. His five wickets for 157 runs enabled him to finish second in the Test averages on Mike Smith's hard-pressed tour to South Africa in 1964—65, but this aspect of his game then lay neglected, despite its potential value to Yorkshire in the one-day competition. Boycott had no pretentions as a wicket-taker, but his reluctance to act as a containing element reflected two things.

He did not want to subject his back to undue pressure and he hesitated to attempt anything without being reasonably sure of reaching an acceptable level of competence. He delayed, therefore, reviving a skill from his younger days. His Nottingham venture satisfied him, but he did not get carried away, holding his fire until the Kent game in which Yorkshire had five specialist bowlers, including young Alan Ramage, a 'green' newcomer. With Kent reduced to 33 for five, Yorkshire rampaged along, until Boycott strangely decided to bowl five accurate if gentle overs.

Although he rationed Kent to five runs, Boycott allowed them to wriggle off the hook and reach 153 — 51 too many for Yorkshire. That did not go down well, nor did the manner in which Kent completed the 'double' with a six-wicket Championship victory. Boycott, seemingly distracted, left Cope and Bore to wheel away without evincing sufficient interest and he then watched while Underwood swept through the Yorkshire second innings, like a forest fire, on an accommodating surface.

The world's deadliest exploiter of the 'terror track' took seven for 43, Boycott hanging on to be the last victim, and his 61 stood out on a card containing only Lumb in double figures among the others. Unfortunately, he made a poor attempt to deal with the real menace, facing only twenty-seven of Underwood's sixty last-day deliveries. The odds swung against Yorkshire because of the conditions and Boycott dodged the responsibility of meeting the biggest threat — or as much of it as possible. His duty was to tackle Underwood and hope that his team-mates scrambled something at the other end to save the situation.

He behaved as though pre-occupied, spending much of

Kent's formality of a second innings with his hands in his pockets. Afterwards he claimed he had merely kept them warm, but that did not count as an acceptable excuse. Whatever the facts, he set a bad example. Folkestone on July 26, however, was the low-water mark for him. Yorkshire continued on the downward path.

Four of the next five Championship outings were lost, the solitary draw rewarding his ninety-ninth century and Old's one hundred in thirty-seven minutes from seventy-two balls, the second fastest in history. The committee did not distinguish themselves in this spell, for with Hampshire injured, third-choice captain Cope wrestled with, among other things, a minor outbreak of food poisoning at Hove. Someone should have found the time to maintain essential contact with a bewildered group of players under a worried leadership.

In keeping with the on-going pattern, results improved when Boycott played. Yorkshire switched the Roses clash to Bradford in a bid to end a depressing stalemate stretched over six years of draws, an initiative rewarded with a five-wicket win, and Boycott's 47 was top score in the first innings when defeat appeared likely. His firm handling of the side in the field also restored a noticeable spirit.

Boycott completed the summer as nearly everyone's favourite. Despite not playing in the first two Tests, he was England's leading scorer with 442 runs for an average of 147.33 and on the domestic front he alone managed 1,000 runs for Yorkshire, his 1,257 bringing an average of 57.22. The county lost four of the six Championship fixtures he missed, drawing two and while his absence was not the sole reason it was the main one.

He headed the Sunday League averages with 347 runs (38.55) and in all the one-day matches only overseas stars Kepler Wessels, of Sussex, and Clive Rice, of Nottinghamshire, bettered his 627 runs for an average of 48.23. Yorkshire went through a dreadful Sunday season, sharing a miserable thirteenth place, yet Boycott did most to contain the disaster.

His 79 not out shattered Worcestershire at Worcester, and Yorkshire got home by six wickets on a testing track, while in an utter humiliation at Huddersfield he had 72 out of 120 as Hampshire romped to victory by 129 runs. Another memorable innings highlighted a run spree at Headingley, where Lancashire failed to defend 223 in forty overs. Boycott top scored with 76 in Yorkshire's reply, holding one end firm while fireworks exploded at the other. He accorded his partners plenty of the strike through a succession of neatly placed singles and the six-wicket success owed as much to his class as the complementary power.

Boycott had nothing to fear from any comparison, yet on September 30, Brennan dropped a bombshell with the opening shots in his campaign to have him replaced. 'It is no good having a fellow who is playing fifty per cent of the time for the Test side,' he declared. 'We need a father figure. Boycott is a great player but to my way of thinking he is not a leader. A captain should be able to sacrifice himself and his own game for the benefit of the side. What I have seen of Geoff Cope gives me the opinion he is the type who would put everything before his own personal achievements.'

A stunned Yorkshire public hardly knew what to make of that and Cope was a shocked as anyone. He put Yorkshire first by undertaking the stock bowling role when it proved too much for Carrick, who as the left-arm spinner was expected to do the job. He sent down most overs, losing some of his spin in the process, but that admirable gesture hardly meant he had outstanding captaincy claims.

Boycott could have argued that others might well have done more to help, particularly in his absence on Test duty.

The records also revealed that Yorkshire won seven of the forty-nine Championship matches from which he had been an absentee since 1970, losing eighteen, but he did not have to defend himself. Plenty were ready to do that, and Connell leapt into the ring, rightly reprimanding Brennan for his outburst by saying: 'I deplore the idea of any individual member of the committee making a public statement on such a matter. I admit that certain committee members have expressed a nervousness at Boycott's continued run as captain now he is back as an England player.'

Ryan joined in, making his bow on October 5. 'I will resign from the cricket committee unless there is a dramatic change in the way things are run,' he said. 'I am a great believer in contact and I accept that we don't maintain a close enough contact with the players in the day-to-day business.'

Here at last an official acknowledged that flaws existed in an operation that some regarded as perfect. He continued: 'We have a great opening batsman, a world-class all-rounder, one of the most consistent middle-order run-makers in the game, a wicket-keeper on the fringe of the Test squad and some of the most exciting youngsters. I think the time to take action is now, when we have plenty of time to do something worthwhile.'

As the demand for internal action gained this voice, the county secretly planned a complete break with tradition and a section of the membership stirred themselves into action. The Reform Group, formed in early October, acted as a focal point for concerted opposition that haunted the committee and eventually team-manager Illingworth, rattling skeletons in the cupboards to cause a lot of heart-searching and the odd sleepless night.

This group announced their intentions with a resolution expressing no confidence in Brennan and requesting the county secretary to call a special general meeting under Rule Three, which requires 'the requisition of not less than two and a half per cent of the members on the books' for such a purpose.

Motivation for the Reform Group stemmed from Leeds-based John Featherstone, who acted as secretary, and Peter Briggs, from Manchester, the chairman. Bob Slicer, a close friend of Boycott's, who gained prominence as a leading force in the National Breakdown Recovery Club, joined them as publicity officer. Later Sid Fielden, from Doncaster, lent a powerful oratory to the Group, functioning as assistant secretary and taking over when Featherstone resigned. Great anger was generated by the head-on collision between the immovable county officials and the irresistible Reformers.

The committee for a while dismissed the group as self-elected rabble-rousers, who had little standing and less knowledge, but in the main the Reformers used their holidays and spent large sums travelling the length and breadth of the country to support Yorkshire. They included enthusiasts undeterred at the thought of getting up in the middle of the night to drive down to Hove, Bournemouth, Bristol or some other far-flung venue. Their interest centred basically on the cricket, but greater involvement sprang from sharing the same hotel as the players, so they did not have to eavesdrop or spy to become aware of divisions.

Once set up as a properly constituted body, their declared aims were to 'improve the lot of the players, improve the facilities, often archaic and inadequate and even disgustingly dirty, at most of the grounds, improve the coaching, scouting and the young player situation, get a more virile and vigorous approach to fund raising and the general public relations work, including better contact with the membership.'

A lot of what they said sounded reasonable and Yorkshire's attitude towards the members often left a lot to be desired, with few committee representatives making the effort to meet their constituents. District get-togethers represented a simple means of keeping the public informed, yet the club dismissed them with a marked lack of interest.

Unquestionably the Reformers saw more matches than the committee so they spoke from first-hand experience. They defended Boycott because they appreciated how much he meant to the team. The club would have been wise to meet them half way, to invite Briggs and Featherstone to an open discussion, but they chose to fight, a tactic which ate deep into their finances, besides bringing an unwelcome spotlight onto the unpleasant areas.

The Reform Group comfortably obtained the necessary signatures and presented an 828-name petition to Lister on the morning of November 10, when the cricket and general committees met. This expressed confidence in Boycott and the lack of it in Brennan, who was away on business!

They did not know that Boycott had already been unanimously reappointed captain at a secret meeting towards the end of October, after which Brennan resigned from the selection committee, and they were also ignorant of the bigger development — the signing of Illingworth as team manager from April 1, 1979. Boycott, too, was in the dark, having no suspicion before that morning of anything of such monumental consequence. Belatedly his views were canvassed, but he resented the short notice and contented himself by

142

insisting that the division of authority and responsibility would need to be clearly defined.

He wanted time to investigate all the implications of the move. It had to be applauded from a practical standpoint, for Illingworth must be an improvement on the committee, particularly as he immediately made it clear that he intended to travel with and supervise the first team, but this necessitated his working in tandem with Boycott. The captain, therefore, should have been brought into the negotiations at the earliest stage since a common understanding between the two was absolutely crucial. The small, senior group who handled the enterprise showed a sorry shortage of sensitivity as their action left Boycott with the impression that his opinion did not count for much.

Connell put on a bold face when the plans were unveiled, admitting that the committee had found increasing difficulty in attending matches owing to business commitments — a charge so resolutely denied in the past. 'Ideally you have one man watching all Yorkshire matches,' he said, accepting seven years too late something others had seen as an obvious requirement if Boycott were to succeed. 'We have discussed the position of a team manager for three or four years, but it was something that could happen only at the right time,' he continued.

'We felt that the running of the club had become so commercial and so highly technical that it was essential we had a full-time expert in charge. We appreciated that the appointment of a team manager in itself was no solution, but considered that if we could get the right man he would carry the county forward. We regard Illingworth as the ideal man. We are putting alongside a very experienced captain a man who has a lot of experience himself and a superb track record. They will work together as a team and I see no reason why they should not work together successfully.'

Connell voiced no doubts about Boycott, added no qualifications about his behaviour in the coming season. He went so far as to stress that the captain's authority on the field was unchallenged. 'The team is his. There is no question of divided power.'

Illingworth echoed the conciliatory tones. 'I see this as the natural extension of my career. I think I have a lot to offer and I have no fears about not getting on with Geoff. I can't see our duties overlapping and obviously neither of us will be looking for confrontation. We have played together and got on well, but no one can expect to go through a season without some disagreement.'

Behind all this shop-window dressing the hard bargaining went on and Boycott, having studied his position, wrote a long letter to the chairman on November 21, stating his main worries — loyalty and the background to Illingworth's appointment. 'The resignation of Brennan from the selection committee goes no distance towards the re-establishment of trust, and my unanimous election to the captaincy does not in any way guarantee that the sniping and lobbying or the public and private creation of dissension will stop,' he said, going on to ask how the committee proposed to deal with the problem.

Boycott remained unhappy about his association with Illingworth, despite a meeting on the Sunday of November 13, when the president, Temple, Crawford and cricket committee member Norman Yardley were present to define the role of team manager and discuss the way in which the two principals could best help each other.

In his letter to the chairman, Boycott, therefore, complained that Illingworth had been quoted as saying that being in control of all cricket matters meant the final say in team selection, although the manager agreed that the captain had the last word in settling the exact eleven from a party of twelve or thirteen.

He concluded his letter: 'I am sure that unless the major problem which I have mentioned is first resolved, the disloyalties and dissensions will continue and that the appointment of Ray Illingworth will not help the situation, but tend to increase rather than diminish the divisions simply because those who are disloyal and still seek my removal from the captaincy will use the divisions of authority, which it is proposed to create, for the achievement of the ultimate purpose. Clearly the position is unsatisfactory in every way and a great deal of further thought should be given to the problems set out in this letter which are inter-related.'

Schooldays – Boycott is pictured in the Hemsworth Grammar School
team, third from the right in the back row,
next to headmaster Russell Hamilton

With the Ackworth club, Boycott is second from the left in the front row.
Third from the left in the back row is his uncle, Albert Speight,
while George Hepworth is second from the right

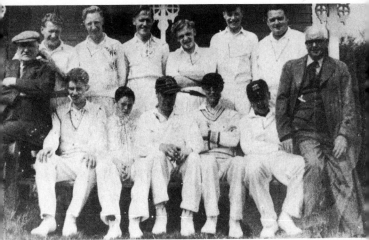

Number 45 Milton Terrace,
Fitzwilliam, where Boycott lived
with his mother
until her death in 1978

Buying his first car,
Boycott compares the vintage
model with his new vehicle

October 1963. (*Left to right*) Boycott, Tony Nicholson
and John Hampshire (*Yorkshire Post*)

Boycott, wearing spectacles, after the victory against Surrey at Lord's in the
1965 Gillette Cup final. (*Left to right*) Tony Nicholson, Phil Sharpe (front),
Richard Hutton, John Hampshire (obscured), Ken Taylor, Brian Close,
Doug Padgett, Don Wilson (rear), Fred Trueman,
Ray Illingworth and Jimmy Binks (*Sport and General*)

Meeting the new chairman. From the left: Don Wilson,
John Hampshire, Geoff Cope, Boycott and Barrie Leadbeater meet
John Temple (centre) at Headingley, 1971 (*Yorkshire Post*)

opposite above: Boycott is mobbed at Headingley in August 1977
after scoring his one hundredth century

opposite below: The three greatest Yorkshire batsmen: Boycott,
Herbert Sutcliffe and Sir Leonard Hutton at Headingley in August 1977

Boycott and the county president Sir Kenneth Parkinson
toast Yorkshire's future, August 1977

Yorkshire secretary Joe Lister (left) receives a petition from
(left to right) Sid Fielden, John Featherstone and Peter Briggs
in October 1978 (*Yorkshire Post*)

Boycott talking to an admiring audience of youngsters

The battlefield of Harrogate. Yorkshire members crowd into conference centre to vote committee out of office (*Yorkshire Post*)

Celebrating victory. Tony Vann (front left) and Sid Fielden and Reg Kirk, with their arms aloft, acknowledge the cheers of their supporters after the Harrogate result had been announced (*Yorkshire Post*)

Facing up to crisis.
Ronnie Burnet (left)
and Michael Crawford
were under intense
pressure from the
moment Yorkshire made
the decision
to sack Boycott
(*Yorkshire Post*)

Standing for the
committee. Boycott
hands in his nomination
papers for the Wakefield
district to secretary
Joe Lister
(*Yorkshire Post*)

Boycott requested a further meeting to go into greater detail, an apparently obvious course, but none was held before his sacking. Thus the bold new blueprint for a brighter future lost much of its relevance while still in draft form. The great alliance proclaimed by the chairman creaked at the joints from the outset.

8 Bitter Conflict

Ironically after reaching the pinnacle of hope and ambition
by leading England in four Tests against Pakistan and New
Zealand in the winter of 1977—78, Boycott went sliding
down what might be called the razor blade of life. The long
and painful journey brought a great player and a great club
into bitter and public conflict, with the participants riding
the swings and roundabouts of fluctuating fortunes. Yorkshire's far from comfortable survival in the face of repeated
onslaughts stood as a tribute to a common will among the
members and supporters, whose patience passed the acid test,
preserving a degree of dignity. Without agreeing with the way
things were run they, at least, stayed loyal to the body of the
club. Public support did not decline, with membership
hovering around the 12,000 mark, despite all the wrangling,
but concern for the continuation of Yorkshire as a competitive
force presented itself in a variety of ways and the Reform
Group did not let sleeping dogs lie.

They put forward another petition in late January 1978,
calling for a special general meeting to debate a resolution of
no confidence in Brennan and Ryan. They called for their
suspension and demanded that all committee members
maintain confidentiality about club business. They also
wanted to set up a select committee of not more than ten,
representing equally themselves and the county, to offer
constructive advice on the constitution, rules and management
of Yorkshire cricket.

Yorkshire could have made a generous gesture which

would have shown them in the right light by offering to put the Reform Club resolutions on the agenda for the annual meeting, but they did not offer this olive branch. Having missed the opportunity for compromise, Yorkshire despatched a letter full of references to Rule Nine and Rule Thirty-six and sentences such as: 'So far as Resolution Six is concerned the members have no power to set up a committee other than the committee referred to in Rule Twelve.' All strictly in accordance with the letter of the law, but the committee misunderstood the spirit on their contract with the membership, who paid the bills and the wages and were referred to as 'the cornerstone of our club' when the treasurer dealt with the balance sheet.

In exercising their high horses, county officials rode rough shod over the feelings of people who reacted by fighting back. Denied what they saw as the democractic processes, the Reform Group adherents made their presence felt at the meeting in Montgomery Hall, Sheffield, where Sir Kenneth Parkinson valiantly tried to unite all parties with a major speech. He admitted that serious problems existed and, while insisting that he expressed a personal view, his analysis was still perceptive.

'I have been giving a lot of thought to the state of Yorkshire cricket since I took over as president in 1974', he said, 'and for many years before that, and the problem is that we do not have a team. In saying that, I am not criticising the captain or any of the players who constitute the eleven men on the field. However good our players are individually or collectively we will not win competitions until we have a committee, staff, members, public and players who are all pulling together at the same time in the same direction for the same purpose.

'What I am appealing for in 1978 is unity from which we can derive strength, loyalty to what I regard as the true cause of Yorkshire cricket. I sometimes think our weakness stems from that passion to do well which can result in sub-standard performances. Individuals get edgy and uptight, organisations become over critical. I am not suggesting that argument and debate should not take place. That is the lifeblood of democracy, but when a majority decision has been taken and leaders have been appointed, we should give them our utmost support. Confidence will then be created and success will surely follow.'

His reference to the 'lifeblood of democracy' drew a response from Brennan, who called out 'Hear, hear.'

'It is eight years since Yorkshire won anything, but it took Lord Hawke ten years to win the county Championship,' added Sir Kenneth. 'In looking back we can feel disappointed, but we can also take comfort, for I believe we may be on the verge of another golden era of Yorkshire cricket. I cannot see much wrong with the way cricket is being played in Yorkshire at the present time, so although there is absolutely no reason for complacency, we can be optimistic at the start of a new season.'

Cricket at grass-roots level was flourishing — in villages and schools, in clubs and leagues and in impromptu matches which littered the county grounds during the intervals, he contended. 'When the urge to play this sort of cricket disappears the first-class game may be finished also, and we in Yorkshire are strong in these manifestations of the love of cricket. We have the players in strength and depth. The number of contracted players is the highest ever and most have played a fair amount of county cricket. No fewer than eleven of our players have been abroad playing cricket this winter.

'So why have we not done better? Maybe we could do with another batsman of the calibre of Boycott or another fast bowler. Maybe this reason or that reason can be suggested, but the problem is that we do not have a team.'

His impression of league cricket may have been rose-coloured, but he hit the target in firing his shots at Yorkshire, stony faces on the platform testifying to the accuracy of his attack. He was no rebel shouting in an attempt to blow down the walls of privilege, but the most respected figure in the club, and when his appeal went unheeded it was not Boycott who turned the deaf ear. On the contrary, he carried on as peace-maker. Boycott regarded Hampshire as his vice-captain from 1975, although there was no official confirmation. 'I have always tried to work with John and keep him fully informed of all the things discussed in committee and my thoughts on tactics and team selection. He has been my right hand,' Boycott said when he heard of plans to demote the number two.

Boycott fought for Hampshire, and, in this context, it has to be remembered that Brennan had wanted to promote Cope, so the batsman who stood second to the captain in ability had critics in late 1977 and early 1978.

The mystery, then, concerns what happened in the next few months to bring so sensational a change in the top-level thinking, for results cannot have counted. Yorkshire climbed from twelfth to fourth in the Championship and from thirteenth to seventh in the Sunday League.

In the Gillette Cup they reached the quarter-finals and the single disappointment came in the Benson and Hedges Cup, with failure to qualify from the zonal rounds. Yet Yorkshire commented in their annual report at the end of the summer: 'Yorkshire's committee has always been aware that very high in its priorities must be: 1 — Creating means for enterprising and successful cricket throughout Yorkshire. 2 — Providing the best possible facilities on the grounds on which first-class cricket is played, having the need to cater for our large membership in all quarters of the county.

'Both objectives require money and the committee, as the accounts clearly indicate, has again made strenuous efforts to provide the finance. It is emphasised, however, that at no time has lack of finance been an inhibiting factor in obtaining and retaining the best available Yorkshire-born players. The committee has always kept a close watch on the remuneration of the players and believes this to be at least as good as that offered by the best of the other counties. Lack of success on the field is, therefore, all the more disturbing. Against this background, the committee decided that after a run of eight years without winning a competition a change in the first-team captaincy is necessary.'

To make any sense at all, that should have been said a year earlier when, instead, Connell trumpeted his great faith in the Boycott—Illingworth combination. After the satisfactory progress on almost all fronts it could not be taken seriously unless Hampshire, who led the side as Boycott's deputy, had brought about the improvement himself. He hadn't.

The Championship records were: Boycott *P*12 *W*5 *D*6 *L*1, Hampshire *P*10 *W*5 *D*3 *L*2, and they supported no particular contention. The Sunday League comparisons were: Boycott *P*8 *W*4 *L*4, Hampshire *P*6 *W*3 *L*3. Identical returns, with two matches abandoned. The Gillette Cup run benefited from Hampshire's century off Durham in the first round and Boycott's top score of 62 against Nottinghamshire, while neither could be blamed in any way for the defeat by Sussex.

This tie degenerated into a ludicrous ten-over farce at Headingley, heavy rain having washed out Yorkshire's original 174 for seven on the first day. Umpires Spencer and Phillipson ruled that there was time on Friday for no more than the minimum contest, from which Hampshire was an absentee due to a shoulder injury sustained in Yorkshire's non-existent first innings.

Sussex, sent in, were contained to 68 for six, but Yorkshire fared even worse. Boycott shrewdly dropped himself down the order, yet Lumb went in first when Athey represented a more logical choice. Selector Sutcliffe advocated the move and Boycott acceded, but the unhappy opener struggled through twenty-three deliveries to score 10. Lumb could not escape censure, although the decision was not his, and Boycott, who came close to losing his temper, unfortunately lashed out in his direction. This flashpoint had repercussions in Boycott being reported to the committee, and failure had other implications as it turned out.

It has to be admitted that 1978 was not one of Boycott's best seasons as captain. He dropped out in the early weeks with a finger injury, and he suffered some aberrations, principally at Oxford in May, when he entered into a trance-like state as an amazing match staggered to a draw. The University were the only first-class outfit in regular action against whom Boycott had not registered a century and this time he chipped a return catch to the obscure Simon Wookey for nought, this unimagined turn of events being the prelude to a massive Yorkshire total of 468 for six.

Carrick bewildered the students, who were well below their inadequate full strength, taking six for 33 in a total of 125. Boycott batted a second time instead of enforcing the follow-on and failed again, being brilliantly caught inches from the ground in the covers for three. Barely breaking stride he departed to the distant nets while his red-faced colleagues, with little appetite for the exercise, piled on meaningless runs and endured the good-natured ribaldry of the varsity wits. Boycott did not return to reality and the pavilion until Yorkshire's lead had grown to the gigantic proportions of 548, and John Claughton, himself the off-shoot of a well-respected Yorkshire cricketing family, coolly steered Oxford to safety.

Boycott erred in ignoring an essential of first-class cricket by putting the winning of the contest second, but the accusation that he batted a second time to try for that elusive century did not hold water. There was never going to be enough time unless he used up the bulk of the last day and a more likely solution to the puzzle was that he allowed his attention to wander, getting too engrossed in his practice.

On the approach to Oxford, Yorkshire's form with the bat caused concern, so it was in his mind to let his team get back in the groove. He just overdid it.

Boycott made 61 out of 222 for eight in the abandoned fixture with Kent and the Pakistan visit to Bradford turned into a forlorn journey as rain washed out the game without a ball being bowled. Yorkshire lost to Warwickshire at Edgbaston, collapsing badly in the second innings to fall 35 short of their 145 target. Boycott, Hampshire and the young left-hander Kevin Sharp were the only batsmen to have got the feel of a decent innings, so it might be claimed that Boycott's decision contained an obscure element of merit, but, on the other hand, the value of practice against poor and weary bowling, was very limited.

In the midst of all this, though, another incident took place that counted against Boycott. During the Oxford second innings wicket-keeper Bairstow discarded his pads and joined the attack, bowling nine overs of steady medium-pace to take one wicket and concede 15 runs while Love stood in behind the stumps. Far from being an empty indication of boredom, this was a meaningful experiment for Bairstow was pencilled in to supplement the bowling for the Benson and Hedges tie at Trent Bridge on the following day. A back strain forced Boycott to drop down the order to number six in the Cup game and he did not consider himself fit enough to bowl his full ration of eleven overs if the need arose.

With both spinners in the side, Bairstow became extra seam insurance. A team meeting took the calculated risk on the grounds that Bairstow enjoyed a reputation as a workmanlike bowler in the nets, boisterously advertising his claims and being eager to try his arm in earnest. Yorkshire lost to Nottinghamshire and Bairstow bowled indifferently, his three overs costing 17, so the benefit of hindsight allowed the official seal of disapproval to set on the idea, backed by the instruction that there must be no repeat. The committee, lacking representation at Oxford, knew next to nothing about the reasoning.

Yorkshire enjoyed mixed fortunes without Boycott, losing badly to Nottinghamshire in the Championship at Worksop, but having compensation in the shape of victories over Lancashire, Worcestershire and Leicestershire, but the political pot simmered gently, stirred by a two-day win over Lancashire in the blistering spring bank holiday sunshine at Headingley. On a wicket of variable bounce, reported as being below standard, Yorkshire comprehensively outplayed Lancashire, Stevenson ripping through the batting with a first-innings' haul of eight for 65. A huge Sunday crowd, gathering to witness the last rites and get a rare taste of the three-day game on the Sabbath, found the proceedings much to their liking.

Equally happy, the committee suddenly decided to 'cap' Stevenson, announcing this honour over the loudspeakers to a roar of delight. Boycott seemed as surprised as anyone, particularly as May is an unlikely month to award a 'cap' and if Stevenson had earned that accolade he could have been given it either at the end of the previous season or at the start of the new one. At the time his seniority settled upon him, he had bowled in only two Championship matches and the inference was that a snap decision had been made during the afternoon. Certainly the Press received very little advance warning.

It magnified the whispers, picking up the well-worn theme about Yorkshire doing better without Boycott. Hampshire allegedly had a casual command of the players' complete loyalty and affection, while his genial appearance and forceful batting made him popular with the spectators. Inevitably, the anti-Boycott campaign lurched to a sudden halt when the demanding Bradford regulars barracked Hampshire for batting throughout the last day against Middlesex.

The professionals appreciated the commonsense refusal to make any sort of declaration. He simply did not have enough time at his disposal to make a game of it and, like Boycott before him, bowed to the dictates of a slow, low wicket, but it suited the politicians better to paint the latter as the dull, coldly calculating leader paying too little attention to entertainment.

Although Boycott's inner fears were coming frighteningly true, possession counted as nine points of the law, so there was a good deal in his favour when the Northampton incident blew up in his face on July 17. Lacking immediate attention, it grew into a cancer, destroying the corporate body of the county club, who never seemed to grasp the magnitude of what happened.

On another wicket short of both pace and bounce, with forcing stroke-play difficult, Northamptonshire advanced by means of steady application to 280 for seven in their first-innings allocation of one hundred overs. Boycott, a bit out of sorts with his own game, battled along in second gear in reply, his first 53 runs accruing from eleven twos and thirty-one singles in just over three hours. Grim stuff, but it did not matter, for Athey aggressively dominated a second-wicket stand of 202 in 208 minutes, so that after eighty-two overs Yorkshire were on 245 for two, well within reach of maximum batting points at 300 and a useful lead.

Boycott also stepped up the pace, his second 50, boosted by seven boundaries, occupying ninety-eight minutes, but the closing eighteen overs of the innings produced only 33 runs. After Boycott departed, Hampshire and Johnson scraped 11 from ten overs. Hampshire received fifty-nine balls from which he attempted only four scoring strokes, including a boundary from a full toss in the one hundredth over, in a most controversial innings which did nothing to improve the side's prospects.

'I could not time the ball. I did what others have done

often enough in the past,' he said defensively, but he 'shouldered arms' continually, making no noticeable effort to hit the ball, and refused Johnson's call for a number of apparently safe singles. Many of the small crowd, unable to work things out for themselves, approached the Press box, situated at the back of the pavilion behind the stumps, in search of information. We had none. Nor had the players who dodged questions at the little bar between the dressing rooms. Their transparent confusion, however, indicated more reliably than any words that this was no conspiracy. The luckless Johnson found himself in the newspaper headlines which suggested he had been party to some secret agreement, although his genuine distress proclaimed otherwise.

There were two important witnesses, Sutcliffe and Sir Kenneth Parkinson, the latter visiting the ground following a board meeting of United Newspapers in the town. Sutcliffe, reluctant to get deeply involved, said: 'I am as mystified as anyone else as to what was going on out there. Certainly we will want some sort of explanation at our usual post mortem. I expected us to get around 350 in these circumstances and there is no doubt that we threw away a batting point. That is a serious matter.' He did not demand an explanation from Hampshire there and then nor take the necessary disciplinary action which should have followed whatever was said.

Boycott did not send home his senior professional because he lacked confidence in the committee. 'What sort of backing can I expect?' he asked, but he, Sutcliffe and Sir Kenneth added up to a formidable triumvirate well able to suspend Hampshire on the spot. Instead judgment was deferred to the end of the week and the longer the delay the more complicated things became.

Compounding the original error, the cricket committee spent over four hours at Bradford and then took the easy way out. Temple, Sutcliffe and Burnet, who replaced Ryan on this body, interviewed Boycott, Hampshire and Johnson, who was completely exonerated, remaining behind closed doors long into the evening.

Their statement hardly justified the long wait. It read: 'The selection committee has considered all aspects of the incident and has conveyed its findings to the players concerned and now considers the matter closed.' No explanation, nothing to calm the widespread disquiet until the Press, filling its real function, elicited the news that Hampshire had been severely reprimanded and warned as to his future conduct. An intended statement contained implicit criticism of Boycott, who insisted that either the president or the chairman be consulted and obtained a ruling in his favour, but it required steely determination on his part to avoid the stigma automatically attached to the incident.

The president had a great deal of sympathy with Boycott at Northampton. I received an invitation to join him for breakfast at the Saxon Hotel on the morning after Hampshire's demonstration and he sought my views on the Yorkshire first innings. I told him I believed Hampshire to be so much in the wrong that public disciplinary action was essential and that it had become clear his annual meeting appeal had failed. I added that he faced the unpleasant prospect of having to assert his authority to bring about what he hoped to achieve by example.

'I was so dreadfully distressed yesterday,' he replied. 'I truly think it one of the worst days of my life. Things cannot be allowed to continue in this way. There must be no more of the kind of thing we had to endure yesterday. I will insist upon that. It was bad, very bad. I am certain we have the players to do better if only we could get everybody working together. What must young Athey have thought after batting so splendidly? I know that certain elements in the club are unhelpful to Boycott and, therefore, to York-shire as a whole, but it is not easy to solve all our problems without attracting more damaging publicity.'

He intended, then, to make an impression in private, but forces were working against his influence. At the heart of the Northampton 'go slow' was the effect on the players, who had seen Boycott's authority and the dignity of his office eroded, and it took hours rather than days for the details of the Bradford meeting to become general property.

Despite a ban on Cope, whose bowling action again fell foul of the regulations, four of the nine three-day games which followed Northampton were won and only one lost. Interestingly, since the committee and Hampshire shared reservations about him, Boycott missed the bulk of the matches leading up to Northampton. He recovered from his finger injury to rejoin his team at Taunton, scoring 48 and 38 steadily and almost leading Yorkshire to victory as Somerset finished with eight wickets down and a deficit of 152 runs. His 49 and 59 off the Essex attack at Chelmsford were similar efforts among the showers which killed the game and he did not shine in either the Warwickshire or Surrey fixtures. They both brought success, though, so Yorkshire were bowling along happily in third place in the Championship table when they arrived at Northampton.

Whatever his faults, Boycott had done nothing to bring about a change in anyone's mind concerning his suitability as captain and it was only back in April he had written to the chairman to underline his own faith in Hampshire, so why the cricket committee should want to associate him in any statement condemning Hampshire is a mystery.

Boycott's slow century for Yorkshire against New Zealand at Headingley followed the disciplinary meeting and on that occasion with a make-shift attack at his disposal, his hopes of doing better than a draw were minimal. Both sides settled for serious practice, which came in useful for Boycott, who compiled a three-hour century at Sheffield as Glamorgan were beaten by an innings and 99 runs.

Rain prevented any play on the first day and eyebrows were raised when he decided to bat after winning the toss. The majority opinion was that he had made a mistake and should have fielded. 'I know what people mean when they say I was wrong,' he said. 'They think that we could bowl out Glamorgan cheaply twice and possibly have to bat only once or one and a half times at worst, but they are seeing only part of the situation. I telephoned the weather men who told me there was a real prospect of overnight rain. The pitch has been covered from all the early rain, so it is firm enough to make runs now, but if it gets wet during the night we shall expect to win by an innings because the ball will turn and I can enforce the follow-on.' That is exactly what happened, Yorkshire making 318 for six and reducing Glamorgan to 122 and 97 in rain-affected conditions that yielded Carrick a haul of ten for 67.

Boycott showed more imaginative captaincy at Southampton, declaring behind on the first innings and top scoring with 20 in the second when a chase for 132 in 105 minutes became a defensive operation closing at 98 for seven. His century at Scarborough as Nottinghamshire were beaten by eight wickets took no more than three hours and forty minutes and he pressed on again in the second innings at the head of a victory bid, but the knives reappeared at the seaside venue in the final match of the summer, although Yorkshire won a contest reduced to a single innings by the weather.

Gloucestershire were dismissed for 161 and Boycott used up 124 minutes and 111 deliveries to score 23 as his side scrambled home by two wickets on the back of Carrick's aggressive 37. Hampshire toppled him from the top of the Yorkshire averages for the first time in sixteen years and with the pair of them separated by only a couple of runs it was readily put about that Boycott's sole aim was a not-out innings to snatch the prize from his rival, who missed the game through injury. Once he got out in the 90s, however, a Yorkshire collapse silenced the knockers. Five wickets fell for 13 runs before Carrick took a hand, so Boycott's painstaking effort hardly needed justifying, but he pointed out:

'The wicket was far from easy and the only way to make runs was to wait for bowling errors. Stovold got 59 for them through working hard and Procter reached 50 because he is a great natural attacker of the ball and hit it so hard that he got away with the odd miscalculation. The rest did nothing. I knew the danger of us collapsing, so I decided to make sure we got a good solid start. If you reach the closing stages with wickets in hand you have a chance. We got to 93 for one and young Athey played super. Without him, me and Richard Lumb, Yorkshire would have lost and Phil Carrick would not have been able to do what he did. It is as simple as that, but I know there are those about who will believe what they want. They don't know enough about cricket though, so they don't bother me.'

By the time September came around, my own feelings, based on casual conversations with players and one or two members of the committee, was that Boycott could be in trouble at the captaincy meeting. The animosity between him and Hampshire smouldered on without exactly bursting into flames and the possibility had to be faced that the latter might leave if Boycott continued in office. Whether that would be a good thing depended on how you looked at it, for Hampshire's batting, was almost as important as the captain's.

That meeting took place on September 29, but on the previous day Sir Kenneth appeared in the offices of the *Yorkshire Evening Post.* I had completed a preview of the deliberations, covering all the possibilities, suggesting the possibility of a change, and concluding with the hope that the Boycott—Illingworth partnership would be given at least one year in which to tackle the problems behind a decade of decline. 'I hope,' said Sir Kenneth, 'that you will have nothing much to write about tomorrow.' I showed him what I had already written and he was less than pleased.

'I intend to make sure that Geoff gets the support he deserves next season,' he said. 'It is clear to me that he has not had much in the past, but this is the right time to make a new start. It is not fair to ask a man to do a job unless you have absolute faith in him. I have that faith in Geoff and I want him and Raymond to have every chance. We can afford no more mistakes. Perhaps standards have slipped and that is something I shall have to put right. There must be no more trouble. Both Geoff and John Hampshire are fine players and it is our job in running the club to get the best out of both of them. We are simply not making the fullest use of all the skills that exist within the county. Internal unrest is responsible, I know, and I want to end it.'

That was straightforward enough, so, taking advantage of this 'inside information', I rewrote the article, forecasting that Yorkshire were ready to employ the twin strengths of their leading figures in the search for a success formula. How wrong Sir Kenneth and I were.

Boycott was on holiday on September 15, telephoning before he left to check whether there was anything I wanted to ask as it would be impossible to contact him for a couple of weeks. We had a normal conversation and when I mentioned the captaincy he said that since nothing had been said he hoped to be reappointed. 'As you know I had some

158

reservations about the team manager's role, but I have a great respect for Illy and now I am really looking forward to working with him,' he said. 'It is a new concept for us both, but we ought to be able to do a lot with the material we have. As captain of England he often asked me what I thought about certain things and sometimes I answered before he put the question because my mind was on the same wavelength. That gives me great confidence now and I am sure we are both man enough to handle the arguments that will probably crop up.'

The solitary cloud in his holiday sky concerned his mother's illness and no one outside his close family can imagine the shattering extent of the blow caused by her death while he was away. To this grief, Yorkshire added the crushing burden of his sacking as captain.

When he hurried sadly home to Fitzwilliam, he discovered a letter dated September 18 inviting him to a selection committee meeting on September 22. The date subsequently became September 28, the day of his return, so he could not attend, but Illingworth was present. Boycott chose to go to the cricket committee meeting on the 29th, despite his bereavement, and, in accordance with practice, left the room when the captaincy came up for discussion. These deliberations take place before lunch and then the general committee are informed of the outcome, which they either confirm or reject. Normally Temple would have told Boycott of his re-appointment immediately the cricket committee broke up, but this time he said that he had to wait for the general meeting, adding that a two-year contract had been recommended.

Following the general committee meeting Boycott received the news that Hampshire had accepted the captaincy. That is a brief summary of the events leading up to the bulletin released in the early evening by Lister. It read: 'The Yorkshire County Cricket Club, after long and careful consideration, have decided that the interests of the club would be best served by offering the captaincy to J.H. Hampshire. The committee very much hope that Boycott will continue to extend his invaluable services as a player and have offered him a two-year contract to continue as such.'

'They are grateful to him for what he has done for the club over many years and as captain during the last eight years.' Shattered, Boycott appealed directly to Sir Kenneth, who could not, however, do anything to overturn the democratic system even if he had wanted to and, according to Connell, the decision had been based on a majority such as would be required to elect a pope. Although Yorkshire were prepared for some reaction, they must have been shaken by the outburst of anger as Boycott went into hiding to dodge the Press corps hot on the trail of the biggest cricket story for years.

To say that he wept is to enter the world of the over-dramatic, but when I contacted him he was in the depths of despair. 'I want to play for Yorkshire and I want to captain them. I can't think beyond that, but I feel let down on all sides,' he said. 'It's impossible for me to consider what to do next at the moment, I am too emotionally upset. I don't understand what has happened since last year, except that Hampshire was censured. Now they want me to play under him.'

He maintained a sensible silence otherwise until appearing on the BBC television Parkinson Show on the night of Saturday, October 7, when he defended himself by attacking the committee. Television is a tricky medium and Boycott did not come over sympathetically.

Referring to the committee, he snapped: 'They are small-minded people — people who think they are always right. The whole thing was a set-up. They knew they were going to sack me, but at least they could have postponed the meeting. They could have allowed my mother to be buried in peace, but they could not wait.' He also called directly to the members to support him. 'If they want me to return as captain they must do something about it. They have got to get together, get off their bottoms and do what they have to do to make it happen.'

He was anxious to reach as wide an audience as possible within the seven days allowed by Test and County Cricket Board regulations for him to make a reply to Yorkshire's announcement, but on October 12 the cricket committee met and voted to send Boycott a letter, signed by Lister, requiring him to appear before them to explain his conduct.

It contained the following closing paragraph: 'It has been reported in the Press that you do not consider that you are required to obtain the club's approval. I take this opportunity of pointing out to you that whatever your contractual position with the club, if you wish to maintain your registration with the Test and County Cricket Board you are obliged to comply with its rules and you are still bound by its rules. I hope, therefore, that I shall have your assurances that you will not act in breach of those rules. I feel that on reflection you will agree that in your own interests as a player you should not prejudice your registration.'

Boycott agreed to make his television appearance in accordance with Section Two of rule 'B' in the TCCB discipline sub-committee regulations, which stated: 'Before making any public pronouncement a registered cricketer must obtain the prior consent of his county cricket club, except in the case of a reply or replies within a period of seven days to any public pronouncement about such registered cricketer made by the Board or any members of the Board, including his county cricket club.'

Confident of being within his rights, he adopted a militant stance. 'I am not prepared to meet anyone under threat,' he informed Lister bluntly, adding: 'If I have written confirmation that any threat is unreservedly withdrawn, I will be happy to meet the general committee with my solicitor in attendance if this can be arranged before my departure.' Boycott, due to join Brearley's party for Australia, had a tight schedule.

Lister replied by saying that he did not look upon his letter as containing any threat. He said the cricket committee were most anxious to meet Boycott 'in order that there should be no misunderstanding whatsoever of your position.' The exchange of letters did nothing to bring the parties closer together even on matters of fact, but a meeting with the general committee was convened for Monday, October 23, at 4.0 p.m.

Boycott, meanwhile, tried to clarify the issue. 'I have said all along that I have nothing to hide and I have regularly asked the committee to publicise the facts. I know I have been criticised for my television comments, but until then the matter was being kept very quiet. It was only after I had criticised the committee that they decided they ought to meet me. I have also said I am quite happy to have the contents of the letters we exchanged made public, but they seem reluctant to do this. I still do not know why I was sacked and I am waiting for some specific reasons.'

Mutch delivered an address a little short of two hours to the general committee, detailing what he and his client regarded as evidence of disloyalty and, after a brief interlude for the committee to dwell on what he said, Connell launched into the official reply. 'Let me say in the first place that this has nothing to do with playing ability. Playing ability is irrelevant except insofar as a player must be good enough to be a member of the team before he can be considered. It is nothing to do with what Mr Boycott has done or has not done. It is to do with what he is. Captaincy requires playing skill, tactical ability and experience, but is above all a matter of leadership and the ability to persuade the other members of the team to play right up to and on occasions beyond their potential.

'This is the quality which in the honest and sincere opinion of the majority of this committee Mr Boycott lacks. He is so dedicated to the perfection and exploitation of his own batting techniques that he is sometimes oblivious to the feelings and aspirations of his team-mates. As a result he cannot and does not get out of his team-mates what is there to be got. You may think that the committee have taken a long time to reach this decision and indeed we have been criticised for this.

'His lack of leadership ability has been the question mark which has hung over his captaincy from early days. It has come up every year — and I would emphasise that the appointment of a captain is made for one season only with no guarantee of continuance — and has been one of the principal factors which has been considered when each year the committee came to decide whether the incumbent captain was the best available, what were the alternatives, and whether the time was right for a change to be made. The feeling has varied from year to year, but this year a substantial majority decided that a change should be made. It was not a personal decision. It was made honestly and sincerely in the best interests of Yorkshire cricket.

'This characteristic of utter dedication frequently leads to an inability to achieve personal relationships and so disqualifies the possessor from leadership, but it is nevertheless the quality which has enabled Mr Boycott to make himself the player which he is. It is because he is so good a player and because of his constant and, I am sure, sincere assertion that all he wants is what is best for Yorkshire cricket that the committee offered him — and have confirmed the offer — the maximum contract given to any of the playing staff, that is to say, two years. The committee hope that Mr Boycott will continue to play for Yorkshire — the general committee are unanimous on this point — and still hope that he may come to see that this is how he can best serve the county. Finally the committee wish to state that the new captain John Hampshire will have their unanimous support.'

This put him one up on Boycott, who never enjoyed that luxury, but two questions remained. If all this were true, how could the committee expect Boycott to fit into the team in any capacity? Why were there so few references to specific cases and so many vague generalisations? Set against all the facts and figures the committee statement was a limp tissue of theory.

Boycott had little left to say, except: 'My first job is to do my best for England and score as many runs as I can. I was highly delighted to hear my playing ability was not in question and that the committee went out of their way to say how highly they regarded me. I reiterate my remarks about the cricket committee, however. I am a Yorkshireman at heart, but can I play with such disloyalty at the door?'

As he flew out to Australia, the Reform Group mobilised their forces and an indication of the passions came in their letter to members which left them open to legal charges for misrepresenting the committee. Thrust and counter-thrust enlivened each day as both sides grappled for the vital middle ground of support. At this point Illingworth entered the debate with a letter to the chairman dated November 10, 1978. Although not due to take up his duties before April 1 the following year, he wrote: 'I have recently returned from holiday and find the controversy about Geoff Boycott still raging. As you know when I was first offered the job of manager I said I would serve with any captain who might be appointed and in particular was perfectly happy to work with Geoff. Up to now I have, therefore, kept out of this row, but as things are developing I think I should now let you know that the players are wholeheartedly behind the committee in the change.'

In publishing this, the committee brought off a master-stroke, winning support from those members who sought to cast their votes in the most constructive manner, but again questions were raised. Why did Illingworth say he would be happy to serve with any captain in the first place? Was the captaincy discussed before he took the job? If so, Yorkshire accorded him a privilege denied Boycott or, for that matter, Hampshire, who had a manager imposed upon them whether they liked it or not. The more cautious members pondered this thoughtfully.

The Reform Group probed into the origins of the letter without getting very far, but, in fact, the background is very significant. Cope, the players' representative, conducted a secret dressing-room poll in August at the request of a committee member and reported back that dissatisfaction with Boycott was prevalent. He did not, however, mention Hampshire as an alternative. At least one member of the ruling body, therefore, knew how the team felt before Boycott was sacked and presumably he did not keep the information to himself. Illingworth telephoned Cope in November to ask if the position was still the same and then put pen to paper.

It should be added that Cope told the committeeman concerned that the players did not really feel it was any of their business, and while a couple indicated they were considering asking for their release, they stayed on with Boycott in the side, so they lacked a burning conviction.

The Reform Group, having gathered the necessary signatures for a second time, demanded a special general meeting in order to put two resolutions:

(1) That this special general meeting has no confidence in the members of the cricket sub-committee and recommends

their resignation from the general committee of the Yorkshire County Cricket Club forthwith.

(2) That Geoffrey Boycott be reappointed captain of the Yorkshire County Cricket Club and be invited to serve as such for the 1979 season.

Yorkshire, legally advised that the requisition had not been framed properly, claimed that the issue was a simple one of confidence and opted to call a meeting of their own to seek a vote on this issue. This was not the same thing at all, however, for members might reasonably have confidence in the committee as a whole while wanting to remove from it those who formed the cricket sub-committee, so the Reform Group took the matter to court.

Vice Chancellor Blackett-Ord, in the chancery division of the High Court at Liverpool, ordered that Yorkshire must hold a special general meeting to consider the Group's two resolutions, awarding costs to the Reformers. Thus Yorkshire faced the expense of two meetings and they acted quickly to incorporate them into one at the Royal Hall, Harrogate, on December 9, when three motions appeared on the agenda, the two from the Reform Group and one from Yorkshire to the effect that 'This meeting has confidence in the committee of the club as now constituted.'

The contestants created an election atmosphere by publishing their manifestos, the committee being first into the field with a three-page circular signed by Connell, who began by defending the committee system. 'It cannot be too strongly emphasised that the committee does not choose itself. The committee consists of members elected either by districts or by the general body of members at an annual general meeting. If members cannot trust the judgment of the committee, which they themselves elect and the membership of which they can regularly revise, the club — indeed any club democratically constituted — becomes impossible to run. In addition to attending numerous committee and sub-committee meetings many members of the committee willingly and freely give of their time in other adminstrative directions.'

So far, so good, although there was no mention of the committee giving their time for watching the team and studying Boycott at first hand. Turning to the captaincy, the statement continued: 'The essential question is "Who is the best available captain of Yorkshire in 1979?" This is the question to which the committee addressed itself and with their knowledge of the facts came to the conclusion that John Hampshire was the man. It is this decision which a group of members, sincere though they may be, seek to challenge largely on irrelevant grounds. Who are they? They are a self-appointed body. They have no first-hand knowledge of first-class cricket nor have they any knowledge of its administration.

'What is known to these members, as indeed to all the world, is Geoffrey Boycott's manifest playing ability and record, his dedication to the game, his immaculate turn-out and his long and loyal service to the county. These virtues deserve every recognition, but are they relevant to the question of captaincy? This appointment is not for past endeavour. It is given to the man who can best lead the team at the present time. Such a man must not only get the best out of the material at his command but on occasions a little more.

'The playing record of the county during the past eight years of Geoffrey Boycott's captaincy, particularly in the one-day matches, has not been good and a substantial majority of the committee believe a change in captaincy to be not only desirable but essential. In this connection it is worthy of note that Yorkshire have had two captains in the sixteen years between 1963 and 1978, during which period every other county has had numbers varying between three and six.

'Furthermore, the interests of the playing staff have to be considered and this was of necessity a prime factor in the minds of the committee. Among its other assets, Yorkshire have a crop of young players at the moment whose potential is as high as any of the overseas stars who have contributed so much to the success of other counties.' Such nonsense hardly deserves comment, but indicates clearly how out of touch with the playing realities the Yorkshire officials were — as the next few years proved.

Connell went on to make a startling admission. 'He has

never been seen to be an ideal captain, though in the early days it was hoped that he might become one. Even when it became apparent that he was not going to develop the necessary qualities, there was the problem of an alternative. Each year the question has to be considered anew and each year there has been the difficult decision to be made as to whether to reappoint and, if not, who should be appointed.'

Hampshire, of course, had been available just as long as Boycott and was capped on the same day. It took the committee a long time to decide he had better claims and their dithering over the captaincy did them little credit. On the subject of Hampshire, Connell continued: 'Much has been made of the Northampton incident. The committee deplored it at the time and reprimanded Hampshire. It was a bad mistake but it was and remains a solitary incident in a long career of faithful service to Yorkshire. The fact that the committee have in the past had occasion to reprimand Geoffrey Boycott has not prevented them from reappointing him.' Still no details. Did Connell really mean Boycott had been so near to suspension as Hampshire? If so, the occasion has escaped the notice of a fairly alert Press.

The further they progressed the more Yorkshire got themselves into trouble, for in trying to explain their failure to invite Boycott to a committee meeting before November 1973, they made no mention of 1971. It was a careless omission. They also challenged Boycott's statement on the awarding of caps in 1976, but not the voting pattern he disclosed, and concluded their appeal: 'If the members on largely sentimental grounds are to call such decisions in question, other than through the regular actions of committee members or at the annual general meeting, the club will destroy itself.'

All this stemmed from the source that had a year earlier proudly proclaimed: 'We are putting alongside a very experienced captain [Boycott] a man who has a lot of experience himself [Illingworth]. I see no reason why they should not work successfully together.' Those with long memories might have wished Yorkshire would make up their minds. Trueman's contribution came through the correspondence columns of *The Times*. He said the deposed captain had no divine right to hold office. 'He had held the appointment for eight seasons during which time Yorkshire's results have been the worst for one hundred years,' he wrote, adding that the county's Championship position has been in double figures eight times since 1878, five of them coming during Boycott's captaincy. 'My only quarrel with the Yorkshire committee is that they put up with Boycott as captain for so long,' he concluded.

As an honest comparison, Yorkshire's longest run without a Championship since Lord Hawke revitalised the club and won the title in 1893 had previously been the nine years between 1950 and 1958. In that spell they finished eleventh and twelfth, despite the formidable presence of Trueman in their ranks. For the most part Surrey were too strong, but in Boycott's case a greater variety of opposition scaled the heights.

Boycott toyed with the fanciful notion of flying back from Australia on a lightning visit to present his own case, but, shelving the energy-sapping project, he relied on a statement of his own. Replying to the county, he said: 'If the club is to prosper this attack must fail for four main reasons:

'First — It is dishonest in that it makes no reference to the disloyalty to the team, the club and the captain throughout the whole of my eight seasons of captaincy.

'Secondly — It blurs the issue, seeking to suggest that the whole question is "Who is the best available captain for Yorkshire in 1979?" The real question is who is responsible for the present state of Yorkshire cricket? That is the vital question and the termination of my term as captain has highlighted this in a way which nothing else could have done.

'Thirdly — The statement is also inaccurate and misleading in a large number of its facts.

'Fourthly — The chairman defends the committee's actions on democratic grounds. How democratic is a club which tries to refuse its members a special meeting after all the procedures have been observed? The members' right to a special meeting exists just so that they can make sure decisions taken in their name are decisions they agree with. It is a safeguard. If the club becomes ungovernable it is because the committee forget that they are elected to reflect the members' views and not their own prejudices.'

Boycott produced figures to show that his record was better than Hampshire's in both the Championship and the Sunday League, adding: 'I venture to suggest that if the team had not lost four Championship matches towards the end of 1977 when I was absent (Hampshire two and Cope two) we should have been in the top four. The chairman makes a special point that the playing record of the club particularly in the one-day matches has not been good, but my record in one-day matches has been more than one and a half times better than Hampshire's and almost one and a half times better than his in the Championship over the five-year period.'

Still on the playing front, Boycott said: 'Both Illingworth and Trueman predicted that it would be ten years after the loss of Close in 1970 before the county was capable of winning a major trophy and recently Jim Laker declared that if Brian Sellers himself had captained Yorkshire over the past seven years they still would not have won the Championship. Had I had the loyalty of my committee in 1974 my "leave of absence" from the England side might never have occurred. Trueman's attitude towards me changed completely when he joined World Series cricket as commentator as anyone can check.' This was not quite true, for Trueman had, as we have seen, expressed concern from Boycott's first season, being consistent in his opposition to his captaincy, and generally a number of former players stood against him.

Dismayed by the Illingworth letter, Boycott dismissed it from the reckoning. 'It must be clear to everyone that the members of the team are completely precluded from joining openly in discussion because they are servants of the committee — they would be fools to join in this debate. They are not free agents. They could put their jobs at risk if they admit to disagreeing with the committee.'

He claimed, too, that one side of the picture had been shown, adding: 'I believe I have been as responsible as any in the development of the potential crop of young players. I do know that in 1976 when I was injured they were urging me to return as quickly as possible. During my absence I was instructed to leave matters to the match captain and I did not have a vote in team selection.'

Turning to the timing of the committee meeting, which Connell insisted could have been rearranged only at a cost of great inconvenience to many, Boycott said he had not been offered a postponement, continuing:

'The chairman says it is not possible to call a truly representative meeting of thirty people "the great majority of whom have to earn their livings" at short notice. When I criticised the running of the club on television on October 7, a full committee meeting was convened at less than a week's notice.'

Querying the committee role in dealing with representations behind his back, Boycott said: 'The general committee have never been fully informed of the situation. They have been pawns of the cricket committee.' He went on in agonising detail over many of the points we have come across on the preceding pages and summed up: 'It gives me no pleasure to fight this battle. Indeed, it has given me little pleasure to fight the many battles which I have had on behalf of the team. Tensions create tensions and defeat concentration on what we should all be aiming for. The Reform Group are right in every respect. Indeed I do not feel their resolutions go far enough, for the whole leadership of the club, with certain honourable exceptions, needs to be removed.'

Stirring stuff, and the special meeting lived up to the liveliest expectations as a packed gathering of over 1,300 squeezed into the Royal Hall and almost escaped the control of the chairman, booing and jeering the pro-committee speakers with such noisy gusto that Mutch requested a fair hearing all round.

All the excitement was superficial, for proxy votes decided the three resolutions, but the committee margin underlined the need for caution. The voting figures on the three motions were:

(1) This meeting has confidence in the committee of the club as now constituted. For 4,422 (proxy 3,952), against 3,067 (2,196). Majority 1,355.

(2) This meeting has no confidence in the members of the cricket sub-committee and recommends their resignation

from the general committee forthwith. For 3,346 (2,401), against 4,216 (3,820). Majority 870.

(3) That Geoffrey Boycott be re-appointed captain. For 2,602 (1,902), against 4,826 (4,279). Majority 2,224.

Those at Harrogate supported the Reform Group by almost two to one and Boycott, on balance, had slightly the better of the exchanges. Members of the general committee might plead ignorance, but the cricket committee had been aware of a dangerous situation and done little. So why did the Reform Group and Boycott lose? There were four things which swayed the outcome, the first being the natural in-built British desire to avoid sweeping change. Many of the proxy voters supported the committee out of a sense of tradition.

The committee, they accepted, had always run the club and if they did happen to be wrong about this, they had been right in the past. Equally, the Reform Group had no real standing and there were understandable fears that if the committee lost the vote chaos would ensue. Good, bad or indifferent, the incumbents at least kept the club running and there was no guarantee that the 'rebels' would do as well overall. Then the Illingworth letter played a part. The committee's biggest majority came on the question of Boycott's re-appointment which can hardly be coincidence. A lot of members felt that if the team wanted a change then that was that. They quarrelled rather with the manner of its implementation. Finally, Boycott's television appearance counted against him. I spoke to numerous uncommitted members in the days immediately after the Parkinson show and no one had a kind word for him. It is possible to contend, therefore, that in those few fateful minutes he actually lost the whole battle.

Still, whatever the pros and cons, the will of the majority had to prevail and Boycott had to live with the result. So did the committee, who had little cause for self-congratulation when over 3,000 members indicated they had no faith in their administration. The ballot contained a warning for them to mend their ways quickly.

Far away in Australia, Boycott, with the England tourists, and Hampshire, playing for Tasmania, came into passing but surly contact, Old and Bairstow doing their best to patch up the differences without too much success. The pair appeared reluctant to discuss the gulf between them. The usually reticent Hampshire permitted himself a few comments. 'It is up to Geoff whether he plays next season or not, but I will insist on his attitude being right. I must admit I have been surprised by the strength of feeling. I expected something, but nothing like this. All the same, I think Geoff has brought the pressures he so readily talks about on himself. My wife and family have suffered a lot, especially with all the arguments about loyalty after Northampton. What I did there was on the spur of the moment. It was not a bid for the captaincy or anything like that, but I don't regret it. The first thing I knew about the captaincy was when I was telephoned and offered the job and I had no hesitation. Those who still want Geoff to be captain have to realise that the game is Yorkshire cricket and nothing and nobody is bigger than that. The sooner we get playing cricket the better as far as I can see.'

That speech, a long one by Hampshire's standards, hardly helped to heal the breach, while Boycott remained dourly entrenched. 'I am the injured party,' he said. 'It is up to Hampshire to make the first move. He has not even apologised for Northampton which is the least he could do in the circumstances. As far as I can see I have nothing to approach him about.' Hampshire, however, actually bowled a few deliveries to Boycott in the nets at Melbourne.

Boycott was unsure about accepting the offer of a two-year contract, although heartened by a massive petition organised by the *Yorkshire Evening Post* in which thousands of readers urged him to play on with the county. 'Of course I want to go back and do my best for Yorkshire. Nothing the committee do can touch the genuine concern I have for Yorkshire cricket and for the ordinary followers who are the strength of the club. I have always said I never wanted to play for anyone else and I simply don't know how to give less than my best, but it's not as simple as that. What sort of reception can I expect in the dressing room from Hampshire and Illingworth. Hampshire has made no attempt to talk things over with me here in Australia and there is no way I am going back to be picked on or pushed about. Seniority has its privileges and I have worked very hard to get where I am today. I will not be taken for granted or made to feel or look guilty.'

He was also subjected to conflicting advice, with some of his friends advocating the hard line of a clean break and a new beginning. Emotionally, however, he shied away from such drastic action, and he chose to stay because he wanted to keep faith with the public and with his ideals. He might also have reflected that the best way to metaphorically spit in the eye of his detractors was to retain his dignity, keep out of any sort of controversy and score as many runs as possible.

'I have learned to live with the people who can see no good in me. They don't matter. They are small-minded, although they can do me a lot of harm and, through me, hurt Yorkshire cricket. Some day the world will see through them. In these sad times for me I have been really encouraged by the support of the people who matter most — the true Yorkshire cricket lovers. At least they are constant and I know they respect me as a player.'

His decision received a mixed reception back in Yorkshire, the average enthusiast's delight contrasting with hunch-shouldered annoyance in one or two areas. Boycott and Illingworth were to get together after all.

9 Hampshire, Old and Hartley

'The committee believes that all members will now unite
solidly behind John Hampshire in his efforts to bring a title
to' the county. In this connection your committee believes
that the county now has the most promising set of young
cricketers for many years and that the members can look
forward with renewed confidence.' With those brave words
Yorkshire ushered in the new era under the direct control of
Illingworth as team manager and Hampshire as captain. The
players, they claimed, also had the change of leadership they
wanted. The portents could not have been brighter and, with
Boycott resigned to the 'back bench', a better team spirit
must surely be the outcome of more enlightened management.

It was all another committee pipe-dream. The predicted
upsurge in the county's fortunes never materialised, although
Yorkshire came within sight of the Benson and Hedges Cup.
They collapsed from fourth to seventh in the Championship
and gained no more than mild satisfaction from reversing the
process in the Sunday League. Their one Gillette Cup victory
was gained against Durham and the season bore a remarkable
similarity to most of those under Boycott. Never hesitating
to give his best, Boycott put all his personal disappointments
behind him to superbly head both batting and bowling
averages in the three-day competition — a feat previously
achieved by George Hirst in 1910.

Not only that, he comfortably finished at the top of the
national averages with 102.53, becoming the only batsman to
break the three-figure barrier twice. In doing so he wiped

174

the smirks off a few faces, for he had been contemptuously written off as a man of the past by the bulk of his critics following a very poor tour of Australia. 'Of course, his eyes have gone. He hasn't been playing well for a long time,' they said. 'It doesn't matter whether he plays for Yorkshire or not, he's over the hill.' He averaged only 21.91 in the Tests 'Down Under' and 26.65 in all matches, soldiering on through the winter without a century and getting very square on to the bowler as he did so.

Was he straining to pick up the ball? He said not, but his friends wondered, and when he decided to sign his new Yorkshire contract he had something to prove. Only he knew how much bereavement and Yorkshire's rejection affected him, however, and while he paid careful attention to each minute detail of his technique, he did not fear the future.

It became a stage upon which he displayed all his glittering talents, nine first-class wickets bringing him almost as much pleasure as his 1,538 runs, and he was delighted to grab a career-best four for 14 in the Headingley Roses match. He and Lumb contributed nine of the eleven three-figure Championship innings and without these two Yorkshire would have been in desperate straits, Hampshire discovering that the cares of captaincy reduced his output of runs. The youngsters failed to live up to their much-vaunted promise.

The usual accusations of selfishness were trotted out as he fought to keep his average above one hundred from the end of June, increasing in volume when he pulled out of the final match through injury, but he could afford to take no notice. He had acquired no taste for sour grapes. 'If I did not get any runs some would say I was deliberately not trying because Hampshire is captain, but when I do well they say I am doing it for myself. I can't win,' he admitted with a wry smile.

Yorkshire actually made one of their worst starts to a Championship season since the war, having to wait until the eleventh game to register their opening win — a run as poor as that in 1974 — and the strains resulted in some sharp exchanges behind the scenes. Hampshire's captaincy leant heavily on the defensive as he wrestled with the problems that so severely taxed Boycott's expertise. The author of the cheerful forecasts in the *Yorkshire Year Book* could profitably have spent a few days gaining first-hand knowledge of the playing strength and the way in which it was utilised.

When Yorkshire at last got off the mark with a nine-wicket victory over Derbyshire at Chesterfield, Boycott scored 167 and 57 not out to exert overall control. Then Middlesex were beaten at Scarborough, and his 76 — 45 more than the next highest score — held things together in the first innings, making it possible for Lumb to win the match in the wake of a generous declaration.

Despite being hit in the eye by a delivery from, of all people, the gentle, medium-paced Johnson in the nets, Boycott also top-scored with 94 in the first innings of the Lancashire fixture, which Yorkshire won by six wickets, so he played a prominent part in three of the five Championship successes. His presence was helpful in every way and it could not be shown that he cost the team points by pursuing his own goals. His 151 not out off Derbyshire at Leeds drew the sting from a burst of exceptional seam bowling by Hendrick, whose figures of one for 41 were an utter travesty. Against almost any other batsman in the world they would have been substantially better and Boycott spent more than his fair share of the innings in the firing line.

Bowlers held the upper hand at Cardiff, Boycott's patient 58 being the highest innings in a washed-out engagement, and he deserved praise at Bradford when Hampshire, winning the toss, inflicted the worst of the wicket on Yorkshire in the Surrey game. He ground out 52 priceless runs and used up important time, being seventh out at 78. His resistance against the new ball enabled Carrick and Cooper to lift the score to 162 after six of the first seven batsmen made 12 between them. Hampshire got himself into something of a muddle on the last day, declaring and then finding Surrey too much of a handful. As they neared their target of 193 in 140 minutes, however, he called up Boycott, who bowled five tight overs for 18 to save his face in a breathless draw.

As ever, Yorkshire seldom sparkled without Boycott and sometimes dawdled along in his presence, being involved in some dreary draws. He enlivened one of these, the Somerset match at Harrogate, with an unbeaten 130 in an opening stand of 288 with Lumb, but Yorkshire stumbled across another snag when he was away. No one fancied the idea of going in first with Lumb, so the trusty Bairstow had to volunteer while his team-mates with specialist batting qualifications — part of such a 'bright crop' — stood back. Far from improving, things deteriorated, reaching a sorry pass when the opening innings for Yorkshire represented an unwelcome imposition.

Nottinghamshire, winning at Worksop by eight wickets, would have impressed their superiority in two days but for Boycott's second innings resistance as he carried his bat for 175, made in six hours. He nearly saved the day for Yorkshire and he definitely saved the home club financially, a large third-day crowd turning up to see if he could perform a miracle.

So on to Cheltenham and Gloucestershire, who had Yorkshire at 54 for five in reply to 288 for eight with Procter recording an lbw hat-trick, but Boycott's patient 95 patched up the cracks making it possible for Carrick to hammer a century as the tension eased and the weather ruled out a positive finish.

Shaky performances against Kent and Sussex while he was away merely confirmed his importance, for the batting creaked and groaned, and, although he had less success in the Sunday League, his 92 provided much-needed assurance in a very edgy scramble in the Gillette Cup. By picking up yet another Man-of-the-Match award, he prevented Durham bringing off a repeat of the Harrogate sensation and if ever Hampshire had cause to be grateful to him it was here. After bowling badly to allow Durham a negotiable 213 for nine, Yorkshire lost two wickets for six and three for 70. Hampshire survived an error, from which he should have been stumped, to score 75 not out, but he knew who had won the contest for him.

Boycott behaved himself impeccably off the field except in two matters. Perhaps it is not surprising that he should be mildly amused when Hampshire got into difficulties that were supposed to be in his own mind, but he showed it too readily, particularly as the presence of Reform Group devotees became a source of irritation to Illingworth and the rest of the players. This unfortunate state of affairs grew out of misunderstanding as much as malice, but the resentment was real enough and it was widely thought that the Reformers presented themselves as a one-man fan club.

Irrespective of their expertise or political views, the Reform Group members remained enthusiasts who supported the team generally while backing Boycott as a special case. Since the players had been used, however innocently, to bolster the committee's action in changing the captain, they had to expect some reproach when performances remained poor, so the arguments continued. Illingworth and the more forceful members of the team challenged the Reformers here and there, which was good since these debates were a channel of communication. Unfortunately, the heat generated turned them into a running sore.

Far more important, however, was the problem over the Benson and Hedges Cup semi-final, in which Boycott was unable to play. Essex edged into the final, thanks to the extra experience of their line-up in a very tight game. Boycott had strained a leg muscle in the Championship game with Somerset and did not bat in the second innings. This raised doubts about his fitness for the semi-final which followed immediately and confusion was multiplied by the lack of rapport between the manager and his outstanding player.

They spent a lot of time apart instead of getting together to assess accurately the extent of the gamble if Boycott played. No one knew what was happening when the party reached Chelmsford, but shortly before the toss, Illingworth left out Boycott. 'I had no choice,' he explained. 'I asked him to run hard and he said he couldn't, so I dare not take the risk of his breaking down. If we go into the tie with him, Essex would be within their rights to refuse us a substitute if anything went wrong. In any case, I would want him to bowl a few overs.' Boycott offered a conflicting version. 'I could not go all out, but I was told I had been left out. I did not say I could not play.'

Yorkshire lost by three wickets and Illingworth defiantly claimed that Boycott would not have made any difference, but this was not a calm, objective verdict. Hampshire and Lumb carved 100 from twenty-six overs for the first wicket, a faster rate than could have been expected with Boycott at the wicket, but the batting order left the middle terribly exposed, and Athey, Sharpe and Love managed 3 between them. Boycott must have been a better bet than anyone of this nervous trio and Illingworth ought to have insisted on his taking part, knowing there was no risk of his giving less than one hundred per cent.

Of the two, however, Illingworth was most entitled to sympathy and he, like Boycott before him, needed a good result or two to guard his back. In proving no more successful as a unifying force he became vulnerable to hatchet men, for not everyone had welcomed him back to the county with open arms. Reg Haigh's anger at his return, for example, matched his fury at Boycott's general conduct. I met him at a private cricket gathering in Huddersfield a few days before Yorkshire announced Illingworth's appointment. 'You'll hear something in a short while that should make your blood boil. It does mine,' he said. 'I can't tell you what it is, I'm sworn to secrecy, but I'll tell you this, the fellow concerned let us down badly before and he's worse than Boycott in my opinion. There's quite a few of us damned angry and, remember this, what's been done can be undone. Mark my words there'll be a lot of trouble yet.'

So the engagement of Illingworth, about which the bulk of the committee knew nothing, did not meet with universal approval.

Hampshire's second season turned out no better than his first. Yorkshire climbed one inadequate place to sixth in the Championship, but they crashed to joint fourteenth on Sundays. They disappeared from the Benson and Hedges Cup in the qualifying stages, losing three of their four games to poor bowling and defensive captaincy as Hampshire spread his field far and wide in an attempt to protect large scores against Warwickshire and Worcestershire.

Boycott had 40 out of 268 for four against Warwickshire at Headingley, where Old unbelievably allowed Dilip Doshi to scramble ten from the game's last over to beat Yorkshire, who went one run better to register their highest total in the competition, 269 for six, at Worcester. Here Boycott, at his superb best, reached 142, another Benson and Hedges record for the county, with one six and fourteen fours, out of 251, but this was not enough either, Worcestershire having four wickets to spare in a comfortable victory march.

He had, in fact, a purple patch in limited-overs cricket, with 66 against Worcestershire in the Sunday League and an unbeaten 37 at Huddersfield as Warwickshire won again. There he retired after losing a contact lens when in full flow and he scored 38 at Middlesborough in an opening stand of 93 from nineteen overs with Athey at the expense of Sussex, but Yorkshire still lost.

In the circumstances, Illingworth's decision to leave him out of the Sunday side as a matter of policy raised a furore. The manager's thinking, which also encompassed Hampshire, though not so directly, was easy to follow in one way. He regarded his senior batsmen as expendable in the hurly-burly of the Sunday League because they were approaching an age when plans had to be made to accommodate their declining physical powers, and Peter Ingham, stepping into Boycott's shoes, made the most of his opportunity. His briskly fashioned sequence of 53 not out, 87 not out, 6, 28, 13, 41 and 47 took the heat out of the situation without solving anything.

To Boycott, the thin end of the wedge appeared and he did not like being dropped for any reason. 'I reckon I am as fit as most and my record speaks for itself. Surely experience is valuable in the Sunday League. Still I had better not say too much.' He did not know it, but he never said a truer word.

Thus another obstacle appeared on the road to understanding between Boycott and Illingworth, who also 'rested' Hampshire on the same grounds from the final Sunday fixture at Canterbury.

A place in the semi-final of the Gillette Cup highlighted the 1980 season and Yorkshire were unlucky to lose the toss to Surrey at the Oval. Batting in conditions that would not have been tolerated in the Championship and intimidated by some very fast, short bowling by Sylvester Clarke, they were held to 135 and beaten by four wickets.

Boycott suffered a relatively lean time in the Championship, playing only thirteen innings and waiting until late August for his first century — 135 at Old Trafford — but he finished in style with 154 not out in the drawn game with

Derbyshire at Scarborough and kept his average over 50 for the eleventh time in succession.

The truth, unpalatable though it may have been to the officials, was that after two years 'under new management' Yorkshire were no better than when Boycott laboured uneasily at the direction of the committee. In some ways they went backwards and the club's good name was sullied at Harrogate in the Festival Tilcon Trophy. Spectators were definitely displeased by the team's performance as they lost to Glamorgan without showing the expected fight.

The players faced a long haul down to Southampton for the Championship fixture with Hampshire on the night of the Tilcon final — Friday — and in losing by ten wickets in the qualifying round they made their preoccupation with other things all too obvious. They stood third in the table, poised to press their challenge, so it could be argued that they got their priorities right, for the Tilcon Trophy had little prestige outside Harrogate. On the other hand, Yorkshire could ill afford to alienate their public. Illingworth, although annoyed, asserted that the competition posed problems and Yorkshire declined an invitation in 1981, leaving the way clear for the Nat-West Cup tie at Canterbury. Bad behaviour also scarred a game for the Cope—Leadbeater joint benefit fund at Otley in 1980.

Overall there were a number of warning signs and the committee might profitably have dealt with another issue.

Boycott devoted a lot of time to negotiating a new contract and in late July he, Hampshire and Old agreed two-year terms. Immediately howls of protest rose from the ranks, the players complaining that this broke with the tradition whereby such matters were settled in September. The squealing reached a sufficient volume for the new chairman, Crawford, who had replaced Connell, to hurry dutifully along to rain-swept Sheffield, where he lightened the gloom of an otherwise uneventful afternoon by promising that in future all contracts would be discussed at the same time. What a change from 1968 when Illingworth was shown the door and invited to take any other dissatisfied cricketer with him.

Step by step, Yorkshire retreated, using Boycott as an excuse for their own short-comings, failing to deal with dressing-room upstarts, and now they no longer had the courage of their own convictions. Instead of reading the Riot Act, Crawford sued for peace and, in doing so, made a mistake. With the readily made exception of Bairstow, whose passion for Yorkshire equalled Boycott's, not one member of the contracted staff had the right to query anything about a trio who stood head and shoulders above their colleagues in ability.

All this unrest harked back to the first year of Boycott's captaincy when his critics shuffled in to moan about one thing and another. The faces altered but the attitudes were unchanging. Had the earlier mutineers been ordered to 'walk the plank' Boycott's prospects of steering the ship into more promising waters would have been enhanced.

Hampshire resigned at the end of the 1980 campaign, sadder but wiser. He did not see eye to eye with Illingworth on team selection nor always on the handling of his resources in the field and clearly grey, undefined areas of command complicated their relationship. By now at least three men appreciated the extent of the rebuilding operation. Lumb and Old spent three games each under the microscope as stand-in captain while Hampshire nursed an injury. These occurred in a run from May 28 to June 24 and their records came out identical – one win and two draws. Neither impressed sensationally nor failed seriously, but Lumb was none too keen to lead a team containing two former captains, so promotion settled on Old. Lumb, however, accepted the vice-captaincy on an official basis, but, like all the best laid plans, this arrangement soon ran into deep water.

Old went straight to Boycott for help, reaching agreement during the England tour of the West Indies whereby he could avail himself of guidance as the need arose. Lumb, beset by a string of broken bones and a bad attack of 'dropsy' in various catching positions, slowly melted into the background. While all this went on, another cloud appeared on the horizon. Old, the subject of some caustic comments by Illingworth in a book, had a reputation for being injury prone and in 1980 received a one-year contract which demanded that he prove his fitness. When he dropped out of two key Sunday games, therefore, he lost a few friends and Illingworth was far from pleased, feeling that his best bowler should have pushed himself harder.

Apart from arguably costing Yorkshire points, Old's injuries added a new dimension to the captaincy. Bairstow took over for the Sunday League games, both of which were narrowly lost, but in the Championship Hampshire resumed command at Cardiff and Trent Bridge while Old answered England's call. Two more defeats ended Hampshire's readiness to be captain and on July 29 at Scarborough Neil Hartley relished the unique distinction of leading out Yorkshire as an uncapped professional. The incident hit the headlines and Bairstow, among others, expressed some doubts about the arrangement.

Whatever might be said about Boycott's reign, it was comparatively quiet. Hartley actually overcame the difficulties admirably, revealing a cool head and a firm grasp of the fundamental principles, but there were objections. In the first place the young Shipley batsman did not command a regular place in the side on merit and he was linked socially with Illingworth's daughter, which raised the indictment that he was being favoured. In fact, conversely, Illingworth considered the move earlier, holding back because he feared the charge of nepotism, but Hartley's lack of seniority raised a few hackles.

Yorkshire, therefore, had four captains in the 1981 season, as they did in 1972, and it would have been five if Lumb had accepted the job at Wellingborough. Disgruntled by then and feeling he had missed too many matches and too many tactical discussions, he stood down in favour of Hartley. With the dressing room knee deep in field marshall's batons, it was too much to expect that no one would trip over them.

Illingworth nominated Hartley as official vice-captain at Chesterfield, but when Old received a second term the county did not name his deputy, returning to the match-by-match arrangement, so confusion reigned once more.

Before that happened, though, one feature of the summer gained remarkable prominence. Boycott, contemptuous of the manoeuvring, contented himself with making runs, although not as many as usual, and minding his own business when not acting as Old's mentor, but he was drawn into the

spotlight almost by accident. The new captain preferred to
field at slip, being both adept and reliable in that position,
but it kept him a long way from his bowlers, so a quiet word
of advice between deliveries was impossible. This magnified
the retiring nature of his leadership and was significant when
Stevenson stood in danger of losing length and line at
Worcester in an exciting climax. Boycott stepped into the
breach. From mid-off he directed activities firmly, demanding
the ball which he handed on to Stevenson, coaxing him into
a more workmanlike rhythm.

Although Yorkshire lost, Boycott demonstrated that he has
few equals at bringing the best out of anyone prepared to listen
and take notice, and he repeated the trick against Hampshire at
Middlesborough, standing in on the last day for Old, who had a
damaged knee, to organise an impressive effort that carried the
side to the brink of victory. He handled severely weakened
bowling resources magnificently, giving an object lesson in the
art of making a lot out of a little and the whole team moved with
a real sense of purpose.

The essence of any cricket correspondent's art is gauging
the mood of a side and learning to read the signs, which are
constantly changing with the composition of the party.
Casual, off-the-record conversations are crucial, not essentially
in the search for exclusive stories, although these are un-
deniably important, but more to keep a complete picture
available. It is helpful to know the way in which the players
are thinking and how they react to the whole variety of
occurrences which make up a summer on the road.

Towards the end of 1981 the underlying note was one of
uncertainty in Yorkshire, with the captaincy in the balance
and Old far from sure as to whether he could look forward to
another year. More than one member of the contracted
squad had in the course of the year agreed with me that
things ran more smoothly on the field under Boycott. They
did not so much stick up their hands and vote for him, but in
the reflective calm of a quiet drink and an amicable discussion
they tended to think that he had done a good job. With the
benefit of hindsight, change had not been for the best
although Old had certainly not been anything like a failure
and also had admirers.

In an attempt to find a solution to the puzzle that had defeated the administrative mind, I wrote an article in the *Yorkshire Evening Post* suggesting a secret ballot among the players. This, at least, I reasoned would give Illingworth and the cricket management committee a pointer in one direction. Whether they took notice was another matter altogether.

'There has been much argument over the captaincy virtually from the time Boycott replaced Close,' I wrote. 'The time has come to sort it out decisively and the only answer is in player power, however unpleasant that expression may sound in the corridors of administrative power. From my own observations, Boycott is re-established as the team favourite, but the way to prove or disprove that theory is via the ballot box.' Since I also indicated that there was a reasonable chance of Old being elected and thus getting a clear mandate to impose his will on events, I regarded this as a constructive proposition. Boycott, who I had sounded out, was eager to serve the county. 'I have given up getting involved in the politics,' he said, 'but obviously if the players wanted me as captain I would be delighted. I am not too modest to think I have nothing left to offer and I am always ready to do what I can, like helping Chris this time.'

Before any action could be taken, however, the Reform Group set the cat among the pigeons, launching their campaign to have Illingworth dismissed. The manager then suspended Boycott for the last two games of the season, both these acts being linked to a policy decision which meant Boycott and Hampshire standing down again on Sundays.

Neither of the senior professionals was happy, but Boycott made the most noise, saying in a television interview that, while he did not want to upset the team, he intended to clear the air with Illingworth once the competitive programme was completed. Boycott's disappointment also concerned a failure to select him for the Scarborough Festival matches, while Illingworth could possibly have held back from a decision which raised tempers. In a spontaneous response, holiday customers at Scarborough, spilled onto the playing area, threatening to delay the start of the match against Northamptonshire.

As Boycott sadly left the North Marine Road ground

through an avenue of well-wishers, Fielden busily collected signatures for the Reform Group's anti-Illingworth campaign, which continued with a series of meetings.

Yorkshire stirred themselves into action, holding a day-long meeting at Headingley, but producing another of their famous statements that did nothing to satisfy either the legion of television, radio and newspaper men squeezed into the pavilion bar or the cricket-minded public.

It read: 'A statement was prepared for issue to the Press and was unanimously approved by the committee. When it was communicated to Mr Illingworth and Mr Boycott and the legal advisers of Mr Boycott, Mr Boycott and Mr Illingworth raised certain objections and Mr Boycott's legal advisers indicated that they considered Mr Boycott had a case of legal argument. In the circumstances, the committee regrets that no statement can be issued now in relation to the suspension of Mr Boycott.

'The committee is nevertheless concerned, as are the members, at the results obtained this season and an in-depth investigation will be instituted forthwith to seek the causes of this and the steps that can be taken to improve upon what to all is an unacceptable record.'

Having waded through all that, Crawford admitted that he might well have advocated caution had he been consulted before the suspension was imposed, going on to plead for tolerance and understanding. 'I appeal to all Yorkshire members to get behind the club and pull in one direction,' he said. 'Let us call an end to the mud slinging, bickering and personal attacks. The longer they go on, the longer success, after which we are all striving, will be delayed.' Fine-sounding words, but the committee immediately put the county's name back in the headlines.

Out of the blue they produced the results of a dressing-room poll, prompted by my suggestion of a ballot. Eighteen contracted players took part at Scarborough, answering the question 'Would you like to have Geoffrey Boycott re-appointed as captain?' There were, said the committee, fifteen votes against and three abstentions. Following Boycott's suspension, Old put two further questions to his colleagues at Hove:

'Do you wish to have Boycott in the side as a player next season?' and

'Do you want Illingworth to continue as cricket manager?'

Ten players did not want Boycott, two did and four abstained, while thirteen backed the manager and three abstained, and the committee continued: 'Whilst the committee is loath to involve playing members of the club's staff, they feel that the views of the contracted players, as volunteered by their representatives on the cricket management committee, should be known.'

The outcome inevitably was further argument, and before the start of the 1982 season the point of the exercise had become lost as Boycott settled back into the side with no signs in the pre-season preparations of any widespread animosity on anyone's part.

It had never been my intention to spark a public election. All I had hoped to do was offer a lead in the decision making and, in publishing the findings of their little investigation, the club did themselves more harm than good, for a lot of members did not think the idea very honourable, while Eric Baines, the Doncaster representative on the committee, resigned.

The action also put unnecessary pressure on the remaining batsmen suddenly shorn of Hampshire's skills. Presumably having made his feelings known about Boycott in the poll, he threw in his hand, seeking release from his contract to join Derbyshire. He refused to explain, but it was generally accepted that he had grown weary of all the aggravation. The thought of a Yorkshire batting line-up without either Boycott or Hampshire sent shivers down the spine which had nothing to do with the autumnal chill, the more so as the five Championship successes in 1981 owed much to an unbeaten century by Boycott at Chesterfield against Derbyshire and hundreds from Hampshire against Leicestershire, Surrey and Northamptonshire. Only at Northampton, where Yorkshire completed the first leg of a 'double' did victory not depend on a healthy contribution from one of the 'elder statesmen'.

As the winter of discontent dragged its weary way through snowstorms, blizzards, drifts and floods, the investigating sub-committee piled up the evidence from dozens of witnesses to Yorkshire's decline, pausing to note Fielden's landslide triumph in the Doncaster district election to fill the Baines vacancy. He swept into office on a pro-Boycott ticket, indicating that there were still many members who appreciated all the opening batsman had done.

After carrying the side as leader, Boycott scored 2,255 runs for a Championship average of 68.30 for first Hampshire and then Old. No one will ever know what Yorkshire would have done without him. All we can say is that in all probability they would have sunk without trace.

10 A Matter of Politics

Yorkshire's commitment to a searching self-analysis in the
confused aftermath of Boycott's suspension at Scarborough
in September 1981 raised the immediate problem of impartiality. Whatever the composition of the sub-committee,
it was going to be difficult to create a group not subject to
preconceived ideas. With the best will in the world, no
member of the full committee could enter into an investigation with a completely open mind, since everyone had
already formed views on the value of Boycott to the club
and, indeed, the majority had voted on the captaincy issue
back in 1978.

To their credit, however, Yorkshire went as far as could be
expected to ward off threatened criticism in naming their
panel, which consisted of:

Reg Kirk, a company director and the Hull representative
on the general committee;

Tim Reed, a Sheffield solicitor and one of the city's three
committee members;

Phil Sharpe, the former batsman, now back with the
county as a member of the Cricket Management Committee
and the representative for York;

Billy Sutcliffe, on the Cricket Management Committee
as a Leeds member;

John Temple, by now an elected member of the committee,
sitting on the Cricket Management Committee;

David Welch, the club treasurer from Rotherham; and

Julian Vallance, another Leeds member on the general
committee.

Sutcliffe soon stood down, his place being taken by Don Brennan, but Yorkshire had done well to appoint four men — Kirk, Sharpe, Vallance and Reed — who were not on the committee at the time of the captaincy row.

They were less inhibited by familiarity with a deeply rooted system of running the club and, therefore, represented the fairest balance available. To this acceptable mix, chairman Crawford added the vital ingredient of a completely independent chairman in Peter Dobson, a sixty-four-year-old Wetherby-based retired accountant who claimed no direct links with cricket and who soon displayed a perceptive and unfettered mind.

Accepting a job which many might well have spurned through fear of the apparently impossible and others would have accepted for the wrong reasons, he set his straightforward guidelines. 'Our aim is simply to consider all the evidence we can gather and then make recommendations aimed at improving Yorkshire cricket,' he said. 'I don't know why I was chosen, except that I have known Michael Crawford for some time and am reasonably well known in Leeds. No doubt, though, the fact that I have chaired a lot of meetings and am clearly impartial was important. I do not think I am being critical when I say that there is a tendency for all long-established bodies to become set in their ways. I want our investigations to go far deeper than just the way in which the team has been playing, so we will be looking at the club as a whole to see if we can find some answers to the obvious questions.'

Dobson thus allayed fears that the county might be ready to accept a 'whitewash' and Crawford gave additional substance to the sub-committee's operation by insisting that as much of the report as possible would be made public.

By the time Boycott arrived home early from India, nursing a virus, the enterprise was running smoothly enough, but his return caused immediate complications. The investigating committee were, of course, anxious to interview him and had written to him back in October. Unfortunately, the letter reached Boycott only a couple of days before he left for Hong Kong on a business holiday trip, so he had no time to fit in a meeting before flying out on a journey that eventually

190

took him to India, where he joined the official England party.

Nor did the opportunity present itself for him to deal with a questionnaire sent initially to Mutch, who acted with full authority on his behalf back in England. A number of people received these questionnaires, but Boycott was in a difficult position. As the Test and County Cricket Board confirmed to the worried solicitor Mutch, they did not encourage tourists to take part in activities outside the tour, rightly expecting complete concentration on the job in hand from highly paid personnel.

Boycott had a lot he wanted to say, but much of it could not adequately be set down on paper — even if there had been scope for him to turn his attentions in this direction. To make any sense, the dialogue had to be two-way, involving an inter-change of thoughts, so that lines of examination could be pursued to a meaningful conclusion. Accordingly, Mutch informed Dobson of the 'state of play'. There the matter rested until illness brought him back to Woolley and provided another lure for the speculators in sporting journalism's richest commodity.

The fact that Boycott had overtaken Gary Sobers's world record Test aggregate shortly before leaving the England party and his eventual involvement in the controversial and unofficial tour of South Africa brought accusations that his health was no more than a convenient excuse for going about his own business, but anyone who spent any time in Boycott's company during that period had no doubt about the position.

He also had a slightly different version of the golfing incident during the Calcutta Test which came as a prelude to his flight back to England. Boycott, who did not feel well enough to field in the Test, said that he had been advised to get some fresh air and that the club he visited represented the only place where he could comfortably relax out of doors. Far from suggesting that other players should join him in a round of golf, he claimed he had merely inquired as to whether he was to make the trip from the cricket ground on his own. 'To say I played golf is ridiculous,' he said. 'I just ambled around two or three holes and felt much better for the gentle exercise.' In fairness to Boycott, too, no one could remember him ever leaving a game of cricket to do anything.

While Boycott contemplated this slur on his reputation, Dobson made efforts to contact him without receiving the response he expected. Shut away in lonely isolation, Boycott spent a long worrying week in bed and three weeks later still showed the signs of physical and mental strain, which explained why he did not feel able to commit himself to a date for a meeting with Dobson and his fellow investigators. He simply could not find the strength to meet this challenge, which, in any case, had to be a waste of time unless he presented himself fit, well and fully alert to all the implications.

That he was clearly not in such a happy state was confirmed by Dr Mohammed Zaman, who treated him. 'Both I and the specialist consider that Geoff has had some sort of virus from which he has failed to make the recovery we hoped. That could be due to the lack of proper rest. Certainly he had to come home from India and we have told him to do as little as possible. It is important that he takes things very easy. I have asked him not to go too far from home. A brief walk around the garden is all right, but nothing more strenuous than that should be attempted, so if he has not ventured any farther to meet people, he is acting on my advice.'

As soon as he felt stronger, Boycott got in touch with Dobson, indicating his willingness to meet the committee, but in the meantime Yorkshire had gone ahead and studied the first report produced by the investigating sub-committee on the adminstration of the club. While convalescing, Boycott must have reflected ruefully on the recommendations which were made public knowledge. There were six:

(1) A reduction in the size of the decision-taking body within the committee.
(2) An increase in the emphasis on, and the resources devoted to, coaching.
(3) The appointment of a chief executive and secretary.
(4) The appointment of a commercial manager.
(5) A review of the policies on grounds and coaching facilities.
(6) Consideration of the role of the Reform Group.

The full committee pondered on these and retired to give them 'very careful consideration', but many, including

Boycott, looked back to 1973, when his suggestion that the county should appoint a managing director raised such a furore. It was not just the idea that he might get the job that gave rise to resentment. The concentration of power in one pair of hands caused concern, but time had backed Boycott again — as it did with regard to the centralising of fixtures.

The sub-committee report did not really come up with much that sounded original. The lack of a commercial manager, for example, sparked off keen debate at the 1981 annual meeting, when persistence from the floor persuaded the county to look into the possibilities. The committee had, though, shown little enthusiasm for action and team-manager Illingworth appeared to be filling the role admirably, so odds were soon being laid against any dramatic change being brought about as a result of the inquiry. Crawford, himself, however, remained very keen on reducing the size of the power base.

Boycott, while nursing doubts about the reception his opinions might receive in certain quarters, felt that he had a very fair hearing from the investigating sub-committee, keeping his comments low key and aiming to be constructive rather than critical. He seemed to be tired of the arguing and the politics, but he could not escape. On the afternoon of Tuesday, 23 February 1982, the news was leaked that the Dobson committee advocated his sacking at the earliest financially convenient moment as the most logical means of restoring the much-discussed team spirit.

The telephone lines in various parts of the county echoed with the consequences of a radio story which resulted from, in the first place, an anonymous letter. This had landed at the offices of BBC Radio Leeds, whose detailed check promptly confirmed the accuracy of the contents. Of the four obvious options — sacking Boycott, sacking Illingworth, paying up both contracts, or getting them to work together — the sub-committee favoured the former. This embarrassing breach of confidence could have come only from an official source and the air was soon heavy with suspicion and rumour.

Yorkshire officials, understandably angry, mounted their own search for the 'mole' who had done so much to destroy the club's credibility, but they lacked the hard evidence to build a case that would stand up even in a kangaroo court. Thus another indication of unreliable elements within the organisation came to the surface and whoever was responsible did Yorkshire a massive dis-service.

The sound of the Supporters' Association guns were muffled so long as chairman Peter Briggs remained in Sri Lanka on holiday, but their recourse to arms could be taken for granted and some worried committee men admitted in private that they were not over-impressed by the investigating sub-committee, despite this body's well-intentioned efforts. There were a number of serious implications, the most important being the likely cost of removing Boycott.

The inevitable special general meeting carried an estimated price tag of around £15,000, while many members would probably resign, particularly if the team did not produce better results in his absence. A referendum represented the obvious step, if only to get an accurate indication as to the feeling about Boycott. One was being held on overseas players, but surprisingly this obvious hammer was not used to crack a decidedly hard nut. Boycott, advised to say nothing, did just that, but he clearly had to plan for the future in the knowledge that he could be unemployed before the start of the 1982 English season.

He believed he had been playing very well in India before being taken ill and his confidence was unshaken. There were some warning signs in a comparatively lean domestic season in 1981, but he did not subscribe to the pessimistic theory that the end of his career was in sight. Instead he argued persuasively that the pattern of the first-class programme made it difficult for a Test batsman slightly out of form to refind his surer touch. The crowded fixture list certainly restricted the number of Championship innings available between one international engagement and the next, and from May 29 to August 8 in that year Boycott played in only two Championship matches.

There was no question of his contemplating retirement, and as he built up his strength again he expressed concern at supposedly authoritative reports implying he would not be chosen again by England. In the circumstances, then, it is reasonable to accept that the sub-committee leak played a major part in his decision to go to South Africa with the party of English cricketers who defiantly crossed the political barriers to continue earning their living.

News of the unofficial visit became common knowledge on Sunday, February 28, and Boycott's participation captured the major attention, to the point at which he was credited — or perhaps discredited is nearer the mark — with making most, if not all, the arrangements. On the other hand, it ought to be remembered that he turned down the lucrative offer from Kerry Packer in 1977, the inference being that things other than money came into his calculations and his sudden departure for South Africa surprised even his closest friends.

The politicians, never afraid to leap in with instant judgements, had a field day, climbing eagerly onto an already overcrowded band-waggon which rumbled along, gathering momentum before running out of control under the whip of hysteria invariably brought about by the mere mention of South Africa. The ludicrous lengths to which the would-be arbiters of universal morality went were neatly summed up by the worthy members of Boycott's own South Yorkshire County Council, who claimed that 'the greatest living Yorkshireman' had besmirched their reputation, but most cricket followers and the level-headed man in the street adopted a far more tolerant attitude.

Boycott and the other 'rebels' were charged with putting the future of Test cricket in danger, of breaking up the International Cricket Conference and of leaving the future of all seventeen first-class English counties in the balance, but the realities were less obvious and not quite so headline catching. The bonds of loyalty holding together the Test-playing nations had been strained almost to breaking point by a series of events stretching back at least to 1976, when an under-19 tour by England to the West Indies had been affected because some of the youngsters had vague South African connections.

England trips to the West Indies in the winter of 1981 and then to India at the end of the year contained further examples of the hard lines foreign governments were prepared to take. The Test and County Cricket Board were forced to take positive

action and decide how much influence they were going to allow
outside sources to exert. A subsequent three-year international
ban was imposed by the authorities to guarantee the tours by
India and Pakistan and thus preserve the solvency of the
counties. The players concerned were surprised by its length
and asked for leniency but financial considerations really
shaped the decision, although there was a touch of irony as
native-born South African Allan Lamb and Chris Smith earned
England caps without threatening the future of the Common-
wealth or Olympic Games.

The Yorkshire Cricket Association which grew out of the
disbanded Reform Group, dismissed the whole business as a
red-herring and concentrated on trying to push the county back
onto what they considered to be the right road. As they were
quick to point out, the most significant development so far as
they were concerned centred on Old's appearance in the same
team as Boycott, a state of affairs which went a long way
towards bringing about a reconciliation that put the players'
poll into the background. Thus, they argued, there was nothing
to prevent Boycott being accepted back in the dressing room.

They also warned the Yorkshire committee that any decision
to dismiss Boycott, either at once or at the end of his contract,
must be put to the members if the club wished to avoid the
expense of a special general meeting, so it was under a
threatening financial cloud that the officials met at Headingley
on March 7 to search for a silver lining. They found one in the
shape of a new sub-committee which supplemented the
administrative team to help the manager with the day-to-day
running of the team.

This was a constructive move, for, in addition to making it
possible for Boycott to stay it revealed an awareness of the
differences involving other contracted players. The three-man
'trouble-shooting' committee comprised Burnet, Trueman and
Sutcliffe, who were to be regularly available to offer advice, and
Yorkshire also decided to make sure that one member of the
Cricket Management Committee attended every away match.
The aim was to improve spirit and confidence and while both
Burnet and Trueman had been stern critics of Boycott, they
made it clear that they were intent on looking forward rather
than back. 'I can assure everyone that we start without

prejudice and that the slate is clean. We simply want to help Yorkshire,' said Burnet.

He had a good track record in this direction, having created unity in 1958 and 1959 as captain, presiding in his second year over a Championship success that ended a barren spell of nine years without a title. Superficially his return to prominence was interesting, but the comparison between two depressing areas illustrated a crucial point.

Yorkshire suffered from a shortage of harmony in the 1950s as well as the 1970s and divisions within the side fed on the lack of success.

11 The Great Revolution

The need for Yorkshire to win a trophy and create circumstances in which players and officials might discover fruitful
common ground had become desperate in the spring of 1982, by
which time Boycott was in a comparatively secure position.
Chris Old clearly found the implication of the players' poll an
increasing embarrassment and did his best to put matters right.
'I organised the poll not at the request of the players but under
pressure from outside the dressing room,' he admitted. 'It was in
my first year as captain and I now know that I might have
handled things better. One thing I want to make clear is that I
was never anti-Boycott. I feel very badly about the whole
business and I would never do it again. It was not in the best
interests of the team or the club and I want to repair the
damage.'

In clearing the air, however, Old gave substance to the doubts
which had surrounded the committee's action in publishing the
results of that dressing room research and it was not long before
Boycott's hand was strengthened further by his appointment, if
not by name, as vice-captain for first-class matches.

This development followed further action by the players,
whose opinions were expressed decisively on a matter they
regarded as very important. At a meeting involving Burnet, as
cricket chairman, and Illingworth it was decided that the senior
professional would stand in if and when Old was not available
for any three-day fixture, while Neil Hartley remained deputy
in the one-day games.

In bringing about this system, the contracted staff knew well
enough that Boycott was senior professional, so it became

obvious that they were ready to accept him as one of their number and had no qualms about operating under his command.

Boycott celebrated in the approved manner by opening the championship programme with yet another century – 138 off the Northamptonshire attack in Siberian conditions at Northampton – but he remained outside the Sunday League scheme of things. Illingworth's forward-looking theory was that Bill Athey and Kevin Sharpe, as younger, more agile performers, should be given an extended run at the head of the innings, but results went against the manager and the team.

A sickening sequence of defeats undermined Old's confidence to the point at which drastic action became inevitable. Yorkshire lost three out of four Benson and Hedges Cup qualifying games, their solitary success being at the expense of Minor Counties, and even then neither Boycott nor his colleagues looked all that convincing. The pattern was much the same in the Sunday League, with only a tied match against Nottinghamshire at Hull bringing any reward from the first six outings, one of which earned two points as a consequence of being washed out without a ball being bowled. Boycott, restored to the ranks at Hull, came in at the fall of the sixth wicket, much to the annoyance of the spectators, and had the chance to collect a mere two runs from two deliveries.

His contribution could be measured in other terms, for it was obvious that Old welcomed his on-the-spot advice, but that came a shade too late to alter the course of history. Illingworth had by then shed the shackles of retirement to test the reaction of his fifty-year-old body to the stresses and strains of active service. He turned out in the one-day friendly against Zimbabwe at Sheffield on June 10 ostensibly to cover a tiresome injury situation, but there was much more to this reappearance.

Impressively, two days after reaching his half-century in terms of years, Illingworth took a wicket with his first ball for Yorkshire since 1968, aided by an obliging batsman who lofted it gently to backward square leg. The vital overall impression was good, too. The veteran offspinner operated tidily, as was to be expected of a man who had taken part in net work since his return as manager, and the seeds of a daring idea took firm root.

Both Illingworth and Burnet were satisfied that he could hold down a place in the team on a regular basis. The next move depended on Old, who had to take a firmer grip on the side and check a decline that had created panic. Instead, he lost his touch completely, the crunch coming at Middlesbrough, where Northamptonshire slaughtered the Yorkshire bowling on two successive days. During the Saturday of the championship engagement and then in the Sunday League they piled up 584 runs for five wickets from 106 erratic overs as Old's desperation showed through. Throughout Monday the year's most sensational cricket story slowly unfolded and on Tuesday Burnet confirmed that Illingworth would take over as captain.

His statement did nothing to disguise the size of the problem, nor did it, in any way, involve Boycott, who, alongside Illingworth, stood as a solid pillar in a crumbling edifice. Burnett said: 'We have, on two previous occasions this season, had long discussions with Chris Old concerning his captaincy of the side. On these occasions we said that it was essential that there be a considerable improvement, particularly in the one-day games, in his tactical approach and in his ability to lift the side when things are not going well. It is patently clear that this has not happened and Chris himself feels reluctantly that a change needs to be made as he and the team have lost confidence.' He also apologised on the committee's behalf for imposing on Old a job for which he was not suited. Nobody, however, saw the need to resign over what had to go down as an official blunder.

Illingworth immediately inspired Yorkshire's first Sunday triumph, with young Paul Jarvis enjoying the heady experience of the county's first hat-trick in the competition as Derbyshire succumbed by nineteen runs. Although the manager rightly earned great credit for restoring some sense of organisation, there could be no doubt that it was Boycott who brought back pride to Yorkshire cricket.

He passed Len Hutton's total of 129 first-class centuries, took a prominent hand in rewriting the county's record books and produced a number of match-winning performances. Those who so consistently claim he is a one-paced accumulator must have missed all the 1982 season.

Boycott began magnificently. He was on the field throughout the whole of the Edgbaston encounter with Warwickshire, who were defeated handsomely by nine wickets. On an unreliable pitch, the home side were bowled out for 158, Boycott claiming a couple of wickets as he covered for a few worrying overs after Old had limped off for treatment. It appeared that Yorkshire would fare even worse as they lost eight wickets for 108 and only the serene progress of the unruffled opener suggested that it might be possible to make runs. Old lent some support, but not until Graham Stevenson arrived, unusually low down the order at number eleven, was the game turned upsidedown.

He and Boycott made 149 in 140 minutes for the last wicket, breaking by one run the record held by Lord Hawke and David Hunter since 1898. It was the first time in fifty years that a Yorkshire partnership for any wicket had been improved and, in providing the bulk of the runs, Stevenson relied heavily on Boycott's experience. His 115 represented the highest unbeaten score by a number eleven in first-class cricket and, surprisingly, it was Boycott who got out, bowled round his legs by Asif Din.

'It was a combination of my brains and Graham's ability,' Boycott said and, while some regarded this as unjustified conceit, Stevenson accepted the truth of the observation. It had been Boycott's calming presence that checked his natural impetuosity.

As had been the case so often, Boycott held things together when the going was most difficult and, in bowing to Old's hostile second innings bowling, Warwickshire also symbolically touched their caps to the master batsman.

Despite this confidence-boosting exercise, there were some unexpected twists and turns along the way as Illingworth wrestled with the steering. A muscle strain forced him to stand down for the Bradford game with Gloucestershire, so Boycott, no doubt savouring the moment, took over the captaincy for the first time since 1978. Unfortunately, fate was toying with him. The match became another millstone around his neck as Yorkshire lost for the only time in the championship and he twice ran out the luckless Richard Lumb.

In the first instance Boycott called for a straight-forward single only to change his mind without warning or reason, leaving Lumb stranded so far from safety that John Shepherd, the bowler, had time to fumble a hurried throw before breaking the wicket. Lumb, understandably annoyed, could hardly contain his anger when, in the second innings, Boycott refused his call for a single to set him up as the helpless victim once more. There could be no excuses, the blame rested squarely with Boycott, who, however, could do little about the outcome of the contest.

The bowlers' footholds at the pavilion end had been badly repaired and the pitch was not really fit on the last day, a factor which ruled out any challenging declaration. With only thirteen runs between the sides on first innings, a draw appeared to be the only logical result. Inexplicably, Yorkshire collapsed, six wickets falling for seventeen runs to steady rather than devastating bowling. Gloucestershire, hardly able to believe their luck, sped to victory as the Yorkshire attack trod with extreme caution at the danger end. No wonder by the end Boycott began to think that there might be better ways of spending his time than being captain on a part-time basis.

All the same, his instinctive reaction to that disaster brought more runs as Yorkshire prospered for a change. Overall they gained five championship victories and in four of them the honours went largely to Boycott, who completed a rare double by being on the field throughout the whole of the second game with Warwickshire.

Yorkshire again won by nine wickets, Boycott chipping in with 176 runs without being dismissed and using the unfailing mixture of skill and patience to dominate bowling on another pitch that presented problems. In passing, it is interesting to recall that Dennis Amiss, with seventy-three and ninety-four for Warwickshire, confirmed that he and Boycott were still technically the best of the English batsmen.

The county approached the high spot of their campaign at Worksop, where success over Nottinghamshire contained two sparkling innings from Boycott – ninety-one when the side stood in danger of surrendering a big first-innings lead and eighty-two in spritely fashion as Yorkshire triumphantly chased 305 in four and a half hours. They completed their first hat-trick in the major competition since 1978 by beating Scarborough by six wickets at Scarborough. Tributes were paid to John Barclay's generous declaration which set a target of 251 in 195 minutes and his attacking approach came as a breath of fresh air with so many other captains opting for safety at the slightest sign of danger, but without Boycott Yorkshire would have struggled. He unfolded an innings of pure brilliance after surviving what looked a very reasonable appeal for lbw from Garth Le Roux's first ball. He hit thirteen fours and one six, carrying the team home with fourteen balls to spare and sharing in the sheer pleasure of success with his colleagues as though there had never been the slightest hint of trouble.

His relationship with Illingworth appeared sound, too, for the two could often be seen in close conversation or sharing a meal in an hotel. The fact, therefore, that Boycott made only sixty-one runs in two innings to help beat Derbyshire at Scarborough could be regarded as a good thing, for the side had to learn to cope without decisive assistance from its distinguished senior members. This was an important point, for, despite the revival under Illingworth, much remained to be done, notably to halt a serious decline in membership and the loss of revenue through falling Sunday attendances.

The club were, in fact, on a tightrope, edging their way towards the solid safety of improved performance. The last thing the committee could afford was any sudden movement that might unbalance the enterprise, for the lack of a safety net meant that a slip could be very painful. Sadly they chose to complicate matters by sacking Old and offering Boycott just a one-year engagement.

Old had not been at his best, but, even allowing for a worthy desire to prune around £60,000 from their budget, Yorkshire could surely have afforded to think again. Burnet admitted: 'I am very sorry indeed about what has happened to Chris, who is a very nice guy and who has served the club so well, but he is a victim of circumstance.

'The committee feel that he has lost a yard of pace and is no longer the strike bowler he used to be. Although he might still do a reasonable job in the one-day competitions it is impossible to find the money in the present economic climate to justify keeping him on that basis.' The man who had been captain until mid-June thus found himself out in the cold, nursing a back strain and wondering just how much injury had counted against him.

Boycott was in a totally different situation, for he had maintained the most acceptable form and a high degree of fitness. In addition, his standing with the public and some committee men guaranteed an uproar were he not to be re-engaged.

Old went on his way to Warwickshire with a hardly a murmur to mark the passing of one of the best seam bowlers since the war. A single unheeded voice was raised on his behalf in committee, but Boycott, albeit innocently, commanded an army of support. Burnet trod cautiously along a path littered with danger as he said: 'I want to make it clear that there is nothing sinister in this decision. There was a 100 per cent agreement that Geoff be offered terms and the voting was 13-6 that they be for one year. He is remarkably fit, but I know of no sport in which a man of forty-two would be guaranteed more than a year's security.'

Illingworth also tried hard to take the sting out of the announcement. 'Geoff's attitude has been splendid all year,' he said, 'and I think he has played more for the side than in previous seasons. I would suggest that if he plays on and maintains anything like this form he will get another contract next year as well.'

Some of Boycott's friends were convinced that this represented the thin end of the wedge, but he defused a potentially explosive situation in the course of a ninety-minute meeting with Illingworth. He signed his one-year contract and Illingworth commented: 'Geoff and I have never been far apart on the tactics. We have differed over other matters, but I think we have a good relationship and I hope there are better times ahead for everybody.'

It might have been thought, as winter closed in, that Yorkshire cricket could hibernate in comfort, but controversy arrived before the snow. In December it was revealed that the committee were seeking to change some of the club's rules, among other things giving some power to an executive sub-committee and making it necessary to command the backing of ten per cent of the membership to call a special general meeting. Sid Fielden and Peter Charles, the Rotherham representative on the committee, led the opposition to these moves, arguing that democracy was at stake. They insisted that the general committee must have overall control and that two and a half per cent of the members had every right to demand a meeting, stressing that this power had been used only once.

The package of proposals were eventually withdrawn, but the exchanges left behind an air of suspicion. The committee were split and Boycott, whether he liked it or not, found himself at the centre of some lively disputes, including a series of accusations about his general behaviour which did not stand up to keen investigation by Fielden, whose background as a sergeant in the police force proved useful.

That some committee men were ready to harass Boycott over what seemed trivial matters – eating the meat and not the bread in some sandwiches, for example – illustrated the lack of trust, although a flicker of hope shone through the gathering clouds as the 1983 season approached.

Burnet had a word of advice for the younger players – still held in such high esteem – at the pre-season luncheon, stating quite clearly: 'You have the opportunity to learn from two of the greatest brains in cricket. Ray Illingworth and Geoff Boycott are perfect examples of professional cricketers in their attitudes to the game.' Even so, the vice-captaincy passed officially back to Neil Hartley. Burnet explained: 'I had a long chat with Geoff in the winter and he confirmed that, while he is keen to help in any way, he no longer nurses any ambitions regarding the captaincy.'

Thus the stage was set before an eager and expectant audience, who found it difficult to follow the ensuing action. The plot became confused as Yorkshire stumbled to the ultimate disgrace of bottom place in the championship while, at the same time, soaring to the top of the Sunday League to collect their first major honour for fourteen years. It was the equivalent of Laurence Olivier forgetting his lines as Hamlet before going off to win first prize in Sale of the Century.

As the catalogue of woe continued, Hartley found himself following in Old's footsteps, for, having begun in high office with matching hopes, he found himself out of the team, unable to scrape together sufficient runs to merit on-going selection.

Illingworth's captaincy came under increasing fire, for his declarations were often negative, but he knew that his bowlers were very vulnerable in tight situations. A crippling Edgbaston defeat at the hands of Warwickshire, who spent most of the last day fighting for survival, emphasised this short-coming.

Boycott, however, had a splendid run, scoring steadily until mid-July, and then going into overdrive. He had centuries in each innings against Nottinghamshire at Bradford, scoring 103 before lunch on the last day, fell sixteen short of 1,000 in August and finished with an average of 55.45.

Presumably the announcement in early June that he had been awarded a testimonial for 1984 served as additional incentive, although the fact that no mention was made of a contract encouraged speculation. The committee remained steadfast. Contracts could not be discussed before October, so Boycott went about his business with a degree of concern for his prospects. This manifested itself from time to time in a careworn attitude. He still believed that the team benefitted from his presence at the crease and a number of examples could be found to support this contention.

Against Derbyshire at Sheffield, his second-innings unbeaten 112 – the sixth time he had carried his bat through a completed innings for Yorkshire – was marked down as 'Just about the best innings I have seen", by Burnet.

It came on a treacherous pitch reported as unfit for first-class cricket, and Boycott's ability to deal with the threats from pace and spin stood out in marked contrast to some wild efforts by the majority of his partners, who lacked matching resolve.

Boycott set standards far beyond the reach of others and even the most demanding assessment of his work revealed no more than minor flaws. His unbeaten 214 off the Nottinghamshire attack at Worksop tended to meander along, while a hard-earned forty-four against Middlesex at Leeds was put together by an excess of hard labour. These innings attracted passing criticism, but Boycott's unbeaten 140 against Gloucestershire at Cheltenham hit the headlines. Here the pitch was easy pace and the bowling limited if determined, but his rate of progress fell way below what was wanted. His century occupied 262 deliveries and in one spell Sharp, who was playing for his place, scored sixty-nine to Boycott's twenty-seven.

The loss of a fourth batting point attracted unfavourable comment and while that in itself did not matter all that much to a side already rushing headlong towards oblivion the implications of Boycott's innings were considerable. It was alleged that he had ignored instructions from Illingworth to get on with it –

an accusation he resolutely denied with impressive conviction.
'I have never in my career disobeyed a captain,' he said. 'I
might have disagreed with some plan and put my own ideas
forward, but in the end the captain is in charge. I honestly felt I
was following the right tactics at Cheltenham, where we
thought we might have to bat on into Monday in the hope that
the pitch would take spin later and enable us to enforce the
follow-on.'

Illingworth refused to be drawn into any public row, but he
could not deny, when pressed, that he was disappointed with the
end product and admitted that he would be bringing Burnet into
the discussions. With any other player a quiet word would
presumably have settled matters, as it had in the case of Athey,
who pursued a snail-like course at Weston-super-Mare in the
previous match. Boycott, a man set apart, found himself at a
meeting with Burnet and, although he remained firmly of the
opinion that no disciplinary element was involved, the news
emerged that he had been 'mildly reprimanded'. Whatever the
rights and wrongs, there could be no doubting Boycott's
all-round value, for he and Illingworth formed the cornerstone
of the Sunday League team.

Illingworth headed the competition's bowling averages, while
Boycott added to the unusual quota of runs by sending down
twenty-seven overs of medium-paced seamers. The pair were by
some distance the most reliable under pressure which jangled
nerves as the county came within sight of the title.

Boycott, indeed, opened the bowling on three occasions and
also took his turn at the 'death', bowling the last overs with the
batsmen hitting out and some specialist bowlers carefully
avoiding the captain's eye.

Even as Yorkshire celebrated at rain-soaked Chelmsford,
where an abandoned game ensured their place at the top of the
table, Athey's future hung in the balance and he did not delay
long in asking for his release. If this came as an unpleasant
surprise to the public, the next news simply shattered the
county's cricket lovers. On October 3 yet another attempt to
reshape the playing policy brought Boycott's sacking. All
wrapped up in a strange package, it caused much head shaking
and anger and it was impossible to imagine in what
circumstances the committee imagined they could push it

through without starting a riot.

Expressing the ill-founded hope that the members would accept that the decision had been taken in the best interests of the club, Burnet explained: 'The committee feel that the time has come to make major decisions. We can go no lower. The rancour and controversy must end. We must now look to the future and give our youngsters the chance to show what they can do.

'With this in mind, we have appointed the ever-enthusiastic David Bairstow to captain them. Ray Illingworth will cease to play championship cricket, except in an emergency and will not of necessity travel with the first team. Geoff Boycott's contract will not be renewed. We realise that this will mean he will not be playing during his testimonial year which is unfortunate, but the situation makes it unavoidable. We wish him every success with his testimonial which was awarded for his services to the club over the last ten years and we will give him every assistance to make it a success.'

In considering all the possibilities the committee had not taken up an offer from Illingworth, who, tired of the abuse he had suffered from representatives of the pro-Boycott lobby, volunteered to leave the club and quit the job of team-manager if the committee would pay up his contract.

They also neglected to underline the point that the full committee, in voting 18-7 on the issue, had been faced with the whole package or nothing. Fielden quickly took up this aspect. 'A request that we should take them one by one was refused at the insistance of Mr Burnet,' he claimed, adding: 'We were faced with a difficult choice. Some, I am sure, voted against Boycott because they wanted Bairstow as captain. I support Bairstow's appointment, too, but I thought the sacking of Boycott more important.'

Those who voted along with Fielden in favour of Boycott being given another contract were Jack Sokell (Barnsley), Reg Kirk (Hull), Charles, Tony Woodhouse (Leeds), David Drabble (Sheffield) and John Turner (Wakefield). From among the ranks came the prominent figures of the opposition – Fielden, Charles and Kirk, with Peter Briggs resuming his place as chairman of an organisation which took a new name – the Yorkshire Members' 1984 Group – at a stormy meeting at

Ossett. They also appointed a new secretary in Tony Vann, a Bradford-based garage owner.

Faced with the threat of a special general meeting, the committee reconsidered, but only Tony Cawdry, from Halifax, changed sides. Preparations for all-out war went ahead and in some lively exchanges spokesmen for both camps over-stepped the mark to bring solicitors into the fray.

The official case rested largely on the need to rebuild. The club's literature stressed that the eleven-man cricket committee, which unanimously urged Boycott's sacking 'comprises some of the most experienced and talented cricketers to represent the county. They have made a combined total of 162 Test appearances for England and have played more than 2,000 first-class matches for Yorkshire.' A glossy hand-out went on to ask 'Can they all be wrong?'

Behind this main thrust came evidence from Bill Frindall, well known as the BBC statistician. The committee claimed: 'He has carried out research of Geoffrey Boycott which supports the widely held view that he is a match-saver rather a match-winner. Bill reveals that of the seventy-two championship matches in which Boycott has played over the last five years only eleven were won, ten lost and fifty-one drawn (seventy per cent). And of the thirty-seven Yorkshire matches in that period when he did not play nine were won, eleven lost and seventeen drawn (forty-six per cent).'

Here, though, they wandered onto dangerous ground and were cut down by a withering response. Roy Wilkinson, the county's leading expert on the facts and figures, delved deeper. 'Rain, bad light and unfit ground conditions so interfered with play that a result was entirely (or almost entirely) out of the question in as many as thirty of those fifty-one matches,' he discovered.

The Members' Group attacked on all fronts, expressing sensible fears about the declining membership – around 14,000 to a little below 10,000 – and about the coaching and scouting. Boycott, meanwhile, refrained from comment. He did, however, have a meeting with county chairman Crawford and Burnet after which he promised in writing to retire at the end of one more season.

This was the biggest gesture he could make towards a

compromise and he did not come to it lightly. It was not, however, taken up, although subsequently an alternative proposal from representatives of the club envisaged his playing in one fixture on each home ground. Rightly this was laughed out of court. In putting it forward the committee did not exactly improve their chances of capturing the minds of the members at the special meeting which had been called for December 3 to discuss three resolutions – Boycott's reinstatement and votes of no confidence in the general and cricket committees – nor did the circumstances in which the great confrontation had to be put back to January 21.

The club, following the pattern of 1978, did not issue notice of the December 3 meeting to those members whose subscriptions were unpaid at the date of the requisition. This put them in breach of their own rules and a High Court writ was taken out on behalf of four such members, who claimed that the meeting would not be valid. The costs soared to around the £30,000 mark. The Members' Group wanted to go ahead with the December 3 arrangements by building in a facility for those who had been disfranchised, but the court ordered a delay judge Blackett-Ord indicating that 'the secretary of the club misread the rules and he and the general committee did not fulfil their obligations under the rules of the club.'

The crushing blow finally fell at Harrogate, where in the impressive setting of the Conference Centre the debate reached a noisy climax. The committee speakers received a cruelly rough reception and they lost all three resolutions. The figures were:

That Boycott be reinstated – for 4,115, against 3,109.

That the members have no confidence in the general committee – for 3,609, against 3,578.

That the members have no confidence in the cricket sub-committee – for 3,997, against 3,209.

The Members' Group were as stunned by the outcome as their opponents, for, despite the encouraging indications of a vigorous canvassing exercise, they expected to be beaten on resolution two. The effects of all their canvassing had to be felt, however, for while they knocked on doors and spread their gospel the committee sat back and did too little.

'We won because we rolled up our sleeves and worked hard,'

said Vann, and nobody argued. Following the honourable course, the committee resigned on the following Monday – a terrible day, ravaged by snow and travel problems which meant that many had to surrender their seats by telephone. Headingley was cut off from the outside world and some thought that this summed up Yorkshire's biggest weakness.

With few exceptions the committee sought re-election – notable casualties were Robin Feather, finance chairman, and Julian Vallance, the public relations chairman – and bowing to the will of the people Burnet, in Harrogate, said he was prepared to back another one-year contract for Boycott 'but not a minute beyond that.' His timing was a bit out. Boycott's willingness to retire had been conditional and his conditions had not been met. Neither he nor his main supporters saw any reason to make further promises and the prospect of playing again for England hovered on the horizon.

Spreading his wings, Boycott suddenly put himself forward for a place on the committee, being nominated in his own Wakefield area in opposition to Dr Turner. This did not go down well, but his options were strictly limited. 'I am sorry to oppose Dr Turner,' he said, 'but I live in the Wakefield area and have always done so. I could not have stood anywhere else without securing an artificial business address and I would not do that. I want to continue as a player, but I see no problem in sitting on the committee at the same time. I note that it has been acceptable in the past.' This was a reference to Lord Hawke, who filled the dual roles of president and captain between 1898 and 1910, although he was in a rather different position to Boycott, who continued:

'I am seeking election because I honestly think I can do the job. I would, if elected, be able to support David Bairstow in committee and help to reflect the players' views. At the same time, I could keep the players in touch with committee thinking. I have considerable experience of the game as it is now and I see no advantage in waiting for several years before trying to join the committee. Too many old players have come back after ten or fifteen years with their minds frozen at the time they stopped playing.'

The Members' Group contested twenty-one places on the committee or, to be more precise, there were twenty-one candidates who, to varying degrees, supported the official party line, set out in a general manifesto. Brian Close stood for one of three places in Bradford, where Bob Appleyard, one of the great bowling personalities of the 1950s, was returned unopposed.

There were many questions in the air. Illingworth, who had been expected to turn out in the one-day competitions, retired for a second time. 'After all my years in the game I do not need the harassment I have been getting from spectators who don't understand the game and are interested only in one man,' he said. Members' Group officials threatened to abolish the post of team manager if they gained a controlling interest and all the bits of the jigsaw lay scattered across the board, blown about by the winds of discord.

Bairstow faced the most testing assignment of any captain in Yorkshire's history as the team embarked on the 1984 programme under new management. Boycott was back in harness, still serving the county and still very much the people's choice.

12 Conclusions

The one fact central to understanding why Boycott and
Yorkshire were unable to live together in harmony is that he
became bigger than the club. Indeed, by the time he was
sacked he had become larger than life. How else, for example,
can you explain a typical piece of nonsense about him,
emanating from so great an authority as Neil MacFarlane, the
Minister for Sport in the Conservative Government in 1981?
This spokesman, commanding respect as the holder of high
office, wrote an article in the Sports Council magazine *Sport
and Leisure*, in which he discussed the growth of violence in
the sporting arenas. It contained the following sentence: 'I
well remember how it all seemed to start — when Geoffrey
Boycott threw his bat.'

So, in addition to being allegedly responsible for the
decline of Yorkshire cricket, it is suggested that Boycott set
the trend for sporting misconduct by one foolish, thoughtless act in far-away Adelaide in 1971. That nothing could be
wider of the mark is irrelevant, Boycott's name grabs the
headlines and, therefore, the attention. Few men, whatever
their occupation, conduct themselves better. His turn-out is
invariably immaculate, his dedication admired universally and
his readiness to communicate with the spectators widely
appreciated, but these virtues do not make very good newspaper copy and are thus ignored.

MacFarlane, of course, is not likely to do much harm with
such a far-fetched theory, but Yorkshire have suffered
enormously from the easy acceptance of ill-considered ideas
and a general failure to come to terms with its most famous

213

son. His genius flowered in a once fertile garden. For example, the county fell out of the top four only four times between 1900 and 1950, but no one else ever bloomed in such splendid isolation. All the other great players had wonderfully able contemporaries, so even the most famous had someone pressing them from just one rung lower down the ladder. Len Hutton stood higher than his post-war colleagues, yet strength existed in depth through such as Willie Watson, Frank Lowson, Lester, Wardle and Bob Appleyard.

Boycott, heading the batting averages for fifteen successive seasons, set himself as a man apart. Hampshire hovered within touching distance, but no real comparison could be made between England's top run-maker and a man with a mere eight Test appearances. Wherever the line is drawn, Boycott comes out on top and Hampshire fits in below. The sacking of Close removed the last challenge from a player of genuine individual genius, and the returns for the leading batsmen during Boycott's captaincy reveal the gap between the leader and the men he led. The figures are:

CHAMPIONSHIP

	COMPLETED INNINGS	RUNS	AVGE
Boycott	159	11,164	70.21
Hampshire	213	8,692	40.81
Lumb	211	6,560	31.09
Sharpe	102	2,987	29.28
Dalton	18	517	28.72
Old	108	3,026	28.02
Love	67	1,870	27.91
Leadbeater	152	3,986	26.22
Sharp	38	980	25.79
Athey	64	1,540	24.06
Padgett	37	864	23.35
Stevenson	65	1,427	21.95
Johnson	122	2,671	21.89
Hutton	78	1,682	21.56
Carrick	108	2,300	21.30
Bairstow	217	4,308	19.85
Woodford	24	470	19.58
Sidebottom	38	646	17.00
Squires	76	1,271	16.72

SUNDAY LEAGUE

	COMPLETED INNINGS	RUNS	AVGE
Boycott	66	3,052	46.24
Hampshire	91	3,534	38.83
Athey	18	487	27.05
Padgett	11	291	26.45
Leadbeater	39	1,028	26.36
Dalton	11	206	18.72
Lumb	57	1,422	24.95
Old	50	1,038	20.76
Love	19	386	20.31
Woodford	22	446	20.27
Johnson	58	1,113	19.19
Squires	35	602	17.20
Hutton	26	444	17.08
Sharp	14	237	16.93
Bairstow	65	1,098	16.89
Sidebottom	16	239	14.94
Sharpe	31	347	11.19

Although his ranking as the outstanding batsman was never queried, the extent of his superiority still comes as a surprise. His Championship average was more than double that of anyone other than Hampshire and he stood as comfortably the most commanding one-day scorer, for added to his Sunday League aggregate were 1,500 Gillette and Benson and Hedges Cup runs at an average of 46.87. With such limited support, it was no wonder that he increasingly felt his presence at the wicket to be crucial, but the lengths to which he went to create this happy state of affairs have been exaggerated wildly.

As captain, Boycott compiled forty Championship centuries for Yorkshire, the matches in question bringing fifteen victories, twenty draws and five defeats which is an acceptable ratio, particularly as close scrutiny unearths little evidence that those twenty draws were the outcome of self-gratification.

The picture is much the same with regard to captaincy, for his presence rarely failed to bring about an improvement in performance. During his period in office, Yorkshire played

166 Championship matches and 128 Sunday League games, thirteen of which were abandoned and do not come into the reckoning. The breakdown is:

CHAMPIONSHIP

	P	W	D	L	% WINS	% LOSSES
Boycott	106	35	51	20	33.02	18.86
Wilson	12	1	4	7	8.33	58.88
Padgett	1	0	1	0		
Sharpe	19	3	10*	5	15.78	26.31
Nicholson	1	0	1	0		
Hampshire	25	8	11	6	32.00	24.00
Cope	2	0	0	2		100.00

* Sharpe was also captain in the tied match against Middlesex at Bradford in 1973.

SUNDAY LEAGUE

	P	W	L	% WINS
Boycott	77	44	33	57.14
Wilson	8	4	4	50.00
Padgett	1	0	1	
Sharpe	4	2	2	50.00
Hampshire	24	9	15	37.50
Cope	1	0	1	

Disappointment over the captaincy did not diminish his enthusiasm for Yorkshire cricket. He continued to score heavily and his was the most obvious dedication. The arguments about his worth in the Sunday League were squashed by sheer ability. From 1979 to 1983 he headed the county's championship averages three times and finished second twice. No one could match that, nor could they consistently outscore him on Sundays.

Boycott's pre-eminence is, therefore, easy to establish, which leaves his personality under the microscope. Here we enter the field of opinion and the trouble is that everybody has one. The mere mention of his name sparks endless argument, for neutrality is impossible to find. People are either for him or against him and that generalisation covers some who have never seen him play in the flesh. We are all subject to instant television expertise, with one Test-match innings providing the basis for a defiantly held view about Boycott in a thousand otherwise open minds.

Shortly after Yorkshire announced their intention to switch the leadership to Hampshire, I met Ron Aspinall, the Huddersfield umpire on the first-class list at that time, socially with a few friends. We were discussing the likely outcome of the row between committee and Reform Group and Yorkshire's prospects if Boycott were to leave when one of the party suddenly exclaimed: 'Well I'm glad he's been sacked, he's always been a rotten captain.' This surprised me, since the person concerned had not, to my certain knowledge, been on a first-class cricket ground for over twenty years. 'I didn't know you had taken to watching cricket,' I said. 'I haven't, but it's common knowledge that Boycott always plays for himself,' came the reply. It is as though people feel that they are expected to be either for or against him in the great debate.

One thing though is clear – he did not endear himself to many of his team-mates at various times, getting off to a bad start as captain, but the complaints were surely something with which the committee should have dealt. When Burnet became captain in 1958 to instil discipline, he had the firm backing of the committee, who sacked Wardle, one of the best bowlers in the country. Equally, Vic Wilson and Close had no qualms about acting positively over differences with Trueman. Although Burnet was a non-starter as a player, scoring 889 runs for an average of 12.88 and taking one solitary wicket, Yorkshire won the Championship for him in 1959. It is doubtful if the 1971 team could have carried him, but Boycott might have made something out of them had he been so confident of unswerving support.

Instead, he had to make do and mend, hamstrung by the circumstances surrounding him. Yorkshire's proud standing had been built on a constant stream of good quality cricketers from what used to be known as the West Riding, and occasionally, other corners of the county, but in 1971 things had changed for the worse, as Close acknowledged shortly before his departure. League cricket was a pale shadow of its former glorious self. The mellow sound of bat on ball which once echoed deep into the twilight of regular net practice had given way to the chink of money dribbling out of one-armed bandits and into the pockets of professionals a long way below county class.

The Huddersfield League, with its importance rooted in the memory of Rhodes, Hirst and Haigh, no longer sent out youngsters into the county game and the Bradford League, once with claims to being the finest in the country, operated on a lower level. Illingworth, as team manager, and Hampshire, as captain, held talks with Bradford officials to no avail as the Saturday afternoon game continued to lose its way in a labyrinth of negative legislation. 'When I was a lad with Farsley, there must have been a dozen left-arm spinners in the Bradford League who could, at a pinch, have stepped up into the Yorkshire side and done an acceptable job. They might not have been world-beaters, but they would not have let any side down,' sighed Illingworth as the sad seventies gave way to the equivocal eighties.

'Now I don't see any and it is just the same with the off-spinners. Peter Whiteley is the only offspinner in the county of anything like Yorkshire standards. I hardly recognise the game any more. I went to watch a junior match and when one side had lost three or four wickets for less than the twenty, the others still had their fielders strung around the boundary. How can a young boy progress in a set up like that?' He was talking in 1981 and the position had been more or less the same for more than a decade, during which Boycott and Yorkshire were not exactly spoiled for choice and the players not overburdened with competition.

On the contrary, Yorkshire's policy with young players revealed a softer touch, kind words, generous promises and encouragement replacing the harsh demands that once kept hopefuls on their toes. Thick velvet wrapped itself round the feared iron fist. This was something else with which Boycott had to contend, while competing against opposition much stronger than any of his predecessors had known. It is an irritating habit of the cricket watcher to regard the golden age as the one which has just ended, the one mistily remembered by the middle-aged and fondly recalled by the elderly, but the undeniable truth is that the English county game had never been so thickly

populated with international talent as it was when Boycott
inherited the Yorkshire captaincy. The following took part in
that ill-starred 1971 summer:

Derbyshire – Chris Wilkins (South Africa) 1,362 runs (34.92).

Essex – Bruce Francis (Australia) 1,563 runs (40.07) and Keith
   Boyce (West Indies) 647 runs (18.48) and 56 wickets (30.23).

Glamorgan – Majid Khan (Pakistan) 685 runs (34.25) and 9
   wickets (46.11) and Tony Cordle (West Indies) 417 runs
   (13.90) and 33 wickets (36.48).

Gloucestershire – Procter (South Africa) 1,762 runs (47.62) and
   62 wickets (19.14).

Hampshire – Barry Richards (South Africa) 1,628 runs (44.00),
   Roy Marshall (West Indies) 1,388 runs (36.52), Danny
   Livingstone (West Indies) 392 runs (35.63), Gordon
   Greenidge (West Indies) 1,041 runs (26.02), John Holder
   (West Indies) 104 runs (17.33) and 18 wickets (25.27), Larry
   Worrell (West Indies) 202 runs (16.83) and 44 wickets
   (29.70).

Kent – Asif Iqbal (Pakistan) 585 runs (48.75), Stuart Leary
   (South Africa) 368 runs (26.28), John Shepherd (West Indies)
   684 runs (22.06) and 52 wickets (33.61), Bernard Julien
   (West Indies) 403 runs (14.92) and 38 wickets (28.34).

Lancashire – Clive Lloyd (West Indies) 1,124 runs (38.75) and
   Farokh Engineer (India) 635 runs (25.40).

Leicestershire – Clive Inman (Colombo) 1,322 runs (45.58),
   Brian Davison (Rhodesia) 1,183 runs (35.84) and Graham
   McKenzie (Australia) 311 runs (18.29) and 81 wickets
   (18.69).

Middlesex – Norman Featherstone (Rhodesia) 921 runs (32.89),
   Sam Black (South Africa) 213 runs (17.75) and Harry
   Latchman (West Indies) 234 runs (16.71) and 77 wickets
   (25.98).

Northamptonshire – Mushtaq Mohammad (Pakistan) 1,246
   runs (31.94) and 44 wickets (24.65), Hilton Ackerman (South
   Africa) 1,258 runs (31.45), Sarfraz Nawaz (Pakistan) 116
   runs (12.88) and 10 wickets (37.70).

Nottinghamshire – Gary Sobers (West Indies) 1,485 runs (46.40)
   and 53 wickets (30.96) and Basharat Hassan (Kenya) 725
   runs (19.95).

Somerset – Hallam Moseley (West Indies) 219 runs (19.90) and
39 wickets (24.94), Kerry O'Keefe (Australia) 376 runs
(17.90) and 71 wickets (23.12).

Surrey – Younis Ahmed (Pakistan) 1,326 runs (37.88), Intikhab
Alam (Pakistan) 178 runs (12.71) and 32 wickets (32.06).

Sussex – Tony Greig (South Africa) 1,138 runs (27.09) and 71
wickets (28.18), Geoff Greenidge (West Indies) 1,192 runs
(26.48), Udaykumar Joshi (India) 121 runs (6.36) and 62
wickets (30.08).

Warwickshire – Rohan Kanhai (West Indies) 1,452 runs (48.40),
Khalid Ibadulla (Pakistan) 368 runs (24.53) and 19 wickets
(28.57) and Lance Gibbs (West Indies) 110 runs (10.00) and
123 wickets (18.84).

Worcestershire – Ron Headley (West Indies) 1,616 runs (43.67),
Glenn Turner (New Zealand) 828 runs (34.50), Basil
D'Oliveira (South Africa) 752 runs (32.69) and 31 wickets
(23.12), Vanburn Holder (West Indies) 251 runs (15.68) and
72 wickets (25.94).

It is possible to select two highly respectable Test teams from
that glittering galaxy and Yorkshire had no respite. Whole new
fields opened up for the other counties, who were quick to exploit
an expanding market in cricketing mercenaries – fast bats and
even faster bowlers ready to hire themselves out to the highest
bidders. Despite regulations aimed at creating worthwhile
scope for the home-grown talent that was being stifled, the
influx of ready-made first-team material left Yorkshire
carrying top weight in the race for honours.

In assessing Boycott as a captain we have to consider this, and
make allowance, too, for the additional burden on the county of
Test calls. In his one full season of domestic competition in 1975,
Boycott lifted Yorkshire into second place in the Championship,
so the obvious conclusion is that with a Procter, a Sobers, a
Hadlee or a Rice in the ranks some trophies must have been
captured. Failing to win anything, Yorkshire fell foul of the
system not Boycott's personal ambitions.

More than anything he was handicapped by poor bowling. By
his own efforts he could prop up the batting, but he had no
destructive bowling talent. Old, his one cutting edge, did not
play in enough matches. Between 1976 and 1978, three crucial

seasons, Old bowled in twenty-one out of 64 Championship fixtures – less than a third – and the rest were not good enough to compensate for that deficiency.

Arguably this is the heart of the matter, for Boycott allowed frustration to get the better of him on occasions, showing annoyance when others fell below the required standards without suffering the agonies he endured. By social inclination he was shut off from the rest of the team, rarely being seen in the bars of the hotels and seldom joining in any of the rituals, and as the age gap widened with a new generation growing up he found himself more remote.

He demanded one hundred per cent application to the business of playing cricket in an age which settled for less in all walks of life and players resented the driving and the scorn. 'Your ability, my brains,' was an expression with which they became all too familiar, but in his defence he did not ask his team to attempt anything that he did not do himself and some were very slow learners. His professional relationships permitted no liberties. 'I can forgive a sportsman anything, so long as he performs to the best of his ability,' he said. 'I can't bear slackness. A cricketer can be a poor fielder, but he knows that so long as he chases the ball after it has beaten him I will encourage him all I can. He might have faults when he bats or bowls, but if he works hard at improving himself, spends hours at the nets and does his best he can count on my support.'

Those sentiments would have merited a stern nod of approval from Rhodes and a gentle smile of agreement from Hirst. Boycott might have been happier playing in their era, which respected the constant search for perfection. Bill Bowes, the genial figure who, through his own career and many years in journalism, bridged the gap between Boycott's Yorkshire and England's greatest all-rounders, recalled affectionately his days as a junior when Colts in the senior side reported to Rhodes at the close of play to go carefully through the catalogue of each day's events.

• Excuses cut no ice when Yorkshire were a power in the land, and when spectators occasionally let the players know they were unhappy with what was happening the reaction was neither encouraging nor well mannered in one or two instances.

The committee found it easy to deal in grandiose phrases such as 'He is too wrapped up in his performance' or 'He is indecisive and lets his indecision be apparent to the team,' but when were they decisive? They denied the need for a team manager and then appointed one, they publicly expressed faith in Boycott and privately talked over their doubts, they censured Hampshire and then made him captain, they gave Old an ultimatum and promoted him as well.

In 1983 they added another charge: 'Boycott has been the centre of factional controversy within the club. That controversy increased in the later part of the season. The new cricket policy was launched against this background. In this context his contract was not renewed and interdependent decisions were taken.' Superficially it sounds all right, but I cannot recall many occasions on which Boycott instigated trouble. Other players, some of them junior, were much more seriously at fault, yet they escaped punishment, so it could be advanced that those charged with running the cricket side fell down on the job. They failed to handle Boycott and let standards slip in less publicised directions.

Sir Kenneth Parkinson was a man of the highest integrity, a leader in many areas of human endeavour and it is not without significance that he stood by Boycott throughout, providing the most admirable example of his efforts to bring about unity. He had no doubt that the captain lacked loyal support, but he could do nothing to change the course of history, finding himself powerless because he cared too much to further split the county.

Boycott can then be forgiven his lack of assurance. When captain he knew nothing was being done about the areas of discontent, so he had to tread warily. Subsequently, he had every reason to think his future with the club could be assured only by his scoring heavily and regularly. The best way of playing for the team is, after all, a matter of interpretation. Scoring more runs than the next man and winning a few games along the way provides a surer basis for negotiation.

Until the late 1970s, the county committee had been almost, if not quite, a closed shop. This unwieldy body is made up of twenty-three people representing seventeen districts who face elections in rota every third year. A facility also exists to permit six others to be nominated by the committee for election at the annual meeting. To that extent it is democratic, but there are snags.

Before the Harrogate revolution many thought it virtually impossible to break through the barriers to get elected, particularly as there was no central fund for this purpose. In the early 1980s it could cost as much as £500 to fight a keenly-contested campaign which tended to discourage potential candidates, however worthy. The situation also created a complacent atmosphere among the fortunate few, many of whom were returned unopposed to office. More importantly, the sub committees were an internal matter and the membership had no control over who got onto the all powerful cricket committee.

Six members of the cricket committee (it became cricket management after Illingworth's signing) who appointed Boycott were in office when he was sacked – Feather, Melling, Sellers, Billy Sutcliffe, Temple and Yardley.

Surely they ought to have shared some of the responsibility, however slight? They chose the captain, sat in judgment and helped, through their representatives, to pick the team. Possibly some committeemen did not like the new type of professional captain, one with ideas that they regarded were above his station, for Yorkshire represented one of the last bastions of the true blue amateur. Boycott, with all his eagerness for innovations and all his opinions, upset the old-school-tie brigade, but none of the side issues was sufficient to justify his sacking as captain. In making him the scapegoat for an unacceptable playing record, the club missed the point and paid the penalty through further disappointment.

Nor did the players who turned against him do themselves any service by using him as an explanation for their own shortcomings.

Boycott's contract required him to serve the club honestly and faithfully and to use his best endeavours to serve its interests and reputation, and he did exactly that, at considerable cost to his own pocket. He rejected a substantial sum from Packer – in his own words six times the amount he received from Yorkshire in the contract that expired in 1978 – because he refused to risk his availability for the county. He also turned down £10,000 from a Sunday newspaper for one article at the time of his sacking. In either case it was easy money with the promise of more to come.

The facts make it clear time and again that Yorkshire needed him more than he needed them. He fought a long and bitter battle because he cared deeply about the county club and because of his pride. He could have simply walked away from all the rows and the back-stabbing, but he thought he was near to achieving something so he fought on. He tried to meet Yorkshire half way in 1978, stating: 'I will be prepared to stand down and play under any captain if Yorkshire do not win a trophy in the next two years under my leadership.' Similarly he went a long way towards compromise in 1983 by agreeing to retire after one more season, thus creating the opportunity for all concerned to save face and money.

The die, however, had been cast and the conflict merely forced the combatants further apart to the detriment of the club, which attracted unfavourable attention because of Boycott's involvement.

Boycott has always been more intent on pleasing himself than anyone else, but, since his standards are the highest, that has been to the advantage of Yorkshire and England, although unswerving involvement to that depth does not win many friends. Strangely, however, although he played his cricket on the percentage basis, balancing the risk and the value in each stroke, he is a crowd-puller and always the centre of attention.

In this connection one true story is worth recounting. On the morning of Yorkshire's Nat-West Cup tie at Canterbury in July, 1981, Boycott joined some friends and colleagues for breakfast to discuss a private matter. Halfway through the meal, two women of late middle-age approached his table and one thrust a piece of paper and a pencil under his nose while he was in mid-sentence. This gesture presumably did away with the need for any social graces such as 'please' or 'excuse me', but Boycott, anxious to be neither overheard nor have his breakfast interrupted, signed his name with his usual care and passed the paper back without comment.

The woman, stiff-backed with indignation, returned the moment he left the dining room to ask: 'Is he always so rude?' Ignoring her own dreadful manners in tackling him so abruptly while he was talking and eating, she continued: 'I'd heard he was big-headed, but now I have seen it with my own eyes. I hope he gets out first ball today.'

Another dissatisfied customer and another chapter in somebody's fantasies about Boycott. It is easy to argue that the polite response should always be on his lips, but being one of the most famous men in the country is not the joy ride that many imagine. Subjected to the unblinking gaze of public scrutiny, he is bound to slip up from time to time, and every man's image is created as much by other people's feelings as his own virtues and vices. Boycott accepts that he is regarded as cold, ruthless and calculating, but there is little he can do as it is impossible to communicate with more than a handful of those his activities touch.

This does not stop him trying, for no sportsman is more patient with the long crocodile of queues for autographs or more ready to explain a point in the right place and the right time. In the formative stages of the 1981 season, Yorkshire's Benson and Hedges zonal tie with Lancashire at Headingley was washed out, which did not matter much because their fates were already settled. Yorkshire had qualified and Lancashire could not join them in the knockout round.

Unfortunately, the blank Saturday, caused by a waterlogged field, turned out to be bright and sunny and Yorkshire made a terrible mistake in admitting spectators. A series of loud-speaker announcements, warning of a long delay but hinting at the prospect of play in the late afternoon or early evening, did little to appease the disgruntled customers as tempers cooked slowly in the mocking heat.

From the point of view of public relations, the whole business was a disaster, as the president fully appreciated. On one of the last occasions I met him before his untimely death later in the same year, Sir Kenneth expressed again his concern with the way the club was run. 'We do not seem to realise how much these people mean to Yorkshire cricket,' he said, waving his stick in an arc to indicate the angry groups of enthusiasts. 'We should be doing something to explain the situation to them more clearly, because we are losing friends.'

Out of all the committee members and players on the ground that day, one man met the challenge. Boycott, while I was still in conversation with Sir Kenneth, emerged from the pavilion and quickly gathered an appreciative audience. He explained that the players were very anxious to get on with things but that conditions were impossible. 'Don't forget, this is our work,' he said. 'We might have had a day off on Monday if we had finished today, but we will lose that now, and I will have to cancel some business appointments. You enjoy your days off work and so do we, so I assure you if there was any chance of playing today we would have been out there now.' He also gave a little lecture on the ground conditions and how to deal with them, so at least a few left Headingley mollified.

Inevitably, his enemies dismissed this as just another bit of glory-seeking, refusing to allow that, whatever his motives, Boycott saved Yorkshire some embarrassment. If, however, all the committeemen and players had followed his example by giving up ten minutes to mingle with the public and put their side of the story they might have restored confidence in the club, so it was them, not Boycott, who should be called into question.

What of the future? Boycott has proved the hard way that he retains an interest in and an affection for Yorkshire and the worst times the club have known cannot be put down to one man. If he played for himself – and those who claim he did produced few examples – he did so when the nature of things made something of a virtue of this vice. If he has been scathing to the less able, he had plenty of cause, for Yorkshire cricket has lacked application to a frightening degree. Above all, he remained faithful to his ideals.

Throughout all the years of anger and argument, bitterness and bickering, his constant theme remained: 'I want to play for Yorkshire and England and I want to captain them both.' No one has the right to quibble at Illingworth and Hampshire for leaving Yorkshire to further their careers elsewhere, but they did leave. Boycott stayed, not for money but because he cared. He has been wrong on occasions, but without him Yorkshire and England would have been the poorer. Perhaps he cared too much and tried too hard, but he succeeded. In the final analysis he stands comfortably in credit – warts and all.

Appendix—Facts and Figures

CAPTAINCY COMPARISONS

Yorkshire completed **166** Championship matches during Boycott's captaincy. Two games in this period were abandoned without a ball being bowled. Sharpe led the side in the tie with Middlesex at Bradford in 1973. The full list of season-by-season results under the various captains is:

		P	W	D	L	BATTING POINTS	BOWLING
1971							
Boycott		17	4	9	4	44	55
Wilson		6	0	2	4	3	18
Padgett		1	0	1	0	0	2
	TOTAL	24	4	12	8	47	75
1972							
Boycott		10	3	6	1	28	42
Sharpe		3	0	2	1	5	7
Wilson		6	1	2	3	6	22
Nicholson		1	0	1	0	0	2
	TOTAL	20	4	11	5	39	73
1973							
Boycott		8	0	5	3	17	21
Sharpe		12	3	6*	2	11	48
	TOTAL	20	3	11	5	28	69

* plus the tied game with Middlesex

1974

Boycott		15	4	6	5	32	54
Sharpe		4	0	2	2	5	15
	TOTAL	19	4	8	7	37	69

1975

Boycott		18	9	8	1	53	60
Hampshire		2	1	1	0	3	8
	TOTAL	20	10	9	1	56	68

1976

Boycott		11	4	3	4	30	32
Hampshire		9	2	5	2	19	35
	TOTAL	20	6	8	6	49	67

1977

Boycott		15	6	8	1	26	40
Hampshire		4	0	2	2	6	16
Cope		2	0	0	2	4	7
	TOTAL	21	6	10	5	36	63

1978

Boycott		12	5	6	1	31	31
Hampshire		10	5	3	2	27	24
	TOTAL	22	10	9	3	58	55

The comparative figures for the Sunday League are:

		P	W	L	
1971					
Boycott		9	4	5	
Wilson		4	1	3	
Padgett		1	0	1	
	TOTAL	14	5	9	2 abandoned
1972					
Boycott		9	6	3	
Wilson		4	3	1	
Sharpe		2	1	1	
	TOTAL	15	10	5	1 abandoned
1973					
Boycott		10	7	3	
Hampshire		6	4	2	
	TOTAL	16	11	5	

1974

Boycott	9	7	2	
Sharpe	2	1	1	
Hampshire	3	0	3	
TOTAL	14	8	6	2 abandoned

1975

Boycott	14	9	5	
Hampshire	2	0	2	
TOTAL	16	9	7	

1976

Boycott	10	5	5	
Hampshire	6	1	5	
TOTAL	16	6	10	

1977

Boycott	8	2	6	
Cope	1	0	1	
Hampshire	1	1	0	
TOTAL	10	3	7	6 abandoned

1978

Boycott	8	4	4	
Hampshire	6	3	3	2 abandoned

BOYCOTT'S BATTING RECORD AS CAPTAIN

FIRST-CLASS

	INNS	NO	HS	RUNS	AVGE
1971	25	4	233	2,221	105.76
1972	17	5	204*	1,156	96.33
1973	16	3	141*	773	59.46
1974	30	5	149*	1,478	59.12
1975	34	8	201*	1,915	73.65
1976	24	5	207*	1,288	67.78
1977	25	3	154	1,257	57.22
1978	22	1	129	1,074	51.14

SUNDAY LEAGUE

	INNS	NO	HS	RUNS	AVGE
1971	9	0	93	443	49.22
1972	9	1	52*	256	32.00
1973	10	2	104*	444	55.50
1974	10	1	108*	363	40.33
1975	14	3	99	666	60.54
1976	10	4	89*	392	65.33
1977	10	1	79*	347	38.55
1978	8	2	40	141	23.50

CENTURY DETAILS

Boycott scored forty Championship centuries as captain of Yorkshire, and on thirty of those occasions made more than half the runs accrued while he was at the wicket. The details are:

	OPPONENTS	BOYCOTT	RUNS SCORED WHILE GB AT THE WICKET
1971	Warwickshire	110	161
	Middlesex	112*	213
	Nottinghamshire	169	307
	Essex	233	369
	Middlesex	182*	320
	Derbyshire	133	239
	Lancashire	169	319
	Leicestershire	151	314
	Hampshire	111	165
	Warwickshire	138*	232
	Northamptonshire	124*	266
1972	Somerset	122*	226
	Lancashire	105	156
	Nottinghamshire	100	153
	Leicestershire	204*	310
	Essex	121	235
	Hampshire	105	188
1973	Lancashire	101	178
	Nottinghamshire	129	219
1974	Derbyshire	149*	251
	Sussex	117	237
	Surrey	142*	343
1975	Worcestershire	152*	278
	Gloucestershire	141	275
	Middlesex	175*	328
	Nottinghamshire	139	263
	Middlesex	201*	376
	Lancashire	105*	219

1976	Gloucestershire	161*	321
	Nottinghamshire	141	287
	Glamorgan	156*	318
	Lancashire	103*	174
1977	Somerset	139*	275
	Middlesex	117	214
	Nottinghamshire	154	309
	Warwickshire	104	237
1978	Warwickshire	115	190
	Northamptonshire	113	267
	Glamorgan	118	206
	Nottinghamshire	129	269

ACHIEVEMENTS

Boycott is the only Englishman to average 100 for a first-class season in England, doing it twice — in 1971 (100.12) and 1979 (102.53).

Scored two centuries in a match *v* Nottinghamshire at Sheffield in 1966 (103 and 105), *v* Nottinghamshire at Bradford in 1983 (163 and 141 not out) and for England *v* The Rest in a Test trial at Worcester in 1974 (160 not out and 116).

Completed his 100th century in first-class cricket while batting for England against Australia at Leeds in August 1977.

Scored a century for England on all six of the regular Test match grounds — Lord's, the Oval, Leeds, Birmingham, Nottingham and Manchester.

Made a century against each of the other sixteen first-class counties. He completed the sixteen in May 1975 when he scored 152 not out for Yorkshire *v* Worcestershire at Worcester.

Highest scores are: 261 not out for MCC *v* President's XI in Bridgetown 1973—74; 260 not out for Yorkshire *v* Essex at Colchester in 1970; 246 not out for England *v* India at Leeds in 1967.

Played in his 100th Test against Australia at Lord's on 2 July 1981.

Became the highest scorer in English Test history on 13 August 1981, when he passed Colin Cowdrey's 7,624 against Australia at Manchester.

Became the highest scorer in all Test history on 23 December 1981 when he passed Gary Sobers's 8,032 against India at Delhi.

Awarded OBE in 1980 Birthday Honours List.

IMPORTANT DATES FOR BOYCOTT

6 July 1959 — Second team debut *v* Cumberland at Penrith.

22 August 1961 — First century for second team *v* Cumberland at Bridlington, 156 not out.

16 June 1962 — First-team debut *v* Pakistan at Bradford.

3 June 1963 — First century for Yorkshire *v* Lancashire at Sheffield, 145.

2 October 1963 — Awarded Yorkshire cap.

4 June 1964 — Debut for England *v* Australia at Nottingham.

17 August 1964 — First century for England *v* Australia at the Oval, 113.

18 January 1978 — Became England captain as deputy for the injured Mike Brearley for third Test *v* Pakistan.

DIETING
MAKES YOU
FAT

GEOFFREY CANNON & HETTY EINZIG

'DEBUNKS EVERY FAD DIET YOU EVER HAVE BELIEVED IN . . . excellent nutritional and aerobic advice for planning the leaner, fitter you!' SUNDAY TELEGRAPH

If you want to lose fat, if you want to feel good, look better and be healthier, *don't diet*. No matter how hard you diet, no matter which diet you choose, the chances are you'll be fatter and less healthy at the end of it. Because dieting doesn't make you thin or healthy –
DIETING MAKES YOU FAT

This bestseller tells you how to get rid of your calorie counter and your excess weight. Now you can eat, drink, be merry – become a leaner, fitter healthier and happier person – and never need to diet again!

'For years I have resisted the awful truth . . . until Geoffrey Cannon put the point so forcibly, in DIETING MAKES YOU FAT.' THE TIMES

'Simple, impressive, and unbelievably up-cheering.' DAILY EXPRESS

HEALTH & MEDICINE   0 7221 2361 2   £1.95

The Book Of
ROYAL
LISTS

CRAIG BROWN & LESLEY CUNLIFFE

What should you serve the Royal Family if they drop in for dinner?

How does the Queen keep her Corgies content?

Which clergyman did Prince Charles throw into the fountain at Balmoral?

What are Princess Diana's favourite sweets?

Which television programmes does the Queen Mother like best?

How can you recognise a Royal racing pigeon?

The Royal Family is no ordinary family, and Royal Lists are not like ordinary lists. Here at last are the answers to all the questions that have intrigued dedicated Royal-watchers, loyal patriots, convinced monarchists and the millions of adoring fans around the world who follow every move of Britain's first family.

THE BOOK OF ROYAL LISTS is the most comprehensive collection of information ever assembled about the British Royal Family and their ancestors. Witty and informed, amusing but respectful, it surprises, charms and dazzles.

HUMOUR   0 7221 1934 8   £2.50

FEELING FIT FOR NOTHING?

GET FIT FOR LIFE

Our 'Enry's fun way to fitness and health

HENRY COOPER

Do you get out of breath running for a bus? Can you touch your toes or does your stomach get in the way?

Whether you are young or old, fat or thin, Henry Cooper has an answer to your health and fitness problems. There are numerous simple, illustrated exercises to help keep your muscles supple and tackle backache, midriff bulge, double chins and the dangers of smoking and drinking.

Keeping fit can be fun; you don't need to spend hours each day doing the same exercises – variety is the spice of life!

By the time you've finished GET FIT FOR LIFE, you'll not only be able to run for the bus, you'll be able to dispense with it altogether!

HEALTH & MEDICINE   0 7221 2498 8   £1.25

A SELECTION OF BESTSELLERS FROM SPHERE

FICTION

THE MISTS OF AVALON	Marion Bradley	£2.95 ☐
THE INNOCENT DARK	J. S. Forrester	£1.95 ☐
THURSTON HOUSE	Danielle Steel	£1.95 ☐
MAIDEN VOYAGE	Graham Masterton	£2.50 ☐
THE FURTHER ADVENTURES OF		
HUCKLEBERRY FINN	Greg Matthews	£2.95 ☐

FILM AND TV TIE-INS

THE IRISH R.M.	E. E. Somerville and	
	Martin Ross	£1.95 ☐
SCARFACE	Paul Monette	£1.75 ☐
THE KILLING OF KAREN SILKWOOD		
	Richard Rashke	£1.95 ☐
THE RADISH DAY JUBILEE	Sheilah B. Bruce	£1.50 ☐
THEY CALL ME BOOBER FRAGGLE		
	Michaela Muntean	£1.50 ☐
RED AND THE PUMPKINS	Jocelyn Stevenson	£1.50 ☐

NON-FICTION

GRENADA: INVASION, REVOLUTION		
AND AFTERMATH	Hugh O'Shaughnessy	£2.95 ☐
DIETING MAKES YOU FAT	Geoffrey Cannon &	
	Hetty Einzig	£1.95 ☐
THE FRUIT AND NUT BOOK	Helena Radecka	£6.95 ☐
LEBANON, THE FRACTURED COUNTRY		
	David Gilmour	£2.95 ☐
THE OFFICIAL MARTIAL ARTS HANDBOOK		
	David Mitchell	£3.95 ☐

All Sphere books are available at your local bookshop or newsagent, or can be ordered direct from the publisher. Just tick the titles you want and fill in the form below.

Name _____

Address _____

_____

Write to Sphere Books, Cash Sales Department, P.O. Box 11, Falmouth, Cornwall TR10 9EN

Please enclose a cheque or postal order to the value of the cover price plus:

UK: 45p for the first book, 20p for the second book and 14p for each additional book ordered to a maximum charge of £1.63.

OVERSEAS: 75p for the first book and 21p per copy for each additional book.

BFPO & EIRE: 45p for the first book, 20p for the second book plus 14p per copy for the next 7 books, thereafter 8p per book.

Sphere Books reserve the right to show new retail prices on covers which may differ from those previously advertised in the text or elsewhere, and to increase postal rates in accordance with the PO.